WHICH WINE?

Which Wine?

The Wine Drinker's Buying Guide

Peter M. F. Sichel

and

Judy Ley

HARPER & ROW, PUBLISHERS

NEW YORK · EVANSTON · SAN FRANCISCO · LONDON

TO

Stella, Mama, Bettina, Alexandra, and Sylvia

WHO ALL HELPED

TO

Audrey, Wendel, Bob, Peggy, Steve,
Sharon, Diane, and Anthony

WHO ENCOURAGED

Designed by Lydia Link

Library of Congress Cataloging in Publication Data

Sichel, Peter M   F
  Which wine? : The wine drinker's buying guide.
  Bibliography: p.
  Includes index.
  1. Wine and wine making.   I. Ley, Judy, joint
author.   II. Title.
TP548.S552   1975   641.2'2   75-6361
ISBN 0-06-013867-X

 76 77 78 79 10 9 8 7 6 5 4 3 2

Contents

PREFACE   ix

INTRODUCTION   xi

PART ONE
BEFORE YOU BUY

What You Need to Know to Purchase Wine   3
    Identifying Wine: The Four Basic Terms   3
    Wine Laws   5
    How to Read a Wine Label   8
    Vintage and Reality   8

The Art of Making Wine   12

Your Wine Merchant   19

PART TWO
PURCHASING: GUIDE TO SPECIFIC
WINE RECOMMENDATIONS

How to Use the Guide   25
    The Tastings   27

Purchase Recommendations by Wine-Types 30

RED WINES 30

French Red Bordeaux, Bordeaux-Style Wines, and California
  Cabernet Sauvignon 30
French Red Burgundies, Burgundy-Style Wines, and California
  Pinot Noir 50
Beaujolais 66
Zinfandel 72
Italian Chianti, California Chianti, and Related Hearty Reds 77
Bardolino and Valpolicella 86
Two California Varietals: Gamay Beaujolais and Napa Gamay 91

WHITE WINES 94

The Chardonnay Grape: French White Burgundies and California
  Pinot Chardonnay 94
The Riesling Grape, German and Alsatian White Wines,
  California Johannisberg Riesling, and Gewürztraminer 107
White Bordeaux, the Sauvignon Blanc and Sémillon Grapes 124
California Chenin Blanc and Wines of the Lower Loire Valley 130
The Everyday White Wines: Non-French Chablis and Sauterne 136
White Wines in the German Style 142
White Wines of Italy, Spain, and Portugal 147

ROSÉS 152

OTHER NORTH AMERICAN WINES 160

U.S. Wines Produced East of the Rockies and Canadian-Produced
  Wines 160

Purchase Recommendations by Price Categories 172

Food and Wine 207

Enjoying Wine with Food 207
Food and Wine Chart 212
Cheese and Wine Chart 215

PART THREE

BACKGROUND

Storage, Decanting, Glassware, and Bottle Shapes   219

How to Give a Wine Tasting   223

APPENDIXES

Acknowledgments   231
Wine as an Industry   234
Words Used to Describe Wine   237
The Best Vineyards and Estates of the German Wine Regions   241
Important Burgundy Estates   248
Some Dependable Bordeaux Shippers   248
Reliable Burgundy Shippers   249
Reliable Shippers of Rhine, Moselle, and Alsatian Wines   250
Alexis Lichine's Suggested Classification of the Grands Crus
  Rouges de Bordeaux   251
Maps: France, Spain and Portugal, and California   256, 257, 258
Bibliography   259

INDEX   263

Illustrations

Some Examples of Wine Labels   *following page 20*
Relationship of geographical place names
    on a German wine label   112
Decanting   220
Traditional Wine Glass Shapes   221
Traditional Bottle Shapes   222
Maps:

        Bordeaux   33
        Burgundy   52–53
        Italy   78
        Germany   109
        Loire Valley   131
        France   256
        Spain and Portugal   257
        California   258

Preface

I was born into a family that has been in the wine business in Germany and France from father to son for five generations. I grew up in this business and have spent thirty years exporting wines from France and Germany under the Sichel label. Since 1941, after arriving in the United States as a refugee from war-torn Europe, I have been conducting my wine business from this side of the Atlantic. With this experience I wanted to write a book on wine in response to the many questions I am constantly asked and to put on record my particular viewpoint. Shortly after I made the decision to embark on this venture I met Judy Ley, who had decided to organize and write a consumer guide to wine in response to the confusion she saw in the marketplace. We decided to combine forces, I to provide the expertise, she the consumer's viewpoint. It turned out that she also provided the energy and enthusiasm without which this book would never have been researched or written. She forced me to define and reassess my knowledge and prejudices and to stay as practical and realistic as possible.

The wine industry is a great fraternity. Without its help we would not have been able to complete the book. Almost all American and Canadian wineries, wine importers, and industry associations were most generous in their help, answering questions, providing information, and offering samples of hundreds of wines. My colleagues in the field of wine, particularly Alexis Bespaloff and Alexander McNally, helped tirelessly with their immense experience and knowledge. We were blessed with many helping hands. Virginia Hilu, our editor, who fortunately was not new to wine, helped with patience and humor. Warren Weaver was invaluable in organizing and revising our original manuscript. Michael Schweitzer helped in earlier editorial efforts, particularly on food and wine combinations. John W. Rapp was our research assistant, with an abiding interest in the subject; he ultimately also became our cartographer. My wife, Stella, and Louise Duncan in the last months of our race with time became full-time editors and research assistants. We would never have finished the book in time without their unstinting help, brains, and sang-froid. Lois Wyatt did endless typing and collating and helped to follow up requests with tact and patience.

In addition to the above, many people gave us ideas and encouragement, and the members of the tasting panels were a tireless group of willing and enthusiastic helpers. These contributors are listed on pages 231–233.

PETER M. F. SICHEL

Introduction

Until as recently as twenty years ago, a European attending an American dinner party would have been surprised to find that he was offered the choice of another whisky or coffee with his meal. Rarely was wine served with dinner, and then more as a kind gesture to a visiting European whose pleasure in wine was understood. Since then America has gone through a veritable wine-drinking revolution. Americans take as much pride at setting a table, preparing fine food, and drinking wine as any culture in the world. They should, for they are exposed to a larger selection of food and wine than any other country in the world. Wine no longer is a quaint Old World drink reserved for rare occasions. It is in the mainstream, it is part of everyday life.

Yet Americans are still very far behind in per capita consumption. There are twenty countries that consume more wine than we do, and they are not only Italy, France, Argentina, and Spain, but even Australia and New Zealand. Though we are low on the totem pole as far as consumption is concerned, we must be at the very top as far as variety of wines is concerned. Every conceivable type of wine from just about any country in the world is available here. This is not so elsewhere. Not surprisingly, the countries that produce and consume wines in enormous quantities usually offer only local products in their stores, and possibly a few choices from the more famous regions within the country. Only rarely do they offer imported wines, and then they are limited to those from neighboring countries. No one has the selection, the overabundance, the "embarrassment of riches," that we have. Such a marketplace is rich, diverse, and filled with intriguing tastes to explore, but the plethora of labels and nomenclature can cause confusion, uncertainty, and misspent dollars, making the right taste pleasure at the right price an increasingly difficult search.

This American abundance can confuse and bewilder, and makes it difficult to choose among over 10,000 available labels. For one thing, how do you know in advance what you are getting? And how do you know which wine you are going to like, and which wines are the good values? You could, of course, find your wine preferences by trial and error over a lifetime, but this would be a rather unwieldy task in terms of time, money, and frustration no matter how many delightful side-effects it produced.

Thus, we have tried to bring some order to this confusion by writing this basic guide to wine buying. We offer here our guidance to help you buy better from whatever your viewpoint, be it wine-type, price, or food. In our efforts to guide you through the confusion of the marketplace we have done as much of the experimenting as possible for you.

After conducting an extensive survey of the marketplace we decided to concentrate on table wine, which we divided into similar types according to taste and style, ignoring traditional geographic limits. This new way of approaching wines enabled us to find the best values of a wine-type regardless of country of origin.

After we established distribution criteria, we held extensive tastings to find the best wines and values for your money. The results of our tastings, our specific purchase recommendations, are illustrated by charts both by wine-type and price. We have answered the basic question of what wine to serve with what food. A long list of foods included in the text is accompanied by specific recommendations. We have also provided you with basic information on wine making and distribution which will help you to find your way in this complex subject.

We think of our book as a daily buying guide, used to save you time, concentrating on wines that cost less than $7.50, most under $3. This book should be with you on all wine buying occasions. With its help you will get the right bottle at the right price and you can explore the wines from Bordeaux to the Napa Valley with confidence.

BEFORE YOU BUY

What You Need to Know
to Purchase Wine

Identifying Wine: The Four Basic Terms

When buying wine you should be familiar with the following four terms:
generic, varietal, regional, and proprietary. You will need them to identify
just about any wine on the market.

GENERIC

Generics are broad general wine-types whose names derive from the place
where the first wine of that type was made, such as Sauternes, Chablis,
Burgundy. Later, when similar wines were made in other regions or countries, in order to enhance their salability the wines were named after the
established wine whose taste they most resembled. As a result, there is an
enormous quantity of wine on the market today from various places, mostly
American-produced, that is called, for example, Chablis, Red Burgundy, or
Rhine. These wines are not to be confused with the original product. Because
the label specifies the country of origin, you will know if you are getting the
regional original or the generic imitation.

Generics have become our everyday wines. Their names may include further information such as Hearty Burgundy or Robust Burgundy or Gold
Chablis, and they usually sell at $1.29 to $2.50 a bottle. Most often made
from several grape varieties, they are not very distinguished wines. Their
makers, however, strive for a consistent style and taste from bottle to bottle.

VARIETAL

A wine sold under the name of the variety of grape from which it is made is called a varietal, such as Pinot Noir or Johannisberg Riesling. In Europe, the laws specify which grape varieties must go into which geographically named wine, as Chablis or Bordeaux. There is no such requirement in the United States. As the industry developed in America, California wineries found they needed a way to distinguish between a finer wine, such as one made exclusively from the Chardonnay grape, and a generic wine, such as California Chablis, which could be made from any grape variety. The Chardonnay grapes could cost up to ten times as much as those used for generic Chablis, and a way had to be found to identify the difference for the customer. To respond to this need, the American producer began to name some wines by the prominent varietal used, such as Chardonnay.

Today this method of identification is popularly accepted by American wineries and is backed by legislation requiring that a varietal wine have at least 51 percent of the grape variety for which it is named. In fact, a further refinement has been to distinguish between top varietals, the most expensive because they are made from grapes that are richer in flavor and more difficult to grow, and mid-varietals, the next level of quality.

The top varietals for red wines are Cabernet Sauvignon, Pinot Noir, Gamay Beaujolais, and Napa Gamay. For white wines they are Chardonnay, Riesling (also called White or Johannisberg Riesling), Gewürztraminer, and Sauvignon Blanc. The principal mid-varietals for red wines are Petit Sirah, Zinfandel, Ruby Cabernet, and Grenache; for white wines, Chenin Blanc, Grey Riesling, Green Hungarian, Sémillon, Sylvaner, and French Colombard.

REGIONAL

Wines carrying the name of the geographic area where they are made, like Pouilly-Fuissé or Châteauneuf-du-Pape, are regionals, and they account for the majority of imported wines. In Europe, where the wine industry has matured over many years, the laws regulating production, labeling, and claims of quality are based on geographic areas and are a buying guide in themselves. Due to individual differences in soil, climate, and the grape varieties used, these areas produce highly characteristic wines.

In California, grape varieties will eventually produce wines characteristic of the areas where they have been planted, just as they do in Europe. Already more wineries are adding regional names to their labels to identify a valley or even a specific vineyard, such as Alexander Valley, a part of Sonoma County in California, or Martha's Vineyard, a vineyard in the Napa Valley.

Regional names are sometimes combined with generics, like Napa Burgundy. Wines with such specific labels are not necessarily better than those labeled California Burgundy or California Chablis, but at least they show their origin.

PROPRIETARY

Proprietary names are brand names. They are featured on wine labels to facilitate their marketing and may be used on wines that can be produced in large quantity and of consistent quality. They, too, can be combined with generic, regional, and varietal names, though American wineries use only the proprietary name, like Paul Masson "Baroque" and Christian Brothers "Château La Salle." Foreign wines with proprietary names usually combine them with regional origin, like "Mouton Cadet" Bordeaux, "Blue Nun" Liebfraumilch, Beaujolais "St. Vincent."

When you buy wine there are a couple of variations to be aware of. Occasionally, you may be confused by wine bearing a varietal name different from the grape variety from which it is made. For example, some California wines are sold as Riesling, but are not made from the Riesling grape that produces the finest German wines, but actually from the Sylvaner, originally a German grape of lesser pedigree.

Sometimes wines are shipped to the United States under a varietal name on the theory that the familiarity of the name will make them easier to sell. Mâcon-Villages, a French regional white Burgundy, is sold here as Pinot Chardonnay-Mâcon, a legitimate addition of a varietal name, since all white wine from the French area of Mâcon must be made from the Chardonnay grape. The U.S. government requires that imported wines with varietal labels be true varietals, barring, for example, Spanish wine named after grapes that do not grow in Spain.

Wine Laws

For centuries, the production and marketing of wine have been controlled by government regulations. The pharaohs' Royal Sealer of the Wine guaranteed the origin and vintage of each amphora. The earliest code of Roman law, the Twelve Tables, dealt with pruning of the vines, a process essential to the quality of wines. In the Middle Ages, the dukes of Burgundy issued edicts outlawing certain grapes and requiring hillside vineyard planting. In current terminology, wine has enjoyed a history of consumer protection.

Today's wine laws are aimed at preventing any adulterations that could be injurious to health and at promoting quality and truth in labeling.

All wine-producing countries have laws controlling the safety of the product. In the United States, some states go so far as to require chemical analysis of the wine. As a result, the consumer can assume that any wine sold through normal commercial channels has met health standards.

Like all laws, wine laws are effective only so long as they make current sense. These laws require periodic revision. There is no denying that abuses occur, and every country has had its wine scandal. Both France and California have recently had cases of an inferior wine being labeled with a higher designation, and some time ago Italy and Germany uncovered frauds in which wine was made chemically, without benefit of grapes. The law worked effectively in prosecuting these cases and protecting the consumer.

Since French legislation has set the pattern for many other countries, let us examine its history and operation. For the first third of the twentieth century, French viticulture was ineffectively regulated, allowing for overproduction. This caused a loss of confidence in French wines, and sales decreased. In 1935 a comprehensive new wine law created a regulatory agency, the Institut National des Appellation d'Origine des Vins et Eaux-de-Vie (INAO). Literally translated, this means the National Institute of the Origin of Wines and the Waters of Life. *Vive la France!* ("Waters of life" are distillates from grapes, such as Cognac.)

The institute, an autonomous body working with the Ministries of Agriculture and Justice, encourages the production of quality wine by mapping out viticultural regions and requiring within them the use of the most suitable grapes. It also enforces many other regulations. The INAO's small army of experts, consultants, and inspectors tries to balance the interests of producers and consumers. As a result, all fine French wine is now designated Appellation d'Origine Contrôlée (A.C., for short). For each wine with an A.C. designation of whatever quality level there is a minimum standard of quality and a set of requirements for growing, making, blending, and labeling, largely organized along geographic lines. Wines that don't shape up cannot have A.C. on their label.

To qualify for an Appellation Contrôlée, a wine must be made from designated grape varieties and no others. Some appellations have only one permitted variety while others may use several, with the proportions specified.

The law dictates how many vines may be planted per acre and how much wine per acre can be produced. Also controlled are the method and extent of pruning as well as the length of time after planting before vines can produce grapes whose wine is eligible for A.C. designation. The law sets the minimum sugar content of the grapes before fermentation and the minimum alcoholic strength of the wine. Sugar can be added before fermentation only with special permission and within certain limits. The winemaker is allowed to correct nature only up to a point.

In 1951 the French government established a new designation just below Appellation Contrôlée, a sort of "junior varsity" for some wines, called Vins Délimités de Qualité Supérieure, or V.D.Q.S. These fifty regions fall short of A.C. standards but are subject to similar regulations. Because V.D.Q.S. wines are not generally well known, they often represent extremely good value for the consumer.

Wine that does not meet A.C. or V.D.Q.S. standards is called *vin ordinaire,* or ordinary wine. *Comsommation Courante* is the official name for *vin ordinaire.* Growers have recently persuaded the government to authorize the name Appellation Simple for *vin ordinaire,* in the hope that buyers might confuse it with Appellation Contrôlée. There are a lot of wine growers in France, and they all have the vote!

The regulations of most other countries are patterned after the French A.C. laws. In Italy, these are called Denominazione di Origine Controllata; in Spain, Denominaciones de Origen; and in Germany the wines are classified as Tafelwein, Qualitätswein, and Qualitätswein mit Prädikat.

In the United States there is no concerted government program to control the quality of wine, but state laws provide many specific guarantees of a bottle's contents. The geographic labeling varies from state to state. Ordinarily, a wine identified with a state of origin must have 75 percent of its grapes grown in that state. In California a more stringent state law requires 100 percent.

The California regulations, the most comprehensive and influential in the nation, require for statements of local origin, such as Napa Valley or Monterey, that 75 percent of the bottle's contents be from the claimed area. Similarly, a wine labeled "mountain" or "mountain grown" must contain 75 percent grapes from hilly or high country, although the law is not clear as to what "high" or "hilly" means. A vintage year must be 95 percent of that year and 95 percent from the district listed on the label, rather than the 75 percent permitted a nonvintage wine. A label may use the name of a grape variety, such as Cabernet Sauvignon, only if the wine is at least 51 percent from that grape. "Estate bottled" means that the wine must come either from vineyards that belong to the bottler or from grapes that were under his control before their harvest. "Produced and bottled by" means that the bottler crushed and fermented a minimum of 75 percent of the wine. "Made and bottled by" requires the bottler to have crushed and fermented at least 10 percent of his own wine. Though the use of certain generic names such as Claret or Chablis is permitted, there are no specifications as to what kind of wine will be labeled with such names.

Many American producers of quality wines are now trying to encourage tighter regulations. Their wines already exceed the legal minimum standards, and they would like to see the industry upgraded as a whole. Such regulations would increase the minimum varietal content, delineate areas of origin, and enable the consumer to identify the wine much more clearly.

How to Read a Wine Label

To familiarize you with the information on wine labels, we are reproducing some examples representing the main categories of wines from California, France, Germany, Italy, and Spain and will comment upon such terms as generic, varietal, regional, proprietary, estate-bottled, shipper-bottled, and winery-bottled.

Vintage and Reality

What determines the quality of a vintage? Most of the fine wines of the world grow under varying and often adverse climatic conditions. It is the struggle for survival that brings out the flavor and character of a wine. Wines that grow under uniform climatic conditions can be pleasant, but they will never have the personality and elegance of those grown in more difficult climes.

California may claim the contrary, but actually there is no fine wine region in the world where all the years are the same and where every year is a "vintage year." Weather creates vintages, and its changes create wines from the merely adequate to the really exceptional. To make the matter more complicated, each type of wine requires different weather conditions. Red usually poses a greater problem than white, while rosé rarely poses any problem at all.

The vintage year of a wine, like the pedigree of a horse, is only a guideline. Luckily for the consumer, vintages are important only in dealing with

2 or 3 percent of the world's wine production. Most of the wines we consume are blended to a standard quality, so that a vintage year is not important, though it does tell us how old the wine is and, therefore, when we should drink it. In the later sections on wine-types, we'll offer guidance on specific vintages.

Though most of the wine we drink is not vintage-dated, a disproportionate amount of the world's vintage-dated wine is consumed in America. This includes the best wines from each country, the great bottles that give the wine world its glamour and mystique. Since they are the fine wines associated with memorable occasions, it is important to have a grasp of the vintage subject.

Each vintage-dated wine has a lifespan all its own, and it exhibits certain aging characteristics that tell experts how its staying power compares with other years. Long after the first tasting, a wine's nature can change. Sometimes a wine that was thought at five years to have a short future will turn out, twenty years later, to be a wine of endurance, still developing character. The mystery in what a wine may become adds immeasurably to its fascination.

The judgment on the quality of a vintage is subjective. Not everyone's estimate would be the same, even if commercial interests, which can cloud judgment, did not abound. To a great extent, the judgment as to vintages is made by people in the wine business. These professional opinions are usually the ones accepted the world over. Most professionals tend to agree on their overall evaluation of a vintage, though some are more careful and cautious than others. Obviously it is tempting to come out with an assessment on the quality of a vintage as soon as possible, but it is also extremely risky. To damn a wine too early can bring financial ruin; to praise it too early can be harmful to the taster's reputation. Both have happened, though by and large, people in the wine business, while not shy of seeking publicity, are cautious of pronouncing judgment too early. The press, however, lives by reporting news, and obviously good news and bad news are more newsworthy than medium news. This must be the reason why so many wines have been apotheosized as the "vintage of the century" since 1959, when the U.S. press discovered that wine was hot news.

Unfortunately, this matter of vintage years becomes even more complex when one considers the whole palette of fine wines. As far as the American consumer is concerned, these include only wines from Germany, France, northern Italy, and some of the northern counties of California.

The northern counties of California usually have a consistent climate in any one year. In Germany, though, there may be a difference between the Rhine and the Moselle, the former vintage taking place earlier than the latter. The weather can change radically and quickly in this country which gathers its grapes later than any other fine-wine–producing country in the world. France, too, grows grapes in so many different regions and climates that the country could easily have a good vintage in Bordeaux and a bad one in Burgundy.

In northern Italy there may be a good vintage in Chianti, a so-so one in the Veneto, and an excellent one in Piedmont. Unfortunately, while our wine snobs go by vintage years, too often their memory retains only the news from one region, good or bad, and they give short shrift to all other regions.

Vintages in Bordeaux are usually more publicized and studied in greater depth by wine enthusiasts than the vintages in any other region. The reason for this is that Bordeaux produces more fine wine than any other wine-producing area of the world. These wines keep a long time, and require considerable time to mature in the bottle. Bordeaux had a poor vintage year in 1963. Rain prevented the grapes from reaching maturity, and, adding insult to injury, the rains made harvesting extremely difficult. The resulting wine had the taste of rotten and immature grapes, and even where a careful selection was made, the wines were, at best, exceedingly light—more akin to rosé than red wines, with none of the characteristics that make the wines of Bordeaux justly famous. The vintage was correctly declared a failure.

In the same year, Burgundy fared a little better than Bordeaux, but Germany made extremely good wines on the Rhine, profiting from a superb Indian summer. Germans have treasured these wines during the last ten years as elegant and stylish. Unfortunately, it was almost impossible to sell these wines in the export market since everyone assumed that 1963 was a bad vintage. It was a perfect case of a little learning being a dangerous thing!

So, we wouldn't think of slighting the champions in the vintage game. The two greatest red Bordeaux vintages since the fabulous 1928 and 1929 vintages were 1945 and 1961. Both vintages made wines of great concentration, the best of which will live into the next century. If you want to put down wines from Bordeaux for aging, the 1966, 1970, and 1971 vintages are the ones to buy. The best of the three is the 1966 vintage, though 1971 in some cases may end up even better. Of the red Burgundies, 1969 and 1971 are the ones to put down, and if you can still find 1966, they are worthy as well. Among the Rhine wines, the two greatest vintages of top wines, meaning Spätlese or better, are 1967 and 1971.

Here you see the complications of the vintage game. In Germany, 1967 was a good vintage; no better, no worse. But a magnificent Indian summer brought forth glorious late-picked Auslese, Beerenauslese, and Trockenbeerenauslese wines that will probably be judged superior to 1971 wines, a vintage that was worthy of being classed as one of Germany's great vintages of the last thirty years. Wines of both vintages from the Rhine of Auslese quality or better are worthy of aging. The great sweet wines of Bordeaux are the only other ones left to recommend by vintage, and here 1945, 1949, 1953, 1967, and 1971 are wines to put down.

To summarize, vintage is only important when you buy:

- Individual château-bottled red wines from Bordeaux, and sweet white wines from Sauternes and Barsac.
- Premier Cru and Grand Cru wines from Burgundy, plus regionals from the more important villages.
- Top wines of the Rhone Valley, Côte Rôtie, Hermitage, and Châteauneuf-du-Pape.
- Chianti Riserva from Italy.
- German wines carrying the designation Kabinett and Spätlese. Do not worry about wines identified as Auslese, Beerenauslese, or Trockenbeerenauslese, which are only made in good, if not great, vintage years.

The Art of Making Wine

It is not necessary to know how wine is made in order to buy it, but it does add to your enjoyment to understand its history. Consequently, you may go directly to the specific purchase recommendations beginning on page 30 and read this section at your leisure over a bottle we mention, or you may read it now before you begin to buy.

Wine is different from any other beverage, and from earliest history to the present time it has been surrounded by mystique and romance. Reserved for rulers and priests in ancient times, it soon became and remained an important part of the cult of most religions. To the Jews, it signified the recurring blessings of the Lord; to Christians, it symbolized the blood of Jesus; and in primitive religions, it was a means of exorcising an evil spirit. More important, it was the only known medicine for centuries, and still has a place in the pharmacology of modern times. Alcohol is but one of its components; minerals and vitamins also contribute to its beneficial effect. It is a basic food without which many Europeans could not contemplate life. When overexporting caused a shortage of wine in Yugoslavia, the government had to cut back on exports to restore the "tranquility of socialist life."

Wine can be made from almost any fruit or plant that contains both sugar for fermentation and acid for balance and flavor, and every winemaker searches for that divine fruit/acidity balance that characterizes the truly great wines.

Grapes grow in almost any temperate climate, and growing them is the only easy aspect of winemaking. They grow on vines, which, like all fruit trees, require constant care and protection from spring frosts, weeds, diseases, marauding birds, and insects.

The vines we are concerned with are members of several species: *Vitis vinifera*, which originated in Europe and is responsible for all the world's fine wines; native American species, of which *Vitis labrusca* is the most important; and hybrid varieties that have resulted from crossing the two. The American vine is hardy enough to survive the winters in eastern North America, but European vinifera is not. This species produces a great number of grape varieties, the most renowned of which are Cabernet Sauvignon, Pinot Noir, Chardonnay, and Riesling.

GROWTH

Dormant during the winter, the grapevines sprout in April, flower in late May or early June, and then produce small grapes which ripen by fall. A careful grower must match his vines to climate and soil. He controls the quantity of production by pruning the vines once a year, and also regularly cuts them back to encourage higher concentration of the growth, and thus the taste of the grapes. He must balance quality and quantity, both essential to his economic survival.

Vines are not commercially productive until about the third year. They reach full productivity at about seven, and continue until thirty. In later life, they bear fewer but more flavorful grapes. In any vineyard, therefore, the ages of the vines should be staggered so as to assure continuity of production and consistency of quality.

SOIL AND CLIMATE

Vineyard soil is important because it feeds the vine and gives flavor to the grape. Minerals in the soil affect the taste of the grapes; for example, the chalky soil of Chablis produces a dry crisp wine, the slate hills of the Moselle impart the taste of cold steel, and Tokay grapes grown in Hungary reflect a trace of the iron in the soil there. The same variety of grape responds differently to different soil and climate. Compare the Cabernet Sauvignon of Bordeaux to the Cabernet Sauvignon of California.

Soil is also important. Soil that is drained well warms rapidly in the sun, and makes the grapes ripen quickly and have more sugar in proportion to acid, a balance that is a critical factor in the quality of the wine. Similarly, rocky or slaty soil absorbs warmth and retains it through the night. Climate is important because the temperature and the amount of sunshine, two different elements, affect the ripening and ultimately the taste. Together, these factors contribute materially to making the Riesling wine of the Moselle, for example, different from the Riesling wine of California. Even

CLIMATE AND WINE

This record of fifteen years of temperature, rainfall, and sunshine shows the ups and downs of making wine in the Bordeaux vineyards of Château Palmer.

Temperature (coverage centigrade)

	Normal	1960	1961*	1962	1963	1964	1965	1966*	1967	1968	1969	1970*	1971*	1972	1973	1974
May	15	17.1	15	13.9	13.9	16.9	14.8	15.5	14	13.9	15.3	13.9	15.7	13.3	16.6	14.8
June	18.5	19.7	18.7	18.9	12.5	18.3	18	18.4	17.8	18.1	17.1	20	16.6	15.6	19	18.7
July	20.1	18.6	19.9	19.5	20.6	22	19.9	18	21.8	20.7	21.6	20.1	22.6	20.3	19.8	20.1
Aug.	20.2	19.9	19.6	20.4	17.8	20.6	19.4	18.8	19.8	19.5	20.2	19	20.1	18.7	22.8	20.8
Sept.	17.9	16.4	21.1	17.9	17	19.8	15.8	19.1	17.4	17.1	17.5	19.1	18	15.6	19	16.8
Oct.	13.5	12.6	14.4	14.3	14.1	11.6	16.2	14.5	15.6	16	15.4	12.7	15	13.5	12.4	13

Rainfall (total millimeters)

	Normal	1960	1961*	1962	1963	1964	1965	1966*	1967	1968	1969	1970*	1971*	1972	1973	1974
May	63.3	88.8	43.6	70.2	42.8	99	37	49	64	56	108	45	103	92	39	72.6
June	61.5	39.3	32.5	11.5	80.4	31	32	112	18.5	31	46	61	98	21	41	10.2
July	55	55.7	28.7	57	32	25	86	47	23	35	29	14	112	5	124	7.3
Aug	60	82	8.5	13.6	97	57	43	50	27	161	30	51	26	133	17	65.7
Sept.	67.9	177	27.6	42.5	70.5	47	213	25	73	97	207	23	92	20	114	128
Oct.	74.5	232	106	61	52.5	231	41	116	101	46	8	33	14	30	89	180

Sunshine (total hours)

	Normal	1960	1961*	1962	1963	1964	1965	1966*	1967	1968	1969	1970*	1971*	1972	1973	1974
May	198	264	235	177	248	254	156	255	200	210	204	224	166	150	221	194
June	230	283	242	347	197	278	201	214	267	237	192	234	164	196	228	249
July	247	205	244	271	267	304	246	206	279	291	320	284	314	254	184	249
Aug.	226	218	227	280	186	255	212	241	235	202	208	260	236	191	235	243
Sept.	175	175	195	216	133	183	130	224	182	170	115	246	229	183	224	146
Oct.	132	108	149	196	168	147	158	112	152	165	201	180	196	133	175	140

* Great vintages.

14

when the vineyards are only five to ten miles apart, like the Côte de Beaune and the Mâconnais in France, soil and climate produce a different Chardonnay in each.

Every part of the globe has certain soil and climatic conditions that favor certain grape types over others, and it is the result of hundreds of years of experience and not of chance that certain wine regions grow certain grape types. In California, however, the same area may grow a number of different grapes, each for bottling under a separate varietal label. Though soil and climate vary there, too, the California wine industry has not yet evolved the close relationship between grape and region that ordinarily develops with time. This, however, is changing, because the highly regarded scientists of the Oenology Department of the University of California at Davis have divided the state into five zones based on temperature. Each of these is regarded best for certain grape types (see map, p. 258).

To illustrate how the relationship of rainfall, temperature, and sunshine affects the quality of a vintage, we include a chart showing how these three factors affected fifteen vintages of Château Palmer, one of Bordeaux's finest vineyards. We have circled the factors contributing most to the success or failure of a given vintage. For instance, in 1961 the high temperature and the long hours of sunshine in September and October, and the paucity of rain in August and September contributed to a great vintage. Conversely, in 1965 the low temperature in September coupled with incessant rainfall made that vintage almost a complete disaster.

THE HARVEST

Grapes are ripe when they have sufficient balance of sugar and acidity; those picked too early will be too acidic, while those picked too late will have too much sugar and too little acidity. For a good wine, it normally takes one hundred days of sunshine from the time the vines flower until the grapes ripen, and a little longer for a great wine. In the old days, the grower determined ripeness by crushing a few grapes in his hands and testing the juice for consistency and concentration. Today this human method has been replaced by the refractometer, which gives an exact reading of the sugar content of the grape.

The timing of the harvest is still a gamble. The grower wants to pick at the perfect moment, but that moment may never come. The last few days of ripening are critical, for if it rains the grapes might be ruined. Even so, the tendency of most wine growers is to take the chance of waiting those few extra days in the interest of the better wine they might produce if fair weather holds.

Picking begins in late August or early September, except in the cooler northern vineyards of Germany, where it can be as late as October. Once the grapes are pronounced ripe, they must be picked as rapidly as possible to avoid rotting on the vine. There are two different kinds of rot: common gray rot, which comes from excessive moisture and produces bad wine, and "noble rot," (*botrytis cinerea*) a beneficial mold on the grape skins that produces a sweet and luscious wine.

Traditionally, the grapes are handpicked and taken to hoppers near the winery, where rotten or broken ones are removed. However, machine picking is gaining in popularity in the United States and Canada. The mechanical harvester is clearly more efficient, fast and clean, but it can be used only if the vineyard is level and planted in uniform rows for this purpose and if the vines are old enough to be sturdy.

The machine shakes the grapes loose from the vines onto a conveyor belt. As they move along, the leaves are blown away and the grapes are deposited in a tank. The only danger is possible bruising of the vines. New York State, where seasonal farm labor is scarce, has taken the lead in mechanical picking, but it is also used in the Monterey Peninsula in California and in eastern Canada. Machines cannot handle selective picking, such as choosing extremely ripe grapes that have the "noble rot."

PRESSING AND FERMENTATION

The grapes must be crushed as soon as possible after they are harvested, before they begin to deteriorate. Those picked in the morning are usually pressed in the afternoon, and they should never be allowed to stand longer than twelve hours.

Now comes the act that changes grape juice into wine: fermentation. It occurs when the yeast that forms naturally on the grapes (or is added artificially) converts the sugar in the grapes into alcohol and carbon dioxide. The carbon dioxide bubbles up, making the juice appear boiling even though it is well below that temperature, and then dissipates. When sufficient sugar has been converted into alcohol, you have wine.

Fermentation also extracts an organic element, tannin, from red or black grape skins. Tannin gives wine its color. It is interesting to note that the same grapes can produce a red, white, or rosé wine. For red wine, the skins are left in contact with the juice throughout the fermentation and removed later. For white wine, the grapes are pressed on the stalk, and the juice alone, without the skins or seeds, is fermented. For rosé, the skins are left in for the first twelve to twenty-four hours of fermentation, and removed when the wine has reached the desired color. Tannin provides not only color but also a taste reminiscent of strong tea that some wine drinkers say "puckers the palate." At the same time, tannin prolongs the life of red wine, enabling it to survive considerably longer than dry white wine.

The first fermentation takes ten or twelve days, and stops automatically when the chemical conversion is complete. If the alcoholic content of the wine goes above 14 percent, it will deactivate the yeast and fermentation will stop. Fermentation takes place at temperatures between 50° and 80° F. Temperature is usually strictly controlled to prevent fermentation from occurring too rapidly and draining the taste of the wine. After fermentation, any remaining yeast must be eliminated, usually by filtration.

Some winemakers may kill the grape's natural yeast with sulphur dioxide in order to replace it with a different yeast that will create a wine more to their liking. Aside from altering the taste, this technique can produce a cleaner, sounder wine. The fermentation of white and rosé wines is often stopped to retain a residual sweetness. A small amount of sugar is left either by adding sulphur dioxide or by filtration or pasteurization. After the fermentation of red wine stops, the juice is drawn off into wooden casks or tanks for aging and maturing. The residue of the grapes and skins is removed and pressed a second time to make a thinner wine, called *vin de presse* by the French. Stored separately, it is often added to the original wine later to reduce its concentration.

In some areas, water is added to the residue left after the first *vin de presse* has been drained off, and a second pressing is made. This produces a very light wine for almost immediate consumption, or it is distilled into a brandy called *eau de vie de Marc* in France and *grappa* in Italy.

MATURING

Newly fermented wine is raw and murky, and only time will stabilize it. A second fermentation, ideally following shortly after the first, converts malic acid in the wine to lactic acid. This, called malolactic fermentation, makes the wine softer. Malic is the same acid found in apples, lactic the one in milk.

The containers used to store the wine while it ages depend on the type and quality of the wine. Generally, fine red wine and very fine white wine are stored in wooden casks for three months to two years after fermentation, the wood being ideal to the development of its full flavor. Since the kind of wood used in storage barrels affects the final product, some winemakers have changed the character of their product by using wood from a region whose wine they wish to imitate. Other wines, such as light white wines and rosés, are stored in glass- or plastic-lined vats or stainless steel tanks. From the completion of the first fermentation until the wine is in the bottle, it must be treated with an enormous amount of care.

As the wine stands, solid particles fall slowly to the bottom of the container. About every three months, when there is a sufficient accumulation of these lees, the wine is pumped or drained off into clean containers, leaving the residue behind. This process, called racking, is repeated a number of times.

During the aging process, air seeps into wooden barrels and causes evaporation. Since air at the top of the barrel tends to cause premature aging, winemakers fill up each container periodically, a procedure they call topping. Nonporous metal and plastic containers, of course, allow no evaporation.

To remove impurities, the wines are either filtered or fined. Filtering is done by pumping the wine through finely meshed filters or kieselguhr, an earthlike substance. Fining is accomplished by adding an inert material that slowly settles to the bottom of the container, taking with it any solids in the wine. For this, beaten egg whites are still used in Bordeaux. There are other materials serving the same purpose, such as gelatine, isinglass, casein, and Bentonite.

How long should a red wine age in wood? Like many other questions in winemaking, it depends on the desired product. A big, heavy wine will need longer aging than a light one. The minimum would probably be for a Beaujolais, bottled within six months of fermentation, often without benefit of wood storage at all. The average for fine wines would be that of a good vintage Bordeaux, left in a relatively small, forty-five-gallon oak barrel for more than two years to shed its acidity before bottling. Aging in wood is important for white wines too, but over a much shorter period, except for sweet Bordeaux and great Burgundies in a great year.

Tasting always determines when the time for bottling has arrived. Generally, the question is whether or not the wine has lost enough of its acidity in the wood, and has developed balance. If it is left too long, the wine can lose its fruit and become dry or woody.

If a wine is bottled before it is completely stabilized, it will throw off a heavy sediment in the bottle. Usually wine is filtered just before it is bottled, and every precaution is taken to ensure that it goes into the bottle under the most sterile conditions. Modern bottling plants resemble operating rooms. This similarity extends even to the white gowns of the workers and the security of the premises. They have little resemblance to the Bordeaux châteaux that still hand-bottle by gravity, but then sturdy red wines are not subject to the diseases of more fragile white ones.

Your Wine Merchant

The serious wine consumer can easily become quite knowledgeable about wines that suit his palate. Nevertheless, one of the joys that awaits him is the discovery of an experienced and communicative wine merchant.

It is always a pleasure to exchange views with someone who shares your interest in any given field. In wines, this interchange between informed consumer and merchant is particularly rewarding. No one can reasonably expect to taste every wine personally. Nor would it be agreeable to do so, even if it were feasible. Let's face it: some wines are execrable at any price, others are inexpensive "sleepers" that may delight you. The merchant serves the valuable function of screening many of the myriad bottles that arrive in your city from the vintners of California, Algeria or Burgundy. He is in an ideal position to steer you away from lemons—or to direct you to his agreeable finds. Otherwise, you would be restricted to a few safe—and therefore expensive—choices.

There is a second problem that is perhaps even more serious: the wine marketplace never stands still. Superior vintages become unavailable, and new ones take their place. The inexpensive find of yesterday is replaced by another of today, and it should be your wine dealer's sworn duty to keep you *au courant*.

The wine merchant has a respectable lineage to uphold. He is not simply someone who sells you packaged goods from a shelf. He can make a hero or a fool out of you. Of course, it is enlightened self-interest for him to do the former, because he will have gained a permanent customer.

Here in brief is what your wine merchant can do for you:

1. Advise you on your purchase of everyday wines and offer choices that are to your taste, inexpensive, and consistently available. He should sell

this wine by the case at a discount—or in even larger quantity if that is still cheaper.

2. Suggest variety in these daily wines, and propose some seasonal changes (a wine that is satisfying in winter is usually too heavy for summer).

3. Take back defective bottles.

4. Advise you which wines to age. Most people cannot afford to buy a great wine at its peak, but your wine merchant can suggest that you purchase a potential great at an early—and therefore favorable—price and tell you how long to age it.

5. Offer you great and near-great aged wines at favorable prices because you will occasionally want wines that rise above the level of mere good value.

6. Encourage you to taste wine at his shop (unfortunately, this is not legal in some states). He can arrange for you to attend tastings with a guest lecturer, such as those conducted by Les Amis du Vin. Membership in such societies, usually available through the better wine stores, will enhance your knowledge and also enable you to take advantage of special sales. And as an added bonus, you can meet fellow devotees.

Of course, it is not akin to adultery if you check the competition from time to time. Another dealer will sometimes be able to offer château-bottled Bordeaux or estate-bottled German wine at a lower price because he bought it directly from a European outlet or from an importer anxious to reduce his inventory. But a word of caution is in order. Some reduced wine is "distressed merchandise" that has spent too much time in the warehouse and is therefore of dubious quality. One way to make sure that specials are not "distressed" is to insist on pretasting them.

An interesting note for those who live in larger cities: some wine stores specialize in specific types of wines, e.g., estate-bottled German, esoteric Italian, or wines from small independent California wineries.

Depending on your geographic area, the wine merchant you ultimately choose may be so remote that you can visit him only occasionally for large purchases and for the good bottles you want to lay away. In that case do not hesitate to buy standard brands from a more convenient liquor store or supermarket. These outlets usually display different products of a single American winery in one place but group the imports by type. Supermarkets enjoy a rapid turnover, so their cheaper, domestic wines are likely to be fresh. This is not always true of their more expensive wines, which are usually only available in a limited selection anyway. Some supermarkets sell wines under their own private label, and you will have to be the judge of their quality and price.

If you live in a monopoly state that restricts sales to state stores, buying

Some Examples

of Wine Labels

A French Château-bottled Bordeaux Label

The name of the estate (called a château in Bordeaux) on which the wine was grown

"Exceptional Growth"— an official classification

Vintage

The Appellation Contrôlée of the Margaux region of Bordeaux

The owner of the château and address

This means that the wine was bottled at the château that produced it

*Country of origin

*Importer

*Alcoholic strength

The shipper who selected the wine and exported it from France

*Type of wine

*Contents

CHÂTEAU D'ANGLUDET

GRAND CRU EXCEPTIONNEL

APPELLATION MARGAUX CONTROLÉE

1970

Société Civile Viticole du Château d'Angludet · Propriétaire à Cantenac

MIS EN BOUTEILLE AU CHÂTEAU

Produce of France

SHIPPED BY SICHEL & FILS FRERES, NEGOCIANTS - BORDEAUX - GIRONDE

SICHEL

Schieffelin & Co. – New York

RED BORDEAUX WINE

PRODUCED AND BOTTLED IN FRANCE

LIQUID CONTENTS: 1 PINT 8 FLUID OZS   ALCOHOLIC CONTENTS 11.5 % BY VOL.

*Information required by the U.S. government.

A Regional Label: A Burgundy from France

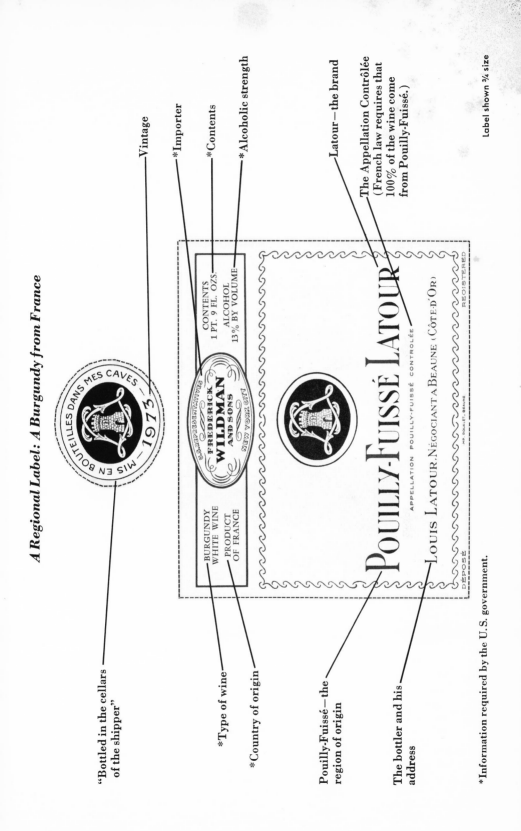

Vintage

*Importer

*Contents

*Alcoholic strength

Latour — the brand

The Appellation Contrôlée (French law requires that 100% of the wine come from Pouilly-Fuissé.)

"Bottled in the cellars of the shipper"

*Type of wine

*Country of origin

Pouilly-Fuissé — the region of origin

The bottler and his address

CONTENTS
1 PT. 9 FL. OZS.

ALCOHOL
13% BY VOLUME

FREDERICK
WILDMAN
AND SONS
NEW YORK CITY

BURGUNDY
WHITE WINE

PRODUCT
OF FRANCE

POUILLY-FUISSÉ LATOUR

APPELLATION POUILLY-FUISSÉ CONTRÔLÉE

LOUIS LATOUR, NÉGOCIANT A BEAUNE (CÔTE-D'OR)

DÉPOSÉ   Mis ROULAT, BEAUNE   REGISTERED

MIS EN BOUTEILLES DANS MES CAVES — 1973

Label shown ¾ size

*Information required by the U. S. government.

A German Regional Label of the Mosel-Saar-Ruwer Region

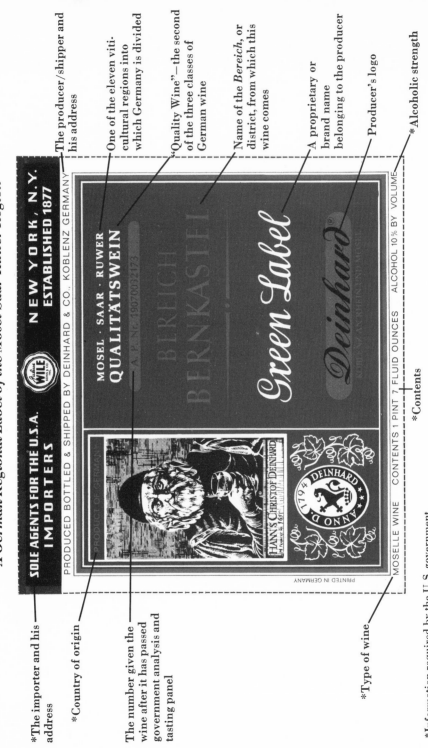

*The importer and his address

*Country of origin

The number given the wine after it has passed government analysis and tasting panel

*Type of wine

*Contents

*Alcoholic strength

Producer's logo

A proprietary or brand name belonging to the producer

Name of the *Bereich*, or district, from which this wine comes

"Quality Wine" — the second of the three classes of German wine

One of the eleven viticultural regions into which Germany is divided

The producer/shipper and his address

*Information required by the U.S. government.

A Proprietary Label for a German Regional Rhine Wine

*Country of origin

The producer/shipper and his address

The number given the wine after it has passed government analysis and tasting panel

*Alcoholic strength

"Quality Wine" – the second of the three classes of German wine

Vintage

A proprietary or brand name belonging to the producer

Liebfraumilch – geographic origin of this Rhine wine

*Contents

*Importer

*Information required by the U.S. government.

A German Estate-bottled Wine Label from an Individual Vineyard

The German equivalent of "estate bottled." It means that the wine was bottled by the grower.

German equivalent of "wine-growing estate"

Vintage
(By German law, a minimum of 75% of the wine must be of the year stated. This will change to 85% in 1976.)

Hipping — the vineyard from which this wine comes

Auslese — designation meaning the wine was made from selectively harvested grapes

The shipper and his address

PRODUCT OF GERMANY

BOTTLED BY — Erzeuger-Abfüllung

Weingut

Franz Karl Schmitt

Nierstein a. Rhein

ESTABLISHED 1549

HERMANNSHOF

Niersteiner Hipping

Riesling Auslese

QUALITÄTSWEIN MIT PRÄDIKAT

A. P. Nr. 4382226/019/72

Shipped by H. SICHEL SÖHNE · MAINZ

R H E I N H E S S E N

1971

Sole United States distributors
S C H I E F F E L I N & C O. · N E W Y O R K
IMPORTERS SINCE 1794

Contents:
1 PINT 7 FL. OZS.

Alcoholic contents:
12% by volume

*Alcoholic strength

*Importer

*Contents

*Country of origin

The producer
(in this case, he is both the grower and bottler of the wine.)

Nierstein — the town from which this wine comes

*Type of wine

Riesling — the grape variety from which this wine was made

"Quality wine with special attributes"— the highest of the three classes of German wine

One of the eleven viti-cultural regions into which Germany is divided

*Information required by the U.S. government.

An Italian Regional Label: A Chianti Classico

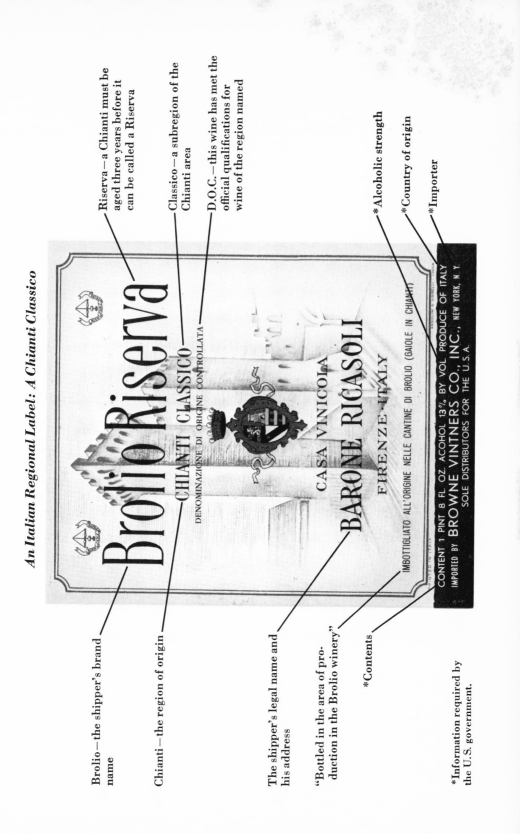

Riserva — a Chianti must be aged three years before it can be called a Riserva

Classico — a subregion of the Chianti area

D.O.C. — this wine has met the official qualifications for wine of the region named

*Alcoholic strength

*Country of origin

*Importer

Brolio — the shipper's brand name

Chianti — the region of origin

The shipper's legal name and his address

"Bottled in the area of pro-duction in the Brolio winery"

*Contents

*Information required by the U.S. government.

A Regional Label: A Rioja from Spain

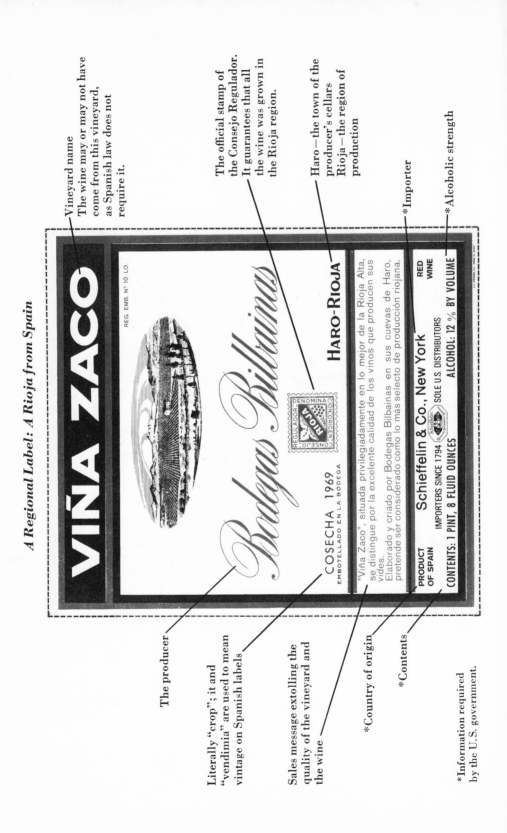

Vineyard name
The wine may or may not have come from this vineyard, as Spanish law does not require it.

The official stamp of the Consejo Regulador. It guarantees that all the wine was grown in the Rioja region.

Haro—the town of the producer's cellars Rioja—the region of production

*Importer

*Alcoholic strength

The producer

Literally "crop"; it and "vendimia" are used to mean vintage on Spanish labels

Sales message extolling the quality of the vineyard and the wine

*Country of origin

*Contents

*Information required by the U. S. government.

VIÑA ZACO

REG. EMB. N° 10·LO.

Bodegas Bilbainas

COSECHA 1969
EMBOTELLADO EN LA BODEGA

HARO-RIOJA

DENOMINACION
CONSEJO REGULADOR
RIOJA

"Viña Zaco", situada privilegiadamente en lo mejor de la Rioja Alta, se distingue por la excelente calidad de los vinos que producen sus vides.
Elaborado y criado por Bodegas Bilbainas en sus cuevas de Haro, pretende ser considerado como lo más selecto de producción riojana.

PRODUCT
OF SPAIN

Schieffelin & Co., New York

IMPORTERS SINCE 1794

SOLE U.S. DISTRIBUTORS

CONTENTS: 1 PINT, 8 FLUID OUNCES

ALCOHOL: 12 % BY VOLUME

RED
WINE

A Varietal Label: A Cabernet Sauvignon from a California Producer

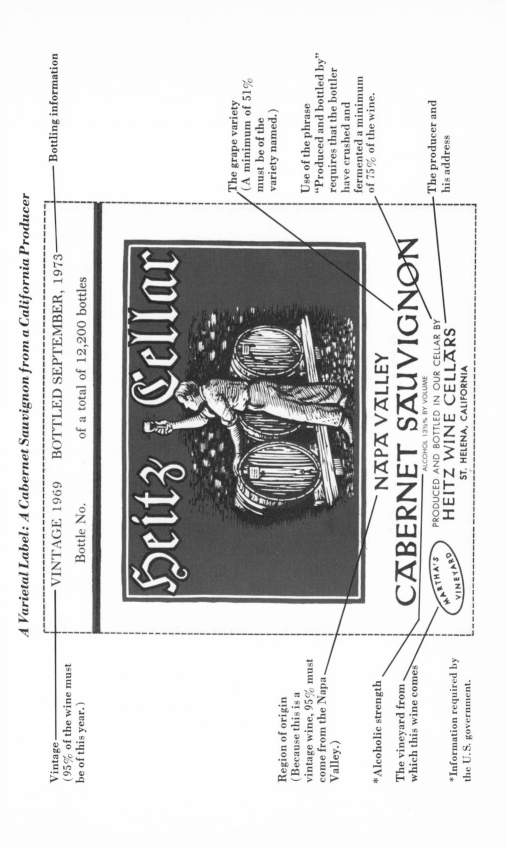

Bottling information

Vintage
(95% of the wine must be of this year.)

VINTAGE 1969   BOTTLED SEPTEMBER, 1973

Bottle No.   of a total of 12,200 bottles

The grape variety
(A minimum of 51% must be of the variety named.)

Use of the phrase "Produced and bottled by" requires that the bottler have crushed and fermented a minimum of 75% of the wine.

The producer and his address

Region of origin
(Because this is a vintage wine, 95% must come from the Napa Valley.)

*Alcoholic strength

The vineyard from which this wine comes

*Information required by the U.S. government.

NAPA VALLEY

CABERNET SAUVIGNON

ALCOHOL 13½% BY VOLUME

PRODUCED AND BOTTLED IN OUR CELLAR BY

HEITZ WINE CELLARS

ST. HELENA, CALIFORNIA

MARTHA'S VINEYARD

A Proprietary Label from a California Producer

A proprietary or brand name belonging to the producer

BAROQUE

PAUL MASSON®

ROBUST RED TABLE WINE

Fine varietal grapes are blended to create this full-bodied red table wine. Rich crimson color and a subtle fruity bouquet are good partners for the robust taste. ❧ Made and Bottled by Paul Masson Vineyards, Saratoga, Calif. Alcohol 12% by Vol.

The producer

The producer and his address

"Made and bottled by" means that a minimum of 10% of the wine was crushed and fermented by the bottler.

*Alcoholic strength

*Information required by the U. S. government.

A Generic, Estate-bottled Label of a California Producer

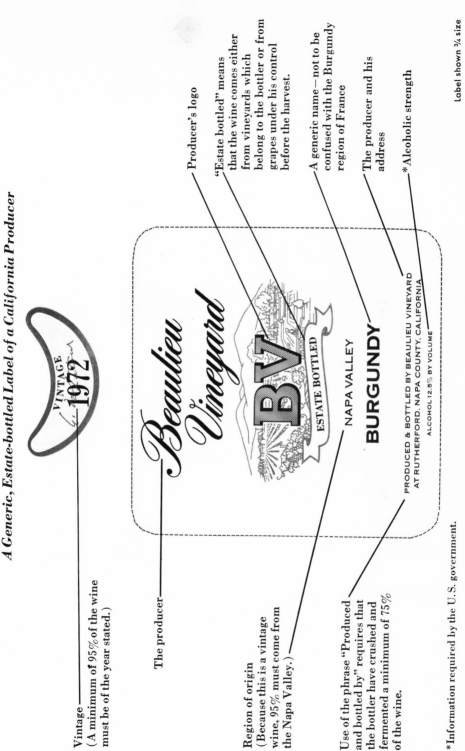

Vintage
(A minimum of 95% of the wine must be of the year stated.)

The producer

Region of origin
(Because this is a vintage wine, 95% must come from the Napa Valley.)

Use of the phrase "Produced and bottled by" requires that the bottler have crushed and fermented a minimum of 75% of the wine.

Producer's logo

"Estate bottled" means that the wine comes either from vineyards which belong to the bottler or from grapes under his control before the harvest.

A generic name — not to be confused with the Burgundy region of France

The producer and his address

*Alcoholic strength

label shown ¾ size

*Information required by the U.S. government.

(Label text)

Beaulieu
Vineyard

BV

ESTATE BOTTLED

NAPA VALLEY

BURGUNDY

PRODUCED & BOTTLED BY BEAULIEU VINEYARD
AT RUTHERFORD, NAPA COUNTY, CALIFORNIA

ALCOHOL 12.5% BY VOLUME

VINTAGE
1972

A Regional Label: A Rioja from Spain

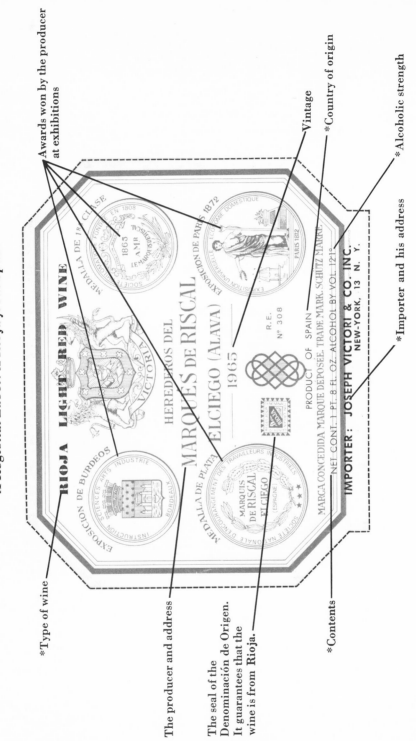

Awards won by the producer
at exhibitions

Vintage

*Country of origin

*Alcoholic strength

*Importer and his address

*Type of wine

The producer and address

The seal of the
Denominación de Origen.
It guarantees that the
wine is from Rioja.

*Contents

*Information required by the U.S. government.

can be a frustrating experience. Some states, such as New Hampshire, operate large self-service supermarkets for wine and liquor offering a wide and ever-changing variety, but others, such as Utah, offer a choice about as varied as a hash-house menu.

Buying wine in the most medieval of the state stores is not unlike filling a prescription in a pharmacy. No product is displayed or advertised. You hand a written request to a civil service clerk, who is not permitted to advise you. In more enlightened states, it is possible to order wines that are not on the approved list but that are sold in the rest of the country—if you buy at least a full case.

Finally, you should be aware that buying wine across a state line and bringing it back into a monopoly state is against the law. If you are caught, it will result, at a minimum, in confiscation of your wine.

GUIDE TO SPECIFIC WINE RECOMMENDATIONS

How to Use the Guide

In this section we present our specific purchase recommendations from three viewpoints: wine-type, price category, and appropriate food. Rather than organize wines in the traditional geographic manner, we have divided them into sixteen types according to taste and style. Within each style, we compare and evaluate wines against one another. For example, our Chianti chapter includes true Italian Chianti, California wines labeled Chianti, and hearty red wines in the same style.

In order to recommend the best wine values generally available, we surveyed the marketplace and established distribution criteria for all American and imported wines sold in the United States. If a wine sold 10,000 cases nationally and/or 1,000 cases in a given market, it was considered to have "general availability." The American wine market is so fragmented that this turned out to be a valid criterion.

Except where otherwise noted, all prices quoted were the retail prices in New York City in the fall, 1975. If you live elsewhere (refer to list of marketing regions, pp. 26–27), prices may be slightly different. Markups, taxes, transportation, and handling charges vary from state to state. Prices should not vary greatly, except in response to normal economic pressures or a fluctuation in crop or market conditions. Usually prices will move in concert with other wines of the same type.

We assumed after tasting that the blends of a winery for their main types would vary little in quality from year to year and it would follow that the quality rankings would remain the same. We will monitor this, of course, for future editions.

Most wines that qualified for our distribution criteria were not vintage-dated, or else vintage was unimportant for their purchase. However, if you find one of our recommended wines in your store that *is* vintage-dated, you can assume it is a good buy, provided you follow our advice on vintage.

Each of the chapters on wine types is presented in the same format. First we give you the characteristics of the type and enough information for you to understand the various wines fitting into the group. Next is a section on vintage, notes on our tastings, and "similar alternatives" to the selections. Each chapter gives you brief food suggestions. The last page in each chapter summarizes the highlights for easy reference. The tasting results appear in chart form; recommended wines are listed according to quality, along with price and distribution information.

On the Tasting Results charts, the ranked wines are presented in three categories: Best Wines at Tasting (BAT), Highly Ranked Wines (HR), and Other Recommended Wines. The wines of this third group are certainly acceptable, sound, and well made. Because the differences in quality are greater within this group, we listed the wines in descending order. Within each of the first two groups, the quality of the wines is close. Therefore, when you see what appears to be a bargain, grab it!

On the left of each Tasting Results chart we give the geographic origin of the wine, its dryness or sweetness (graded *D* for dry, *SD* for semi-dry, *S* for sweet, and *VS* for very sweet), its producer, the name of the wine, and its price. The distribution information is given on the right-hand side of the chart. At the bottom of the chart, when appropriate, we have listed fine wines with very limited distribution but certainly worth seeking.

We have divided the United States into twenty-nine marketplaces, which are coded in the charts as follows:

1. Los Angeles Metropolitan Area
   (Los Angeles–Long Beach)
   (Anaheim–Santa Ana–Garden Grove)
   (Riverside–San Bernardino–Ontario)
2. New York Metropolitan Area
   (New York–Nassau–Suffolk)
   (Jersey City, Newark)
   (Hartford–New Britain–Bristol)
   (Bridgeport–Stamford–Norwalk–Danbury)
3. San Francisco–Oakland
   (San Jose, Sacramento)
4. Chicago
5. Detroit
   (Grand Rapids)
6. Philadelphia–Pittsburgh
7. Boston
8. Miami–Fort Lauderdale
9. San Diego
10. Cleveland
    (Cincinnati, Columbus)
11. Washington, D.C.–Baltimore
12. Seattle–Everett
13. Portland, Ore.
14. Dallas–Fort Worth–Houston
15. Denver–Boulder
16. Tampa–St. Petersburg
17. Jacksonville

18. Milwaukee
19. St. Louis
20. Buffalo–Albany–Rochester– Syracuse
21. Atlanta
22. Minneapolis–St. Paul
23. Fresno–Stockton–Bakersfield

24. New Orleans
25. Providence–Warwick–Pawtucket
26. Honolulu
27. Las Vegas
28. Norfolk–Virginia Beach– Portsmouth
29. Phoenix

For example, if you live in Chicago, you would look for a 4 in the distribution columns to see if a recommended wine is available. Wines listed under "General Availability" sell at least 1,000 cases in a given market; those under "Limited Availability" are sold in the coded cities but sell less than 1,000 cases.

Recommended wines from each chapter, regardless of type, are listed later in the book by price categories. If you are interested in a dry white picnic wine for $2.50, for example, you would simply pick one from the white-wine chart at that price.

There is also a third group of charts, which list appropriate food and wine combinations in greater detail than in the individual chapters on wine types.

If you are unable to find a specific wine on our list, it's either because it did not qualify by distribution or quality or because we overlooked it. Write us[1] if you want us to review a wine you like for our next edition. We will continue to sample new products, and we welcome suggestions.

If you have any fears that you will be left hanging, forget them. By the time you finish this book, virtually all your questions will have been answered. Our intention is to take the mystery out of wine selection. We hope that as your confusion regarding wine lessens the enjoyment you take from it increases.

The Tastings

Before we describe how we went about our tastings, we should state right away that one's judgment at a tasting is subjective and that description is a serious problem. Not everyone uses the classic wine vocabulary in the same way (see Appendix, p. 237).

By writing the importers and producers who we believed handled wine in sufficient quantity to meet our distribution criteria and by scrutinizing

1. Peter M. F. Sichel and Judy Ley, % Harper & Row, 10 E. 53rd St., New York, N.Y. 10022.

the regional *Beverage Media* listings (the monthly trade book of the wine and spirits industry), we compiled a list of qualified wines and computerized the information. From this vast store of facts we selected three thousand wines and, to the dismay of our dentists, proceeded to taste them over a period of eight months.

Our tastings focused on the various wine types we had in mind for this book. Some of the groups worked well, and some did not. For example, we put Gamay Noir, Gamay Beaujolais, and Zinfandel together with French Beaujolais. This grouping proved incompatible, so we ended up dividing it into three separate groups and retasting each. Sometimes so many wines had to be tasted for one wine-type that we had to hold two or three tastings, which included the winners from the previous tasting. We generally tasted forty to sixty wines at a time, which is a tremendous number, but it can be accomplished with a maximum of concentration, a carefully set-up environment, and hard work.

The tastings were blind. We knew only the wine category we tasted. The bottles were covered and distinctive ones decanted to ensure their anonymity. The wines were grouped by price categories, so we could concentrate on one and find the best values in the lot before moving on to the next. At the end we tasted the winners together.

Our panels were composed of professionals and thoughtful consumers, whom we defined as those who drink wine and think about it. Usually we had six to eight people, divided equally between professionals and consumers. We purposely kept the group small to ensure its workability. We balanced the panel as well as we could to avoid inherent taste prejudices; for example, when tasting red Bordeaux and California Cabernets, we had a group of people accustomed to drinking both French and California wines. In all, sixty people assisted us. The "thoughtful consumers" did well. They could tell which were the best, medium, or worst wines. They couldn't tell exactly why they categorized them as such, but the professionals who worked with us could.

In rating the wines, we used a simple grading system of one to ten. Within a price category we would pick out the two or three best wines of the group. As a base for our number rankings, we started with the question of whether the wine was acceptable or if we would send it back in a restaurant. If we came upon a "bad" bottle, we tried a second one. We had two samples of each for just this purpose, either supplied by the industry or purchased by us. After the tasting, we discussed our rankings and recorded the scores, and when there was a controversy, retasted.

We held our tastings in New York, California, and Canada. Outside

New York we used control bottles selected from our New York tastings. For example, the best bottles of Zinfandel from the New York tasting were used as a reference in California.

After we arrived at our recommendations, we again sent forms to the producers and importers seeking exact price and distribution information on the wines listed here. The industry was of enormous help, and we have tried to be as thorough and accurate as possible working in an inexact science.

Purchase Recommendations by Wine-Types

RED WINES

French Red Bordeaux, Bordeaux-style Wines, and California Cabernet Sauvignon

Bordeaux, France

Regional appellations:
    Bordeaux and Bordeaux Supérieur
    Médoc and Haut-Médoc (Margaux,
      St. Julien, Pauillac, St. Estèphe,
      Moulis, and Listrac)
    St. Emilion and Pomerol
    Graves

Spain

Rioja

California

Generic: Claret
Varietal: Cabernet Sauvignon

The great romantic reputation of Bordeaux wine is based on a handful of prestigious châteaux that have made superb wines for many centuries. Their names alone—Lafite, Mouton, Latour, Haut Brion, Margaux—conjure up visions of sparkling crystal, elegant ladies, and heirloom red wine, a world where royalty accepted only the best.

In today's world, the finest red wines are Bordeaux and California Cabernet Sauvignon. Burgundy devotees may challenge this statement, but the quantity, quality, and variety of the Bordeaux-style products of both countries are generally judged superior, and Cabernet Sauvignon is certainly undisputed king of the California red wines. We consider these wines together because they are similar in style and share some of the same grape varieties. The other wines we have included are:

- California wines called Cabernet, whose principal ingredient is Ruby Cabernet.

- California wines called Claret, which are everyday wines similar in style to California Burgundy and California Chianti. The Clarets are usually less smooth and more tannic than the Burgundies, but not as tannic as the Chiantis.
- Red wines from the Rioja in Spain.
- A miscellaneous collection of red wines from other countries that are related by taste.

RED BORDEAUX

Vineyards in Bordeaux are called châteaux and are usually owned by one family. The oldest châteaux date from the 1500s. They were owned by the parliamentarians of Bordeaux and by merchants rich from newly won French colonies. During the French Revolution they fell into disrepair because so many of their customers were on the English side of the British naval blockade. Most of the Médoc châteaux were built between 1830 and 1880 by wealthy merchants, who included such bankers as the Rothschilds, the Foulds, and the Pereires. One of the worst disasters in wine history struck between 1860 and 1880, in the form of a plant louse called *phylloxera* that was accidentally imported from the United States. It devastated the French vineyards, and the cause of the blight was only recognized after it had destroyed two and a half million acres. Since then the fortunes of the great Bordeaux estates have reflected the fortunes of the times.

Château production costs have always been incomparably higher than those of the small peasant grower because château owners cater shamelessly to their grapes (even to planting a rosebush at the end of each row of vines). At harvest time, the châteaux choose only the ripe, healthy grapes and ferment in wood or stainless steel under careful temperature control. Sometimes the owner sits up all night supervising the fermentation, like a husband waiting for the birth of his first child. Châteaux age their wines in small wooden casks, often a fresh set for each vintage. After preliminary aging, a rigid selection is made of the wines that will go into the final blend. The blend is aged until most of the wine has spent at least two years in wood. Often the wine is bottled by gravity alone, lest disturbance from a pump alter its noble character.

Though the public associates Bordeaux wine, particularly red wine, with the names of the great châteaux, their production is only a very small part of the total Bordeaux output. At most, the wines of only two hundred châteaux are familiar to the informed consumer, and usually no more than two dozen are known to him by name, some of these being wines he could rarely afford to drink. The famous and expensive châteaux that have built a reputation over many generations could obviously bring their wine to market without many middlemen, but this is not so for the thirty thousand other growers in Bordeaux. They need the services of the two hundred Bordeaux shippers who do business out of vast cellars and offices overlooking the port. Many of the shippers originally came from the area to which the wine was shipped, as their non-French names make evident: Johnston, Barton, Lawton, Kressmann, Eschenauer, Maehler, Schroeder, Schÿler, and, of course, Sichel. They buy enormous amounts of young wine from small growers, mature it, blend and bottle it, and identify it by their name and the name of the Bordeaux district from where it came. Without them, Bordeaux could never have become a synonym for the world's finest wines.

In 1974, 168,410 acres of Appellation Contrôlée vineyards were under cultivation in the valleys of the Garonne and Dordogne rivers, producing over 24 million cases of red wine and over 12 million cases of white. This makes Bordeaux the largest producer of A.C. wine in France.

Bordeaux is divided into twenty-nine regional appellations, with the wine of each area legally defined to meet certain minimum standards. Since these appellations are based on geography, you might wish to refer to the map of Bordeaux (p. 33) as we explain them. To simplify your understanding of Bordeaux wines, we have grouped the appellations into four broad taste categories. The wines with the designation Bordeaux or a related appellation are the simple basic wines of Bordeaux, whereas the three other categories, Médoc and Haut-Médoc, St. Emilion and Pomerol, and Graves, comprise the fine wines, with each of these appellations having its own champions.

BORDEAUX AND BORDEAUX SUPÉRIEUR

Of the twenty-nine different appellations, fourteen are usually sold not under their own appellations but as Bordeaux or Bordeaux Supérieur and include such appellations as Côte de Castillon, Côte de Blaye, and Premières Côtes de Bordeaux. If well made, they are light and pleasant, but have no great depth, complexity, or individuality. They are good basic red wines, one-dimensional representatives of the Bordeaux taste category.

MÉDOC AND HAUT-MÉDOC

Wines grown in the Médoc region have considerably more style and elegance than the simple Bordeaux. The southern part of the Médoc is the Haut-Médoc, an area with even better soil conditions. Within the Haut-Médoc

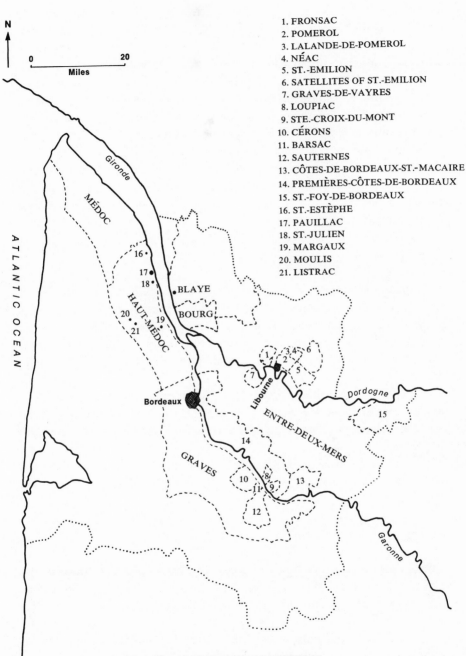

1. FRONSAC
2. POMEROL
3. LALANDE-DE-POMEROL
4. NÉAC
5. ST.-EMILION
6. SATELLITES OF ST.-EMILION
7. GRAVES-DE-VAYRES
8. LOUPIAC
9. STE.-CROIX-DU-MONT
10. CÉRONS
11. BARSAC
12. SAUTERNES
13. CÔTES-DE-BORDEAUX-ST.-MACAIRE
14. PREMIÈRES-CÔTES-DE-BORDEAUX
15. ST.-FOY-DE-BORDEAUX
16. ST.-ESTÈPHE
17. PAUILLAC
18. ST.-JULIEN
19. MARGAUX
20. MOULIS
21. LISTRAC

N

0   20
    Miles

ATLANTIC OCEAN

Gironde

MÉDOC

HAUT-MÉDOC

16
17
18
BLAYE
20
19
BOURG
21

Bordeaux

1
7
2
3,4
5
6
Libourne

ENTRE-DEUX-MERS

Dordogne

15

14

GRAVES

10
8
11
9
13

12

Garonne

WINE PRODUCING REGIONS OF BORDEAUX

six communities make styles of wine differing from the ones made in the total area and therefore invariably sell their wines under their more prestigious names of origin. It is in these six communities that we find almost all the famous châteaux that have made the reputation of the Haut-Médoc. These communities, often called parishes, include Margaux, making wines generally softer and smoother than the others of this area; St. Julien, making wines less soft but with great elegance; Pauillac, where the elegance is coupled with more body; and St. Estèphe, the fullest wines of the area, but which also have more astringency, requiring a longer time to mature. The other two communities, Moulis and Listrac, make wines with more substance but less elegance. Despite the fact that it is across the river and not part of the Médoc region, the wines of the Côtes de Bourg are very similar in style to those of the Médoc.

ST. EMILION AND POMEROL

St. Emilion makes the softest and roundest wines in Bordeaux and the fastest to mature. Wines similar in style, but of less substance, are made in its satellite villages of Lussac, Montagne, Parsac, Puisseguin, Sables, and St. Georges. All these appellations appearing on a label will be hyphenated with St. Emilion (Lussac–St. Emilion) and alert you that the wine is similar to St. Emilion but not as full.

Pomerol, where the wines are even heavier and fuller than the ones made in St. Emilion, is as highly ranked as St. Emilion. Pomerol also has a satellite, Lalande de Pomerol, which makes wines similar in style, but with less finesse.

The two appellations of Côtes de Fronsac and Côtes de Canon-Fronsac, neighboring St. Emilion, make wines similar to St. Emilion and often every bit as good.

GRAVES

The last area is Graves, where the wines are a little fuller than those of the Haut-Médoc but lack their elegance. Only the very best are every bit as fine. The lesser wines here mature faster than their counterparts in the Médoc.

Bordeaux is confusing, since people often buy familiar château names rather than wines with geographic appellations. We want to stress that the only control over quality and origin of a wine in Bordeaux is the regional appellation, not the château name. Even though a famous château might figure prominently on a label, it tells you only where the grapes were grown, where the wine was made, aged, and bottled. It, like its less famous neighbors, must each year pass a test for the right to use the appellation of the area. If the wine of the château fails that test, it can still gain the right to a lower appellation, but no longer uses the château name. To give you an example: Château Latour is in the parish of Pauillac. Should it fail the test for Appellation Pauillac Contrôlée, it can still apply for the test of Haut-Médoc (the next lower appellation and the larger area that includes Pauillac), and (unthinkable thought) should it fail that test too, it could still apply for one entitling it to the name of Bordeaux Supérieur or Bordeaux. However, when château wines are declassified, they usually end up in shippers' blends of regional wines.

All red wines grown in Bordeaux under the Appellation Contrôlée regulations are made exclusively from the following five grape varieties: Cabernet Sauvignon, Cabernet Franc, Merlot, Malbec, and Petit Verdot. Each variety fares better in one soil than in another. For instance, the Cabernet Sauvignon prospers more in the Médoc, and the Cabernet Franc in St. Emilion. Both shy producers per acre, they make wines which are rather tannic and have great finesse, especially the Cabernet Sauvignon. The Merlot, which produces more generously, makes soft, full-bodied wine with little acidity. It is the predominant grape variety in Pomerol, often being used there exclusively. Most of the plantings in Bordeaux are from these three varieties, the Merlot usually being paired with one of the Cabernets in any given vineyard.

The other two varieties are planted only in small quantities, with the thought of having their juice make up for certain deficiencies in the main grape varieties in certain years. The Malbec, a generous producer, yields a round, soft, and rather neutral wine, whereas the Petit Verdot produces a wine of high acidity and high alcoholic content. The separate production of these grapes gives the winemaker the choice he needs to make a balanced and complete wine. Added to this is the fact that the different grapes ripen at different times, making their separate fermentation possible and the final blending easier.

BORDEAUX-STYLE WINES

RIOJA

Spain's finest table wines, called Rioja, resemble Bordeaux more than any other wine-type. They are not made from the classic Bordeaux grapes, but the climate and the vinification and aging techniques give them much in common with Bordeaux.

The 40,000-acre Rioja region in north-central Spain takes its name from the Rio Oja, a tributary of the Ebro. The alluvial soil along the Ebro is too rich to produce a good wine, so grapes in Rioja are grown on less fertile hillsides farther from the river. The three subregions, Rioja Alta, Rioja Alavesa, and Rioja Baja, each produce a distinct style of wine.

Most experts agree that the Rioja Alta produces the best wines, robust, with a moderate degree of alcohol, but we prefer Rioja Alavesa, a fruitier, better-balanced wine from the smallest of the subregions. The Rioja Baja has a much drier climate, making its wines coarser and less acid than their distinguished cousins to the northwest. Because it must be drunk young, most Rioja Baja is restricted to local consumption and does not normally leave the country except as a blend with Rioja Alta.

A government regulatory agency guarantees the authenticity of the Rioja wines with a seal, but this means a good deal less than a French appellation. It does not mean that the wine comes from the subregion on the label, only from the larger region, nor does it guarantee that certain grape varieties are used. In practice, all these wines are Rioja Alta, Rioja Alavesa, or a blend of the two, with, very rarely, a small amount of Rioja Baja added.

The grapes traditionally used are Tempranillo, Graciano, and Mazuelo, indigenous varieties unfamiliar to non-Spanish wine drinkers, and Garnacha, which is apparently the Grenache of France. Riojas are made from a blend of various grape types, in a handful of large wineries called *bodegas*, which buy grapes and young wine from the vineyard owners.

Rioja wine production has been influenced by the French. When the phylloxera epidemic devasted their vineyards late in the 1800s, wine growers from Bordeaux and elsewhere in France emigrated to the Ebro Valley and brought their techniques with them. The subsequent improvement in Riojas was one of the few beneficial results of the disastrous wine blight.

Since that time, however, change has been slow. Most Rioja producers still age their wines in wooden barrels for many years, sometimes for decades, resulting in a woody, oxydized taste that appeals to Spaniards but not the export market. In recent years, some Rioja producers have cut back their aging in wood to two or three years, and their success in foreign sales may result in a trend.

CLARET

For hundreds of years, a light red wine named Clairet was shipped from Bordeaux to England in casks. They drank it within a year after arrival, because wine had to be drunk before it spoiled. Before the science of aging developed, Clairet was palatable in its youth, light in body and texture, with little acidity. A rosé named Clairet is still made in Bordeaux.

The British changed the name to Claret, and still use it as a generic name for the wine they import from Bordeaux, which is no longer light in body or color. The name Claret has been adopted by all the countries that make wine lighter and shallower but similar in style to Bordeaux.

The California Wine Institute describes Claret as a "light-to-medium-in-color wine, tart, of light or medium body." Most California Claret is made from the Ruby Cabernet grape, a plentiful cross between Carignan and Cabernet Sauvignon, which makes wine of fair quality. It is dry and pleasant with no ambition to complexity or style.

CALIFORNIA CABERNET SAUVIGNON

More than 70 percent of all the Cabernet Sauvignon grapes in California are planted in the cooler northern counties of Monterey, Napa, and Sonoma. Some varietal wines are made exclusively from these grapes, but most Cabernet Sauvignon varietals on the market are a blend. In California as in Bordeaux, the second grape is most frequently Merlot, from those same cool counties; it appears rarely as a varietal by itself. Every winery keeps its blending formula secret to prevent imitation of a successful wine, so we do not know which other grapes may be used in varietals labeled Cabernet Sauvignon. Likely candidates besides Merlot are Zinfandel and Ruby Cabernet.

How these producers age their wines has an enormous effect on both their cost and quality. Glass-lined tanks or vats of concrete or stainless steel are regarded as neutral containers, preserving the fruit of a wine, while small wooden casks play a more active role in developing the character. Old wooden casks soften a wine faster, and new ones impart additional acidity but also bring out depth and complexity in the wine. Some producers compromise on aging by blending cask wine with wine aged in large containers.

The wines made almost exclusively from Cabernet Sauvignon are tannic and harsh in youth, requiring a long time to develop in the bottle. In due course, these wines show great elegance and style, but they may take ten years to mature.

An increasing number of California wineries place geographic names on their labels, such as Napa, Sonoma, Monterey, North Coast Counties, Russian River, Alexander Valley, and Pinnacles. Once the present plantings of Cabernet Sauvignon in these areas have reached the maturity essential for character, in perhaps seven years, most of the wine will be made from local grapes and geographic differences in taste will develop, similar to those between the different Bordeaux appellations.

Vintage

Opinion as to when a Bordeaux should be drunk varies from country to country. The French prefer theirs young, with some astringency, fruit, and vigor. The British like theirs old, showing some of the dryness and delicacy of old age; they are annoyed, however, when we refer to this condition as the first blush of death. The Spanish like theirs so old that even the British would reject them. The Americans are in between, preferring a little more age than the French but regarding astringency as a fault.

A word of warning about Bordeaux vintages is in order. The world-famous châteaux have limited production, so greed sometimes induces them to engage in marketing practices that pride should have prevented. Sometimes they label wine from a thin and undistinguished year with the château name or charge exorbitant prices for a decent but not first-class year.

An example: 1963, 1965, and 1968 were rainy years in Bordeaux, with insufficient sun. The grapes were neither ripe nor healthy, many even rotten when they were pressed. Careful selection could have produced a decent thin wine, but many of the famous châteaux, including the acknowledged greatest, bottled a significant portion of their harvest under their names and sold the wine at high prices. Among those victimized were new markets like Japan, which could have only gained a very bad impression of Bordeaux. In general, do not buy château wines from 1963, 1965, or 1968 unless they sell for the same price as the regional Bordeaux appellations.

In 1969, there was just enough sun to give the wine a good color and a not-bad bouquet. The grapes were only partly ripe, so most of the 1969 Bordeaux are somewhat hollow and nasty; their unpleasant acidity disappears with aging, but the lack of fruit remains. This vintage has been selling at a little below the cost of a good year, but should be barely more than a regional wine. Recently, however, prices have started to come down significantly, showing a better relation between price and quality, but they still sell for twice the price of 1970 wines from little-known châteaux of the same area, although, in most cases, the latter are vastly superior. Our advice is to try an unknown Bordeaux from a good year rather than a famous name from a deficient year. Don't buy a case without trying a bottle, unless your wine merchant is more trustworthy than some of the châteaux owners.

In California, we do not have the châteaux to deal with, but the difficulty of separating another kind of fiction from fact. The publicity proclaims that "every year is a vintage year," which is a little California hyperbole, if we may say so. In the Central Valley, with its beautifully laid out irrigation trenches and miles of vines, most years may be good, but this is certainly not the case in the more temperate northern counties of Napa and Sonoma. Though the very finest varietal wines have been made only in small quantities up to now, we believe that with the new plantings enough will be produced to satisfy the great demand for fine wines. As they are produced in larger quantities, vintage years will become as important for a Cabernet Sauvignon from California as it is for a Bordeaux château wine today. Though we are only at the very beginning of "vintage consciousness," the lovers of California wines have long known that 1968 was by far the best year for Cabernet Sauvignon, and most other wines from that year are treasured as much as 1961 from Bordeaux.

We were fortunate in obtaining opinions from Robert Mondavi and Joe Heitz on the Napa Valley vintages, and we want to point out how much we value their judgment. Here is a simplified assessment:

1966—Good year, with well-balanced wines
1967—Lean year, the wines very light in body and character
1968—Outstanding year, the wines having great concentration and balance
1969—Very good year, especially for Cabernet Sauvignon
1970—Good, but not as good as 1968 and 1969
1971—Lean year, the wines light in body
1972—Good year
1973—Very good year
1974—Probably above average, but too early to judge

Vintage information for French and California wines is related to price categories:

Under $4 a bottle. Vintage is probably not important. The California wines are generally nonvintage, and ready to drink when purchased. The French Bordeaux are made to be consumed young and will also be ready to drink when you buy them.

From $4 to $6. Vintage is still of little importance for the California Cabernet Sauvignons; we did not find that those carrying dates were superior to undated wines from the same maker. Although some profit from aging in the bottle, most of them are sold ready to drink. As for Bordeaux in this price range, wines carrying a regional appellation, such as Médoc, St. Emilion, Margaux, or St. Julien, are likely to be ready; they are blended for early consumption. If you find château wines in this bracket, check them against the vintage chart on this page.

Above $6. These wines, both French and American, benefit from aging, so drinking them young would be a waste, albeit interesting. For these more expensive Bordeaux, be guided by the vintage chart. Finer California wines should not be drunk until they are five years old, and more is preferable. It depends a good deal on the style of the wine; Joe Heitz's wines are so big and sturdy that you may not live to see them at their peak, but Robert Mondavi's show an elegance and style rather early, about five years after vintage.

The Rioja wines of Spain require some explanation but little advice. The Spanish word for crop is *cosecha,* and a wine labeled Cosecha 1970 should contain only wine of that vintage. A wine labeled Riserva 1970 will be a blend of vintages of several years that have been aged in wood; it need not contain any 1970 wine at all, but theoretically should be in the style of the year. But watch out—1959 was a disaster for Rioja, a fact that has not deterred one Rioja producer from shipping a Riserva 1959 to this country in an attempt to capitalize on the excellent reputation of that vintage elsewhere.

VINTAGE CHART—RED BORDEAUX*

Vintage Year	Description of Vintage	When to drink
1974	Average-quality crop, good color, sound wines, good fruit, early maturing	1977–1981
1973	Good crop, light, elegant wines with character, early maturing	1976–1984
1972	Light sound wines, lacking in elegance, St. Emilion best of crop	1976–1983
1971	Outstanding, classic big wines, concentrated and long	1977–1992
1970	Excellent crop, with fruit, charm, and character	1975–1990
1969	Light wines, generally lacking character and charm	Until 1979
1968	Bad crop, thin wines, almost rosé	No longer drinkable
1967	Pleasant light wines, a little lacking in fruit, yet sound	Until 1976
1966	Outstanding vintage, big, complete, long, well-balanced wines, great character	Until 1991
1965	Bad crop, very light anemic wines, better than 1963 and 1968	No longer drinkable
1964	Big wines, some lacking acidity, great variations in quality	Until 1984
1963	Bad crop, generally only suitable for rosé	No longer drinkable
1962	Pleasing, clean wines with great character and charm	Until 1980
1961	Superb crop, one of greatest of this century, great concentration, perfect	Until 2000

* This is a general guide when to start drinking a vintage and until when. Small wines will mature quicker, and greater wines might live longer. Underlined vintages should be put away for aging.

Tasting Notes

We tasted this group in several sessions, the last being limited to the more expensive Bordeaux and Cabernet Sauvignon from California. The top category is so rich in diversity that you could find any style you wanted: deep and complex, light and elegant, or sturdy and long. You could spend the rest of your days mining this lode, which is what the enjoyment of wine is all about.

We found that we were able to group the Bordeaux and Cabernet Sauvignon from California into three distinct price and taste categories:

Under $4 a bottle. This covers wines from Bordeaux labeled Bordeaux or Bordeaux Supérieur; wines that bear such names as Cabernet, Cabernet-Merlot, or various brand names such as Club Claret and Mouton-Cadet; some shippers' St. Emilion and Médoc wines; and château wines from Côte de Blaye, Côtes de Bourg, and other of the lesser regions. All these wines have some astringency, good style, usually are ready for drinking when you buy them, and some of them have a little elegance, but generally lack strength, meaning that the taste of the wine does not linger on your palate as you swallow it.

The California wines in this category have more fruit and softness than their French counterparts, do not have the French astringency, but generally lack elegance, their softness ending in a slightly bitter aftertaste.

From $4 to $6. The French wines in this group include both regionals, such as Margaux or St. Julien, and smaller châteaux from the Médoc, Graves, and the Côtes de Bourg. These have more taste than their less expensive brothers in the above category, the astringency has turned to elegance and length, and they show the polish that comes from wood aging. Those from St. Emilion, Pomerol, and their satellites have a richer texture, more flesh and roundness. The California Cabernet Sauvignons in this category also show their aging in wood, have more substance and spice as they move up in price, and have definite elegance and balance. They are somewhat bigger than the French wines and generally not as elegant.

Over $6. As you can imagine, we could hardly wait to taste this category, and we found: (*a*) only a few of these qualified for our distribution criteria because they are made in such small quantities, and (*b*) there was very little difference in the quality of the wines from California and France. They are all wines of individual character showing the style of the winemaker, the vagaries of the weather, and the idiosyncrasies of the grape region. It is a category where price usually increases with quality, but your own taste will dictate your choice of what to buy. In Bordeaux, they are mostly pedigreed château wines, coming from the Haut-Médoc, Graves, St. Emilion, and Pomerol, rarely from one of the satellite appellations. In California, they are made by very small or very select wineries.

RIOJA

We found the less expensive, younger Riojas more to our taste than the older ones made in the traditional Spanish method of lengthy aging in wood, which dries them out, tires them, makes them astringent, and turns them brown. The Riojas under $4 can be as good as Bordeaux or California, but are more astringent, spicier, and wilder in taste. They are never as soft and finished as the California product, never as balanced as the French.

CLARET

The generic Clarets we tasted, wines for everyday consumption, were not as good a value as the popular generic Burgundies, because they are less friendly and appealing, being rather astringent.

Similar Alternatives

Zinfandel.

Congenial Food

In France, Bordeaux is the classical wine for lamb and lamprey, the latter an eel-like fish that prospers in the rivers around Bordeaux and is invariably cooked in red Bordeaux. We can add that all the wines discussed here are best with roasts, steak, game birds, hard cheeses, and pork; Rioja is the traditional wine for suckling pig and country ham. Peter drinks Bordeaux with everything, particularly roast fowl. The bigger wines of Pomerol and California go well with all game as well as all beef dishes.

Notes to Remember

- California Claret is not as satisfactory a daily wine as California Burgundy.
- Rioja under $3.50 is a pleasant wine, particularly if it is not over five years old. The older and more expensive Spanish wines are dried out and not to the North American taste.

- Under $4, Bordeaux have more astringency and elegance than California Cabernet Sauvignon. The California wines are softer, and often a little bitter at the end. In this category, Bordeaux wines are labeled Bordeaux, Bordeaux Supérieur, Médoc, St. Emilion, Côtes de Bourg, small châteaux from all these regions, and Graves.

- From $4 to $6 both Bordeaux and California wines have taste and style, with the California wines being richer and fuller, the Bordeaux more elegant and stylish. Names for Bordeaux wines in this category are regionals from Margaux and St. Emilion, châteaux from Médoc and St. Emilion, Pomerol and Graves.

- Over $6, both California and Bordeaux produce wines of great individuality which must be judged by themselves. There is a wine for every taste. In this category, it is worthwhile buying younger wines and aging them yourself. Select from our lists of recommended châteaux in the Appendix (see p. 251) and the vintage chart.

Tasting Results

FRENCH RED BORDEAUX, BORDEAUX-STYLE WINES, AND CALIFORNIA CABERNET SAUVIGNON—$2.59 & UNDER

Region/ Country of Origin	Dry/Semi-dry/ Sweet/ Very sweet	Producer	Name of Wine	Price	DISTRIBUTION AVAILABILITY BY CITY*		
					General	Limited	None
Best Wines at Tasting							
Calif.	D	Paul Masson Vineyards	Rubion	$2.25	All except→	6, 12, 13, 16, 17, 18, 19, 20, 21, 22, 23, 24, 25, 27, 28	
Highly Ranked Wines							
France	D	A. de Luze	Club Claret	$2.29	2, 4, 5, 14, 19		6, 13, 15, 25, 26, 28, 29
France	D	Dulong	Ecu Royal Claret Reserve	$1.99	All except→	7, 10, 13, 14, 15, 16, 17, 18, 21, 22	6, 9, 12, 19, 23, 24, 26, 27, 29

France	D	Leonard Kreusch	Le Chat Noir Rouge Velouté (½ gal.)	$3.99	All except→	10, 12, 13, 16, 17, 19, 21, 22, 23, 26, 27, 29	6, 9
Calif.	D	Charles Krug Winery	Napa Valley Claret	$2.48		All except→	6, 7, 14, 15, 16, 17, 18, 19, 20, 21, 24, 25, 27, 28
Yugoslavia	D	Adriatica	Cabernet from Istria	$2.59		All markets	

Other Recommended Wines

Calif.	D	M. LaMont Vineyards	California Ruby Cabernet	$1.99	All except→	3, 9, 25	All others
Calif.	D	Almadén Vineyards	California Mountain Red Claret	$1.85	All markets		
Calif.	D	California Wine Association	Fino Eleven Cellars California Claret	$2.09		All except→	14, 15, 16, 17, 21, 27, 28, 29
Argentina	D	Norton	Mendoza Malbec	$2.50	6	2, 11, 13, 14, 15, 20, 25	All others
France	D	Calvet	Calvet Réserve	$1.99	2, 3, 4, 7, 20	1, 8, 9, 11, 14, 15, 16, 17, 21, 27	All others

* See pp. 26–27 for city code.

45

Tasting Results

FRENCH RED BORDEAUX, BORDEAUX-STYLE WINES, AND CALIFORNIA CABERNET SAUVIGNON — $2.60 to $3.59

Region/ Country of Origin	Dry/Semi-dry/ Sweet/ Very sweet	Producer	Name of Wine	Price	DISTRIBUTION AVAILABILITY BY CITY*		
					General	Limited	None
			Best Wines at Tasting				
France	D	Prats	Médoc	$3.39		All markets	
France	D	A. Delor	Cabernet Sauvignon (A.C. Bordeaux)	$3.49	1, 2, 4, 7, 8, 10, 12, 13, 21, 26	All others	
France	D	Austin, Nichols (importer)	Château Guiraud-Cheval-Blanc (A.C. Côtes de Bourg)	$3.25		All markets	
			Highly Ranked Wines				
France	D	Cruse	Bordeaux Roc Rouge	$3.49	1, 2, 4	All others	
			Other Recommended Wines				
France	D	Alexis Lichine	Cabernet Sauvignon	$2.69		All markets	
Chile	D	Viña Undurraga	Cabernet	$2.69		All markets	

Origin		Producer	Wine	Price			
France	D	Prats	St. Emilion	$3.59	All markets		
Calif.	D	California Wine Association	Fino Eleven Cellars California Cabernet Sauvignon	$3.35	All except→		14, 15, 16, 17, 21, 27, 28, 29
Calif.	D	Almadén Vineyards	California Cabernet Sauvignon	$3.10		All markets	
France	D	Barton & Guestier	Prince Noir	$3.49		All markets	
France	D	Alexis Lichine	Médoc	$3.29		All markets	
Argentina	D	Schenley (importer)	Valmont Cabernet Sauvignon	$2.99		2, 4, 8, 10, 11, 12, 14, 16, 20, 21, 23, 28	All others
France	D	Pierre Cartier	Cartier St. Emilion	$3.59		All markets	
Calif.	D	Paul Masson Vineyards	California Cabernet Sauvignon	$2.99	All except→	6	
Calif.	D	Widmer Vineyards	Sonoma/Napa Cabernet Sauvignon	$3.50	20	←All except→	1, 3, 12, 13, 15, 19, 21, 23, 24, 26, 27, 29
France	D	Tytell	Médoc	$3.59		All markets	
France	D	Tytell	St. Emilion	$3.49		All markets	
Argentina	D	Trumpeter	Cabernet-Malbec	$2.99	1, 2, 3, 4, 9, 12, 15, 20, 21, 29	7, 13, 23, 27	All others
France	D	Barton & Guestier	Médoc	$2.99		All markets	

* See pp. 26–27 for city code.

Tasting Results

FRENCH RED BORDEAUX, BORDEAUX-STYLE WINES, AND CALIFORNIA CABERNET SAUVIGNON — $3.60 & OVER

Region/ Country of Origin	Producer	Name of Wine	Dry/Semi-dry/ Sweet/ Very sweet	Price	DISTRIBUTION AVAILABILITY BY CITY*		
					General	Limited	None
		Best Wines at Tasting					
Calif.	Robert Mondavi Winery	Napa Valley Cabernet Sauvignon	D	$6.59	1, 2, 3	All except→	6, 10, 16, 17, 19, 28
Calif.	Korbel & Bros.	California Cabernet Sauvignon	D	$3.95	1, 2, 3	All others	
Calif.	Souverain of Rutherford	Napa Valley Cabernet Sauvignon	D	$7.92		All markets	
France	Ginestet	Pomerol	D	$6.59		All markets	
		Highly Ranked Wines		(L.A.)			
Calif.	Freemark Abbey	Napa Valley Cabernet Sauvignon	D	$6.00		All except→	5, 6, 17, 18, 20, 27, 28
France	Austin, Nichols (importer)	Château Simard (A.C. St. Emilion)	D	$5.49		All markets	
France	Sichel	My Cousin's Claret (A.C. Bordeaux)	D	$3.69		All markets	
France	Ginestet	Médoc	D	$3.98		All markets	
France	Sichel	St. Emilion	D	$4.10		All markets	
France	Dourthe Frères	Grande Marque Bordeaux (A.C. Bordeaux)	D	$3.79		All markets	
		Other Recommended Wines					
Calif.	Louis M. Martini	California Mountain Cabernet Sauvignon	D	$3.99	All except→	14, 16, 17, 19, 21, 22, 24, 25, 28, 29	6
Calif.	Parducci Wine Cellars	Mendocino County Cabernet Sauvignon	D	$4.99	1, 2, 3, 4, 11, 14	←All except→	5, 6, 10, 19, 26

Calif.	D	Beaulieu Vineyard	Napa Valley Cabernet Sauvignon	$4.75	1, 3, 6	←All except→	16, 17
Calif.	D	Simi Winery	Alexander Valley Cabernet Sauvignon	$4.95		All except→	6, 8, 16, 17, 20, 25, 28
France	D	La Bergerie	Mouton-Cadet (A.C. Bordeaux)	$3.99	All except→	5, 9, 12, 17, 18, 19, 20, 22, 23, 28	
France	D	Ginestet	St. Emilion	$4.59		All markets	
France	D	Cruse	St. Emilion "La Garderie"	$4.79	1, 2, 4, 7, 11	All others	
Calif.	D	Cresta Blanca Winery	California Cabernet Sauvignon	$3.90	1, 3, 4, 9, 18	←All except→	6, 7, 8, 16, 19, 24, 25, 26, 28, 29
Calif.	D	Weibel Champagne Vineyards	California Cabernet Sauvignon	$3.95	1, 2, 3, 4, 9, 11, 21, 26, 27	All others	
Calif.	D	Sonoma Vineyards	Sonoma County Cabernet Sauvignon	$3.99		All markets	
Calif.	D	J. Pedroncelli Winery	Sonoma County Cabernet Sauvignon	$3.99	1, 3	2, 4, 7, 9, 10, 12, 13, 14, 15, 22, 23, 24	All others
Calif.	D	Pedrizzetti Winery	Cabernet Sauvignon	$4.79		1, 2, 3, 4, 7, 9, 10, 12, 13, 18, 20, 23, 24	All others
France	D	A. Delor	LaCour Pavillon Médoc	$3.99		All markets	
Calif.	D	Beringer Brothers	Napa Valley Cabernet Sauvignon	$4.79		All markets	
Calif.	D	Christian Brothers	Napa Valley Cabernet Sauvignon	$3.65		All markets	
France	D	Ginestet	Bordeaux Vieux (A.C. Bordeaux)	$3.98		All markets	
France	D	Cordier	Médoc	$4.00		All markets	
Spain	D	Marqués de Riscal	Rioja	$3.98	1, 2, 3, 4, 5, 6, 7, 8, 10, 11, 14, 16, 20	All others	
Spain	D	Paternina	Gran Riserva (Rioja)	$5.35		All markets	
France	D	Dubroca	St. Emilion	$5.75		All markets	

* See pp. 26-27 for city code.

NOTE: We found two California wines in very limited distribution to be of outstanding quality: Sterling Vineyard, Merlot; Oakville Vineyards, Cabernet Sauvignon.

French Red Burgundies, Burgundy-style Wines, and California Pinot Noir

France

Regionals: Red Burgundies
Côtes-du-Rhône
Côte Rôtie
Châteauneuf-du-Pape
Corbières

United States

California
Varietals: Pinot Noir
Pinot St. Georges
Petit Sirah
Carignan
Generics: Burgundy
Wines called Mountain Red
New York State Red Wines

Other Reds

Regionals from Piedmont, Italy
Dāo, Portugal

Burgundy is the red-velvet wine, gorgeous, sensual, and showy. The wines that carry its name are round, pleasant, and easy, conjuring up a feeling of fullness and warmth, softness and smooth drinking. As if this were not enough, Burgundy even has a rival, which adds immeasurably to the fascination of each. Bordeaux, the other classic French red wine, has more tannin and harshness in youth, a complexity you must seek to find, and an infinite elegance that gains with age. Burgundy, on the other hand, is richer in texture, fuller and warmer in both "nose" and taste, with an assumption of sweetness that never comes. The richness and fruit of a Burgundy appear immediately, without the Bordeaux tannin that must be overcome to reach the full treasure.

Comparisons between these two great wines often reach toward the poetic. Bordeaux have often been defined as masculine wines, and Burgundies as feminine. If the music of Bordeaux is Bach, then the music of Burgundy is Brahms, Schumann, and Mendelssohn. If Bordeaux is El Greco, Burgundy is Renoir. Making a cultural leap to the argot of Marshall McLuhan, Burgundy is hot and Bordeaux is cool.

A major difference between the two wines, fiercely extolled by the champions of each, is the fact that Bordeaux is longer-lived and takes longer to reveal its mysteries than does Burgundy. This was not always so; we have tasted sixty- and seventy-year-old Burgundies that had life and substance. In recent decades, the wines have been made to mature more rapidly.

In spite of Bordeaux's more important and distinguished wine production, it has never gained the universal popularity of Burgundy. In an effort to share its success, a host of wines that never saw the duchy of Burgundy and are not made from Burgundian grapes are named Burgundy. Their producers, indulging in the sincerest form of flattery, aspire to imitate the real thing. The final resemblance may be slight, but these wines are closer in texture and style to Burgundy than to Bordeaux.

In this chapter, we have included the whole "Burgundy range": the true French Burgundies, important red wines of the Rhone Valley in France and the Piedmont in Italy, the better and lesser California Burgundies, and, finally, a miscellany of related red wines made in Spain, Portugal, and Israel.

FRENCH RED BURGUNDIES

The red wines of Burgundy come from a valley southeast of Paris, forty miles long and perhaps two miles wide, called the Côte d'Or, the Golden Slope. Aside from the lesser regional products that appear under various names rarely seen in America, this area makes only about 2 million cases of wine a year under a wide range of village and vineyard names, which is only about 10 percent of the Bordeaux production. All these wines are made exclusively from the Pinot Noir grape. Here in its original home, this grape variety, coupled with ideal soil and climate, brings forth one of the great wines of the world.

Burgundy vineyards, unlike those in Bordeaux, are divided among many owners, with each grower usually having only a few rows of vines in different vineyards. Only two dozen owners have enough property to establish their names as prestigious growers and bottlers. Shippers buy Burgundy in small lots, age it, blend a consistent product, and market it under the better-known village names. There are a few growers who have attained a world-famous reputation, such as Domaine de la Romanée-Conti, Comte de Vogüé, Prince de Merode, and Comte de Moucheron, but they are the exceptions. Their production is small compared to the better-known Bordeaux châteaux, and is sometimes spread over several vineyards in several communes.

The names of wines in Burgundy, like all other fine wines in France, are governed by Appellation Contrôlée law, which here not only sets standards for quality, based on geographic areas, but even classifies wine by quality. The best vineyards are accorded the distinction of Grand Cru, the slightly less distinguished ones that of Premier Cru.

The vineyard area of Burgundy has three main subdivisions: the Côte de Nuits in the north, the Côte de Beaune in the central area of the valley, and the Côte Chalonnaise in the south. The Grand Crus come from twenty-one vineyards in the Côte de Nuits and one in the Côte de Beaune. They are identified only by the vineyard name. These are important wines of

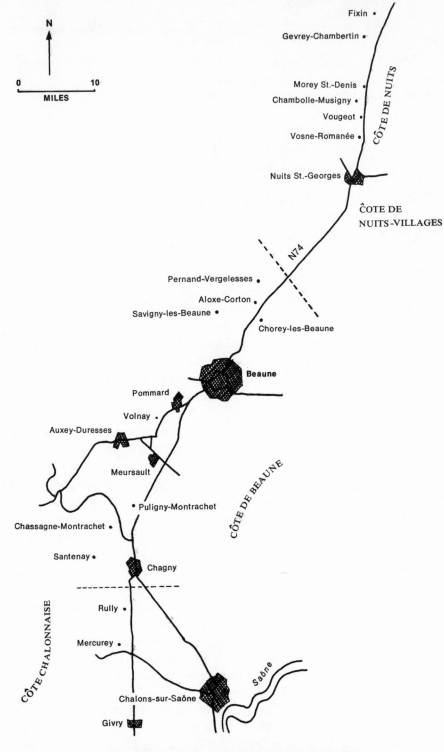

N

0   10
MILES

Fixin •

Gevrey-Chambertin •

Morey St.-Denis •
Chambolle-Musigny •
Vougeot •
Vosne-Romanée •

CÔTE DE NUITS

Nuits St.-Georges •

CÔTE DE
NUITS-VILLAGES

N74

Pernand-Vergelesses •
Aloxe-Corton •
Savigny-les-Beaune •
Chorey-les-Beaune •

Beaune

Pommard •
Volnay •
Auxey-Duresses •
Meursault •

CÔTE DE BEAUNE

• Puligny-Montrachet

Chassagne-Montrachet •

Santenay •
Chagny

CÔTE CHALONNAISE

Rully •

Mercurey •

Saône

Chalons-sur-Saône

Givry •

WINE PRODUCING REGIONS OF NORTHERN BURGUNDY

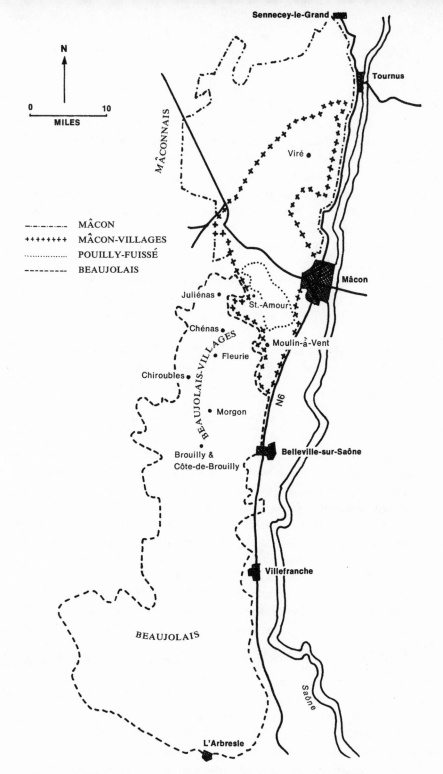

MÂCONNAIS

—·—·—·—·—   MÂCON
++++++++   MÂCON-VILLAGES
··············   POUILLY-FUISSÉ
— — — — —   BEAUJOLAIS

Sennecey-le-Grand

Tournus

Viré •

Mâcon

Juliénas •

St.-Amour

Chénas •

Moulin-à-Vent

Fleurie

BEAUJOLAIS-VILLAGES

Chiroubles •

• Morgon

Brouilly &
Côte-de-Brouilly

Belleville-sur-Saône

N6

Villefranche

BEAUJOLAIS

Saône

L'Arbresle

WINE PRODUCING REGIONS OF SOUTHERN BURGUNDY AND BEAUJOLAIS

53

elegance, depth, substance, and, above all, individuality. Like all great wines, they are long-lived. (See maps, pp. 52–53.)

There are barely 100,000 cases of Grand Cru wine produced in the Côte de Nuits, and half of that comes from the three largest vineyards: 25,000 cases from the Clos de Vougeot, 12,500 from Echézeaux, and 12,000 from Charmes-Chambertin and Mazoyères-Chambertin, which are considered one vineyard. The smaller Grand Cru vineyards each produce between 400 and 5,000 cases under such world-renowned names as Bonnes Mares, Chambertin, Chambertin Clos-de-Bèze, Chapelle-Chambertin, Clos de la Roche, Clos St. Denis, Clos de Tart, Grands Echézeaux, Griottes-Chambertin, La Tâche, Latricières-Chambertin, Mazis-Chambertin, Musigny, Richebourg, La Romanée, Romanée-Conti, Romanée St. Vivant, and Ruchottes-Chambertin. The single Côte de Beaune Grand Cru vineyard, Corton, is at the northern edge of the region and produces about 35,000 cases.

These Grand Cru wines are of limited availability and invariably expensive. The wines bearing village names, however, are produced in greater quantity and are more germane to our purpose. The community names for such red Burgundies are:

Côtes de Nuits: Chambolle-Musigny, Gevrey-Chambertin, Morey St. Denis, Nuits St. Georges, and Vosne-Romanée.

Côte de Beaune: Aloxe-Corton, Auxey-Duresses, Beaune, Chassagne-Montrachet, Chorey-les-Beaune, Côte de Beaune-Villages, Pommard, Santenay, Savigny-les-Beaune, and Volnay.

Côte Chalonnaise: Givry and Mercurey.

Many villages have joined the name of their most famous vineyard to their own to give their other wines more prestige; for example, Chambertin, a Grand Cru vineyard, was added to the village name of Gevrey.

The best village wines carry the name of their Premier Cru vineyards. Such wines carry the communal name first, then the designation Premier Cru followed by the name of the vineyard, like Vosne-Romanée Premier Cru Les Suchots. (Sometimes the vineyard name is *not* preceded by Premier Cru.)

Generally, the wines of the Côte de Nuits have more substance than the lighter, quicker-maturing wines of the Côte de Beaune. The wines of the Côte Chalonnais are sturdy but lack some of the elegance and finesse of those grown in the vineyards to the north.

It is more useful to know the good shippers of Burgundy than to recognize the small number of Burgundy estates. The shippers do their difficult job with competence and sophistication. Though a few of them, like Jadot,

Reine Pédauque, Louis Latour, and Moillard-Grivot, have large vineyard holdings, they all make far better wine than most of the growers from whom they buy young wine or grapes. We have listed in the Appendix those we regard as reputable and consistent (see p. 249).

The production of Burgundy is fragmented, and only a few of the many appellations are produced in enough quantity to be generally available here. Most Burgundy shippers will have a majority of the following appellations, which we list in rising order of quality, in their selections:

- Bourgogne Passe-Tout-Grains, which is made from Gamay and Pinot Noir
- Pinot Noir or Bourgogne Rouge
- Côte de Beaune-Villages
- Côte de Nuits-Villages
- Santenay
- Savigny-les-Beaune
- Mercurey (at 230,000 cases, the largest appellation)
- Chassagne-Montrachet (Though this is better known as a white appellation, the village also produces red wine in some quantity, often sold as Côte de Beaune-Villages.)
- Volnay
- Beaune
- Aloxe-Corton
- Gevrey-Chambertin
- Pommard (often overpriced due to its popularity in the export market)
- Vosne-Romanée
- Nuits St. Georges
- Chambolle-Musigny

Some of the wines bear the label of the Hospices de Beaune. This means that the vineyards that produced the wines were deeded to the Beaune old-age home, the Hospices. They invariably carry the name of the vineyard donor, such as "Cuvée Dr. Pestes," as well as the communal appellation or Premier Cru vineyard designation, if any. These wines are usually very fine, though overpriced. Because they are auctioned before a national television audience, the consumer buys not only the wine but also pays for publicity and makes a contribution to charity.

Some wines are sold under the elaborate label of the Confrérie du Tastevin, an old Burgundian wine brotherhood, the label being accorded to wine that wins approval by a tasting panel. The labels also bear the communal appellation and the name of the shipper.

BURGUNDY-STYLE WINES

RHONE VALLEY

The wines of the Rhone, long associated by proximity and tradition with the wines of Burgundy, are grown south of Burgundy and Beaujolais in a more consistently hot climate. The area produces 14 million cases of pleasant, round, smooth, and rather aromatic wine under the appellation Côtes-du-Rhône.

In France, Côtes-du-Rhône has become a popular replacement for Beaujolais and lighter Burgundies, and we think it is one of the best values in French wine today. It is largely made from Grenache and Syrah grapes. Three villages in the Côtes-du-Rhône—St. Joseph, Cornas, and Gigondas—make wines of more character and style, and sell them under their communal appellations.

Three other areas make wines of distinction and individual character. Côte-Rôtie produces 16,000 cases of a powerful, violet-scented wine; Hermitage 20,000 cases of a deep-colored, strong, long-lived, and aromatic wine made entirely from the Syrah grape. Its satellite, Crozes-Hermitage, produces about 20,000 cases of a wine which is similar but less concentrated and powerful than its noble namesake.

Probably the best-known wine from the Côtes-du-Rhône is Châteauneuf-du-Pape, a powerful, alcoholic, and aromatic wine from vineyards strewn with rocks, which reflect the hot sun against the grapes. About a dozen grape varieties go into the 800,000 cases produced each year, each contributing its spice, flavor, and body.

CALIFORNIA

Plantings of Pinot Noir are now extensive enough to produce 1.8 million cases of wine bearing that varietal name. About three-quarters of this comes, in equal shares, from the cooler counties of Napa, Sonoma, and Monterey. The rest is from San Benito, Santa Barbara, and, to a lesser degree, Mendocino. As they develop, we expect these wines to take on regional characteristics, as the wines of the Côte de Nuits and the Côte de Beaune have. At present, California Pinot Noir lacks the rich texture and fullness of the great French Burgundies. Maybe it will develop more character as the vines gain age. Another grape variety, Pinot St. Georges, makes a varietal that resembles Pinot Noir, although experts claim the grapes are not related.

The Petit Sirah grape is produced in small quantities and is likely to become more important in the future. Grown almost exclusively in the cooler parts of Monterey and Sonoma, it makes a rich, full-bodied, and aromatic red wine, possibly with more character than Pinot Noir. The noted Professor Maynard Amerine of the University of California at Davis considers it a better grape for California than the Pinot Noir. We concur.

The wines labeled California Burgundy, Mountain Red, or Red Wine are an important category both because of the quantity sold and the relative quality; it is the most popular red-wine type in the United States and, at under $2.50 a bottle, represents good value for money. Different grape varieties are used to make these wines. The main variety is probably Carignan, the most widely grown red-wine grape in California, which is also grown in Spain, Algeria, and southern France. It produces large quantities of fairly neutral wine in the hot and irrigated areas of California. Zinfandel is sometimes added to give it character and spice.

Each winery has its own idea of what kind of wine should be labeled Burgundy. Some make more than one style, as the Burgundy and Hearty Burgundy of Gallo, and some wineries market a Burgundy with a degree of sweetness. Carignan also is sometimes sold as a varietal. It tends to have good acidity but is a little wild in taste.

ITALY

The wines of the Piedmont—Barolo, Barbaresco, and Gattinara—have not yet received wide recognition in this country, partly because their quantity is limited. Though they do not closely resemble French Burgundy, they fit this category more closely than any other. They are scarce and pricy, and have a loyal following among devotees of Italian wine. Only perseverance finds them in America, in the stores of the few merchants who pride themselves on their selection of Piedmontese wine.

The Nebbiolo grape dominates winemaking in the Piedmont region, just east of the French border and Barolo is probably Italy's finest wine. It is a big, alcoholic wine, harsh and austere in youth with a tarry taste which gains elegance and delicacy with age, reminding its aficionados of roses and wild violets. For us, it never quite loses its austerity, maybe because it has been enslaved too long in wood. To qualify for its name, Barolo must be aged at least two years in wood and cannot be sold until it is three years old. At four, it can be called Riserva; at five, Riserva Speciale.

North of Barolo is the even smaller area from which comes Barbaresco. It is just a little lighter than Barolo. Barbaresco can be sold after two years, one in wood. After three years it can be called Riserva; after four, Riserva Speciale.

In the neighborhood of these two limited regions, large amounts of less expensive wines, with names like Nebbiolo d'Alba and Nebbiolo di Canale, are produced from the same grapes. They also have a characteristic tarry taste that makes them particularly good with the rare white truffles that also grow in this area.

Farther north near Lake Maggiore, Gattinara is made from the same Nebbiolo grape. Sometimes rivaling the best Barolo in quality, it must be aged at least four years, the first two in wood. This part of the Piedmont also produces a varietal, Spanna, another name for Nebbiolo but with no geographic designation, which lacks the quality of Gattinara, is often dry and coarse, and is less expensive.

Vintage

Among the fine French Burgundies, the wines bearing the name of the Côte de Beaune villages should be ready for drinking three years after the vintage and those from the Côte de Nuits after five years. Both should improve for at least five more years if they come from good vintages.

Wines labeled Premier Cru or carrying the name of a Premier Cru vineyard are normally longer-lived and bigger wines than those carrying only communal village names. Grand Cru wines are, by definition, still bigger, and should never be drunk before they are five years old. They will certainly improve for another six to ten years after that, again if they come from a good vintage.

The vintage chart gives you our best estimate of when the big Burgundies should be drunk.

Among the finer Côtes-du-Rhône wines, Châteauneuf-du-Pape and Crozes-Hermitage are palatable after three years and improve for at least ten years after that, evolving from a heady, alcoholic wine to one with more distinction but less apparent power. Hermitage and Côte Rôtie should really be aged five years before drinking, and will improve for at least another five.

In California, the Pinot Noir and Petit Sirah varietals that cost more than $5 follow about the same maturing schedule as the wines of the Côte de Beaune: three years from vintage until drinking, and about three to five years of improvement during aging after that.

Pinot Noir under $5 a bottle generally has enough aging when it reaches the market and should be drunk soon after purchase. This also applies to the lesser French wines in this category, such as Pinot Noir, Pinot Noir-Gamay, Bourgogne, Bourgogne Grand Ordinaire, Côte de Nuits-Villages, and Côte de Beaune-Villages.

Vintage information is of little or no use for the following wines, which

VINTAGE CHART—RED BURGUNDY*

Vintage Year	Description of Vintage	Côte de Nuits When to Drink	Côte de Beaune When to Drink
1974	Average vintage, some good wines, rather light, early maturing	1977–1981	1976–1980
1973	Large crop, light wines, select carefully	1976–1980	1975–1980
1972	Large and good crop, full-bodied wines, aging quickly	1976–1980	1975–1980
1971	Small and excellent crop, concentrated, long-lived wines	Until 1985	Until 1981
1970	Large and good crop, light, quickly maturing wines	Until 1980	Until 1980
1969	Great year, big, complete, complex wines	Until 1983	Until 1980
1968	Bad crop, wines almost rosé	Too late	Too late
1967	Light, elegant year, great charm, quick maturing	Until 1978	Until 1976
1966	Big, powerful wines, slow maturing	Until 1980	Until 1977
1965	Bad crop, rosé wines largely for local consumption	Too late	Too late
1964	Good wines, rather fat, but lacking acidity	Until 1976	Until 1976
1963	Very light wines, only marginally better than 1965 and 1968	Until 1976	Until 1976
1962	Wines of great elegance, charm rather than body	By 1975/76	By 1975/76
1961	Excellent year, big wines, great concentration	Until 1980	Until 1977

* This is a general guide when to start drinking a vintage and until when. Small wines will mature quickly, and greater wines might live longer. Underlined vintages should be put away for aging.

are ready for consumption when they reach the market: American Burgundy, Red Wine, Mountain Red, Carignan, New York State Red, Côtes-du-Rhône, Languedoc, Corbières, French red wine without appellation, Dão and Spanish, Chilean, and Israeli red wines.

The Piedmont wines need several years of aging to develop properly. Barolo needs the most, but just how much is in dispute. A good Barolo should never be drunk younger than five years, and it should continue to improve for twenty. Barbaresco and Gattinara mature somewhat faster, but additional aging is worth it. These Italian wines are particularly dark when young, taking on an orange cast with age. They should be opened several hours before serving even when old. Though not every year is perfect, there are very few unacceptable ones.

Tasting Notes

We tasted the wines in two price categories: under $3.50 and above. To fill out the lower, less expensive end of the Burgundy category, we tasted a mixed bag of wine from Languedoc and Corbières in southern France, French reds without any identified origin, two Dãos from Portugal, and some New York State reds from hybrid grapes. Most of these wines came in the familiar Burgundy-style bottle and had names or labels indicating that this was the market in which they intended to compete. In the lower category, we liked almost equally the wines from California called simply Burgundy, Côtes-du-Rhône, and Dão from Portugal, as well as some less expensive Pinot Noir from California. They were all pleasant for daily drinking, though with little distinction.

The higher priced category was more complex, particularly since few wines considered top wines from California or France fit into our distribution criteria. In this higher category, the best wines were undoubtedly Châteauneuf-du-Pape from the Rhone, individually made Petit Sirah from California, and some premium or superpremium California Pinot Noir. The Châteauneuf were preferred by the tasting panel over Pinot Noir. The Pinot Noir all seemed a little sweet; by comparison, the Châteauneuf seemed truer. Above $7.50 we tasted a lot of wines which did not meet our distribution criteria and which we therefore do not mention here, largely to define the difference between top California Pinot Noir and French Burgundies.

Similar Alternatives

This is virtually an all-inclusive category, but you might try Cru Beaujolais.

Congenial Food

Red meat, game, soft and smelly cheeses, spicy dishes.

Notes to Remember

- Under $3.50 there are a lot of pleasant wines from California labeled simply California or Napa Burgundy that are good buys. Côtes-du-Rhône is the best buy in imported wines at this price.
- Between $3.50 and $7 we found Châteauneuf-du-Pape the best wine available. California Pinot Noir, though pleasant, does not have the personality. California Petit Sirah is our next choice in this price category.
- French Burgundies have a burnt bouquet, but generally more elegance and style than the Pinot Noir from California, which seems a little sweet and soft.
- Burgundies are difficult to buy, and you must taste them before buying a case. Names and vintage years are often deceiving.
- Look for the following names on French Burgundy bottles if you want good value for money: Mercurey, Côte de Beaune-Villages, Beaune, Gevrey-Chambertin. Be sure to consult our vintage chart.

Tasting Results

FRENCH RED BURGUNDIES, BURGUNDY-STYLE WINES, AND CALIFORNIA PINOT NOIR—$3.50 & UNDER

Region/ Country of Origin	Dry/Semi-dry/ Sweet/ Very sweet	Producer	Name of Wine	Price	DISTRIBUTION AVAILABILITY BY CITY*		
					General	Limited	None
			Best Wines at Tasting				
Calif.	D	Beaulieu Vineyard	Napa Valley Burgundy	$2.99	1, 3, 6	←All except→	16, 17
Calif.	D	Charles Krug Winery	Napa Valley Burgundy	$2.48	1, 2, 3, 4, 5, 9, 12, 13, 23	All others	
			Highly Ranked Wines				
Calif.	D	Paul Masson Vineyards	California Pinot Noir	$2.89	All except→	6	
Calif.	D	San Martin Vineyards	California Mountain Burgundy	$1.59	1, 2, 3, 7, 9, 11, 14, 15, 19, 20, 23, 28	←All except→	5, 6, 10
Calif.	D	Paul Masson Vineyards	California Burgundy	$2.15	All markets		
Calif.	D	Paul Masson Vineyards	Baroque	$2.25	All except→	6, 12, 13, 16, 17, 18, 19, 20, 21, 22, 23, 24, 25, 27, 28	
Portugal	D	Grão Vasco	Dão	$2.99	All except→	9, 12, 14, 15, 16, 17, 18, 19, 22, 23, 25, 26, 27, 29	
France	D	Sichel	Côtes-du-Rhône	$2.89		All markets	
Calif.	D	Pastene	Red Burgundy, California	$1.33	2, 7, 11, 20		All others
Calif.	D	E. & J. Gallo	Burgundy of California	$1.59	All markets		

Tasting Results (continued)

FRENCH RED BURGUNDIES, BURGUNDY-STYLE WINES, AND CALIFORNIA PINOT NOIR—$3.50 & UNDER

Region/ Country of Origin	Producer	Name of Wine	Dry/Semi-dry/ Sweet/ Very sweet	Price	DISTRIBUTION AVAILABILITY BY CITY*		
					General	Limited	None
Calif.	Sebastiani Vineyards	Northern California Mountain Burgundy	D	$1.65	All except→	6, 10, 20, 25	
Calif.	J. Pedroncelli Winery	Sonoma County Burgundy	D	$2.39	1, 3	2, 4, 7, 9, 10, 12, 13, 14, 15, 22, 23, 24	All others
Calif.	Simi Winery	North Coast Carignane	D	$3.00		All except→	6, 8, 16, 17, 20, 25, 28
Calif.	California Growers Winery	California Burgundy (L.A.)	D	$0.99	1, 3	12, 13, 23	All others

Other Recommended Wines

Region/ Country of Origin	Producer	Name of Wine	Dry/Semi-dry/ Sweet/ Very sweet	Price	General	Limited	None
Calif.	G. & D.	Fior Di California Burgundy Scelto Burgundy, California	D	$1.39	All except→	2	14, 15, 19, 21, 24, 26, 27
Calif.	Italian Swiss Colony		D	$1.59	All markets		
Calif.	B. Cribari & Sons Winery	Cribari California Burgundy	D	$1.39	All except→	6, 18, 28	
Calif.	Fetzer Vineyards	Mendocino Carmine Carignane	D	$3.25	1, 3, 15	All others	
Calif.	Cresta Blanca Winery	California Petit Sirah	D	$3.30	1, 3, 4, 6, 9, 18	←All except→	7, 8, 16, 19, 24, 25, 26, 28, 29
Calif.	Almadén Vineyards	California Pinot Noir	D	$3.10	All except→	23, 25	
Calif.	Sonoma Vineyards	California Petit Sirah	D	$2.99	1, 3, 4	←All except→	6, 12, 25

Origin	Code	Producer	Wine	Price			
Calif.	SD	Pastene	Mellow Burgundy, California	$1.33	2, 7, 20, 25	All others	All others
Calif.	D	Louis M. Martini	California Mountain Red Wine	$2.39	1, 3		
Calif.	D	E. & J. Gallo	Hearty Burgundy of California	$1.69	All markets		
Calif.	D	M. LaMont Vineyards	California Burgundy	$1.89	1, 2, 3, 4, 6, 10, 13, 18, 20, 22, 23	9, 25	All others
Calif.	D	Louis M. Martini	California Mountain Burgundy	$2.59	1, 2, 3, 4, 5, 8, 9, 11, 12, 13, 23	All others	
Calif.	D	Christian Brothers	California Burgundy	$2.59		All markets	
Calif.	D	F. Korbel & Bros.	California Burgundy	$2.50	1, 2, 3, 4, 19, 20, 29	←All except→	6, 12
Israel	D	Carmel Wine Company	Avdat Red Wine	$2.29		All except→	5, 6, 8, 9, 12, 13, 16, 17, 21, 23, 29
France	D	Chanson	Côtes du Rhône	$2.59		All markets	
France	D	Delas Frères	Côtes-du-Rhône	$2.99	All except→	11, 12, 14, 15, 16, 17, 18, 19, 22, 23, 25, 26, 27, 28, 29	
Calif.	D	Souverain of Alexander Valley	North Coast Burgundy	$2.95	All except→	5, 6, 8, 10, 13, 16, 17, 21, 24, 26, 27	
Calif.	D	Parducci Wine Cellars	Mendocino County Burgundy	$3.15	1, 2, 3, 4, 11, 14	←All except→	5, 6, 10, 19, 26
France	D	Calvet	Domaine de St. Georges, Côtes-du-Rhône	$3.50		All except→	5, 6, 10, 12, 13, 19, 28, 29
France	D	Thomas Bassot	Pinot Noir Réserve des 3 Glorieuses	$2.99	2, 4, 11, 21	28	All others

* See pp. 26–27 for city code.

63

Tasting Results

French Red Burgundies, Burgundy-Style Wines, and California Pinot Noir—$3.50 & Over

Region/ Country of Origin	Dry/Semi-dry/ Sweet/ Very sweet	Producer	Name of Wine	Price	DISTRIBUTION AVAILABILITY BY CITY*		
					General	Limited	None
			Best Wines at Tasting				
France	D	Chanson	Châteauneuf-du-Pape St. Vincent	$6.45		All markets	
France	D	Delas Frères	Châteauneuf-du-Pape Saint Esprit	$5.99	1, 2, 3, 4, 5, 6, 7, 8, 10, 13, 20, 24, 27, 28	All others	
Calif.	D	Christian Brothers	Napa Valley Pinot Saint George	$3.99		All markets	
Calif.	D	Beaulieu Vineyard	Beaumont Napa Valley Pinot Noir	$4.68		All except→ 5, 6, 8, 10, 13, 16, 17, 21, 26, 27	16, 17
Calif.	D	Souverain of Rutherford	Napa Valley Petit Sirah	$5.00	All except→		
			Highly Ranked Wines				
Calif.	D	Weibel Champagne Vineyards	California Pinot Noir	$3.95	1, 2, 3, 4, 9, 15	All others	
Calif.	D	Louis M. Martini	California Mountain Pinot Noir	$3.99	All except→	6, 10, 14, 16, 17, 18, 19, 21, 22, 24, 25, 28	

Other Recommended Wines

Origin		Producer	Wine	Price	Markets	Markets	All others
Calif.	D	Llords & Elwood	Velvet Hill Pinot Noir, California (L.A.)	$4.50		1, 3, 7, 9, 12, 15, 21, 23, 26, 27, 30	All others
Calif.	D	Sonoma Vineyards	Sonoma County Pinot Noir	$3.99	1, 3, 9	←All except→	6, 12, 25
Calif.	D	Christian Brothers	Napa Valley Pinot Noir	$3.65		All markets	
Calif.	D	Wente Bros.	California Pinot Noir	$3.79		All markets	
Calif.	D	Simi Winery	North Coast Pinot Noir	$4.70		All except→	6, 8, 16, 17, 20, 25, 28
France	D	Sichel	Châteauneuf-du-Pape	$4.89		All markets	
Calif.	D	Mirassou Vineyards	Monterey Pinot Noir	$5.49	All except→	1, 2, 3, 4, 8, 14	
Calif.	D	San Martin Vineyards	California Pinot Noir (L.A.)	$3.50	1, 2, 3	←All except→	5, 6, 10
France	D	Chapoutier	Châteauneuf-du-Pape La Marcelle	$5.99		All markets	
France	D	Cruse	Châteauneuf-du-Pape	$5.19	1, 2, 4, 7, 11	All others	
Calif.	D	Parducci Wine Cellars	Mendocino County Petit Sirah	$4.29	1, 2, 3, 4, 11, 14	←All except→	5, 6, 10, 19, 26
Calif.	D	Souverain of Rutherford	Napa Valley Pinot Noir	$6.00	All except→	5, 6, 8, 10, 13, 16, 17, 21, 24, 26, 27	
Calif.	D	Parducci Wine Cellars	Mendocino County Pinot Noir	$4.99	1, 2, 3, 4, 11, 14	←All except→	5, 6, 10, 19, 26

* See pp. 26–27 for city code.

NOTE: We found the following wines in very limited distribution to be of outstanding quality: Ridge Vineyards, York Creek Petite Sirah; Hanzell, Pinot Noir; Schenley (importer), Domaine Gerin.

Beaujolais

The wine whose name is soft on the ear and gay on the palate.

ORIZET[1]

France

Regional: Beaujolais

Beaujolais is at its best when enjoyed young, and has all the qualities associated with youth, including gaiety. It has a voice of its own, a fully-formed shape, and tolerates an extensive cuisine. Having turned its youth into an asset, Beaujolais has become one of the most popular wines in America. The wines of Beaujolais have the fruit and lightness of white wines, and lack the usual acidity and astringency of the reds. They should be drunk slightly chilled.

Beaujolais comes from a large region south of Burgundy and just north of Lyon, the culinary capital of France (see map, p. 256). The region forms one viticultural area with Mâcon, a district better known for its white Burgundies than its reds (see pp. 52–53, which include white Beaujolais). The soil of the Beaujolais region is granite and clay, rather than the limestone of its neighbor, the Burgundy region, and rolling hills give the vineyards ideal drainage and good sun exposure. Most Beaujolais is made entirely from the Gamay grape, rather than the Pinot Noir, the main grape of red Burgundy. There is, however, some Pinot Noir in the highest-quality Beaujolais, called Cru Beaujolais. The output is large, varying from 75 million to 180 million bottles a year depending on the weather.

The wines of Beaujolais are officially classified by the A.C. laws of France into four categories, listed here in ascending order of quality:

1. *Beaujolais.* It meets the minimum standards for use of the name.

2. *Beaujolais Supérieur.* This is somewhat more restricted in production, and has a slightly higher alcoholic content. Despite its name, Beaujolais Supérieur is no better than Beaujolais. For all practical purposes, the wines are identical, although the Supérieur is permitted slightly less production per acre and must have 10 percent of alcohol instead of the 9 percent for Beaujolais. Although this should make a difference, it does not. The similarity of the two wines is so great that we tend to regard with suspicion anyone who markets a Beaujolais Supérieur, because the label in fact does not denote a higher-quality wine. A number of reputable shippers have succumbed to the ploy of the Supérieur label in the hope that the consumer will go for the Supérieur rather than the Beaujolais. Keep this in mind when you go to the liquor store.

1. L. Orizet, *Les vins de France* (Presses Universitaires de France).

3. *Beaujolais-Villages.* This can only come from one of the thirty-five designated villages in an area where production is even more restricted. It is a real step up from the Beaujolais and the Beaujolais Supérieur. These wines definitely have more elegance, balance, and character than the two lower and more plentiful appellations.

4. *Cru Beaujolais.* The best and most distinctive of this group, it is so highly regarded that it may be sold as red Burgundy, an honor denied the lesser wines of the region. It comes from nine villages: Brouilly, Côte de Brouilly, Chénas, Chiroubles, Fleurie, Juliénas, Morgon, Moulin-à-Vent, and Saint Amour. The name of the village from which the wine comes appears on the label by itself. Each of these villages, and especially Morgon and Moulin-à-Vent, produces wine with individually identifiable characteristics. Some of these wines age well, particularly Moulin-à-Vent and Morgon, unlike the other Beaujolais.

The French have the dubious privilege of drinking enormous amounts of Beaujolais in its early adolescence. The grapes are harvested in September, and on November 15 the new vintage, called Beaujolais-Nouveau, is shipped to Lyon and Paris, decanted into carafes without even benefit of bottling, and consumed chilled by its legion of admirers. The wine is purple, heady, and slightly effervescent, and goes to the head faster than a wine that has been properly stabilized. Like the German Federweise, we find Beaujolais-Nouveau unpleasant, a half-fermented wine that achieves in the stomach of the drinker the maturity that should have been accomplished in the barrel. Its only indication of merit is its many French followers.

In the United States, drinking Beaujolais-Nouveau has been an even poorer bet, despite the promotion campaigns of enterprising importers. What is possible in France, with vineyards close-by and quick consumption assured, is rarely achievable here. Even aboard a chartered Air France jet, this wine just does not travel well, and the retail merchant should shelf-date it, like supermarket milk, keep it under constant refrigeration, and throw it away if it is not sold in four months.

Vintage

Beaujolais is one of the most difficult wine-types to buy intelligently, one reason being that the quality varies much more widely between vintage years than for other wines. When the grapes have not fully ripened, the wines are thin and acid rather than fruity and round. Unfortunately, Beaujolais is one of the few fine wines priced according to the degree of alcohol. The grower earns more if the alcoholic content is high, so that in years when

VINTAGE CHART—BEAUJOLAIS

Vintage Year	Description of Vintage	When to Drink
1974	Uneven, some good and fruity, firmer than 1973	Until 1977
1973	Good, light	Until 1976
1972	Uneven, lacks essential fruit	Until 1976
1971	Good	Until 1976
1970	Very good	Too late

the grapes have not fully ripened, vintners often add an inordinate amount of sugar before fermentation to bring the alcohol level up to the highest point permissible. This makes for a wine that has more alcohol than taste, more bite than fruit.

The delays of book publication make it difficult to provide up-to-date information on a wine that must be drunk young. At this writing, the best Beaujolais year available is 1973, which has fruit and freshness and should still show some of this character well into 1976. The 1974s are light, but some of them should still be good in 1976.

The 1972 Beaujolais vintage included some unripe grapes, and thus some of it shows an undesirable harshness and lack of fruit. The safest thing to do is avoid the year. When this book appears, the 1974 and 1975 Beaujolais should be the most drinkable, but make sure it comes from a reputable estate or is shipped by a reputable shipper. In any case, don't drink Beaujolais more than three years old, except for the Cru villages of Morgon and Moulin-à-Vent, which are generally good from 1963 on.

Tasting Notes

The panel had great difficulty with Beaujolais despite efforts to buy all the major imports available. A mid-1974 tasting of 1971 and 1972 vintages judged the Beaujolais largely old or tired or acid, but we had more luck in a second tasting of 1972 and 1973. Yet even then, some of the less successful shippers of Beaujolais had older vintages still in the stores. Though the wines were correct, they lacked the fruit and charm so essential to this category. As with Chianti, a shipper who has a better turnover of his inventory is likely to have a better Beaujolais on the shelf.

If you buy a recent vintage from a shipper mentioned in the Tasting Results, you should have a Beaujolais worthy of the name. If you buy a vintage more than three years old, you may have a passable red wine but you are more likely to be disappointed.

In September 1974, during our Beaujolais tasting, we tasted a 1973 Beaujolais-Nouveau that was still being sold in New York. It was cloudy and faulty. In a better-informed market the merchant would have withdrawn it from his shelves.

In February 1975, just as we were preparing our manuscript for the printer, we found a Beaujolais-Nouveau in this country which was not just acceptable, but also pretty, and had more substance than the others we had tasted. It was shelf-dated, carrying the following legend on its neck label: "This wine should be consumed before March 1975." The wine was a Beaujolais-Villages 1974, Tirage Primeur (another word for Nouveau), shipped by Prosper Maufoux and imported by the House of Burgundy. This year it will be available in New York and in the future in Ohio, Chicago, and San Francisco. Is this called drinking your words?

Similar Alternatives

The French regard Côtes-du-Rhône, a relatively modest Burgundy-type wine, as an adequate and less expensive alternative (see previous section). Although it lacks the full fruit of Beaujolais, it is fresh and round, and is probably the best value among French red wines available in the United States today.

The lighter Zinfandel (see next chapter), from the northern coastal counties of California, is probably equally suited as a replacement for Beaujolais. Although lacking some of the fruit, it compensates with spice and freshness.

Congenial Food

Slightly chilled Beaujolais is an all-purpose wine that goes with almost all dishes. A light wine, it is better with fowl, veal, hard cheeses like Gruyère, and cold dishes than with heavier food like beef and game. The fuller and richer Morgon and Moulin-à-Vent are the only Beaujolais well suited to heavier food like boeuf bourguignon. The fresh Beaujolais-Nouveau, with its contrived heady fullness, is drunk each November by the French to wash down just about any kind of meal.

Notes to Remember

- Know the four Beaujolais appellations and buy Cru Beaujolais or Beaujolais-Villages whenever possible.
- Don't spend more for Beaujolais Supérieur than for Beaujolais.
- Buy only a vintage Beaujolais (now 1973 or 1974), and if you are in doubt, buy a Beaujolais from a good shipper.
- Drink Beaujolais within three years of the vintage. The exceptions to this are the Cru villages of Morgon and Moulin-à-Vent, which are generally good from 1963 on.
- Unless you're going to Paris, avoid Beaujolais-Nouveau.

Tasting Results

BEAUJOLAIS

| | | | | | DISTRIBUTION AVAILABILITY BY CITY* | | |
Region/ Country of Origin	Dry/Semi-dry/ Sweet/ Very sweet	Producer	Name of Wine	Price	General	Limited	None
			Best Wines at Tasting				
France	D	Louis Jadot	Beaujolais-Villages Jadot	$3.98	All except→	6, 9, 12, 13, 18, 22, 23, 24, 25, 26, 28	
France	D	Sichel	Beaujolais	$3.25		All markets	
France	D	Chanson	Beaujolais-Villages St. Vincent	$3.79		All except→	4
France	D	Browne Vintners (importer)	Château de la Chaize, Brouilly	$3.99		All markets	
France	D	Chanson	Beaujolais	$2.95		All markets	
France	D	Schenley (importer)	Château de Buffavent (Beaujolais Supérieur)	$3.99	All markets		

Highly Ranked Wines

France	D	Louis Latour	Beaujolais Supérieur	$3.95	All markets
France	D	Reine Pédauque	Beaujolais	$2.99	All markets
France	D	Piat	Château de Saint Amour	$4.49	All markets
France	D	Excelsior (importer)	Château des Tours, Brouilly	$2.99	All markets
France	D	Jaboulet-Vercherre	Beaujolais Garelle	$3.69	All markets

Other Recommended Wines

France	D	Joseph Drouhin	Beaujolais-Villages	$3.99	All markets
France	D	Pasquier Desvignes	Marquisat Beaujolais-Villages	$3.99	1, 2, 3, 4, 7, 8, 9, 11, 14, 15	All others
France	D	Cruse	Beaujolais	$3.55	2, 7, 8, 11, 14, 16, 17, 20, 24	All others
France	D	Bouchard Père et Fils	Beaujolais Supérieur	$3.99	All markets
France	D	Barton & Guestier	Beaujolais St. Louis	$3.29	All markets

* See pp. 26–27 for city code.

Zinfandel

California

Varietal: Zinfandel

The origins of Zinfandel, like its exotic name, are shrouded in mystery, but the taste makes a clean-cut statement. It is fruity, spicy, and distinctive. It ranges from light and fruity to deep and full-bodied, from common to aristocratic, ranking next to Cabernet Sauvignon as California's finest red wine. In addition to all these qualities, when well made and priced right it is one of the best buys on the market.

Zinfandel is a member of *Vitis vinifera*, the European family of grapes. It is grown only in California, and among red-wine varieties there it is second in production only to Carignan, an undistinguished blending grape. Just as the Riesling grape is ideally suited to bring out the most from the soil and climate in Germany, Zinfandel is compatible with conditions in California. Not only unique in taste, Zinfandel ranks as one of the most versatile wine grapes in the world.

According to the California Wine Institute, Zinfandel grapes are planted over more than 27,000 acres. About a third of this is in the cooler coastal areas of Mendocino, Monterey, Napa, and Sonoma, the rest largely under irrigation in the hotter Central Valley. The differences in climate and irrigation make for an enormous range in both the volume of production and the style of wine produced. In the cooler climates, where there is little or no irrigation, an acre will produce about 250 cases of wine, while the warmer, irrigated vineyards can yield twice that much. Wine from the low-yield vineyards has much more varietal flavor, concentrated in fewer grapes, and will, like all wines made from noble grapes, improve with age. The wines made from high-yield, irrigated vineyards also have a definite varietal character, though they are lighter in texture and are best drunk young. With such large plantings, in different climatic zones, and with various methods of aging, there is a veritable cornucopia of different styles and flavors under the name of Zinfandel.

Much of the Zinfandel crop never appears under its own name but is used as a blending grape for California Burgundy, port, and rosé, and probably California Claret. We will deal only with red wine labeled Zinfandel, which we feel can be categorized in three styles:

1. *Regular Zinfandel.* This wine is suitable for everyday use and is sold by the gallon and half-gallon as well as by the bottle. It is usually light ruby in color and not overly acid, with a flavor slightly reminiscent of black-

berries. It is often made wholly or partially from grapes from the warmer areas, which accounts for the lack of acidity and relatively slight varietal taste.

2. *Premium Zinfandel*. It is sold principally, but not exclusively, by the bottle. The labels generally indicate the place of origin as one of the cooler climate areas—Napa, Sonoma, Mendocino, or Monterey—or might even specify a smaller area such as Pinnacles or Russian River. These wines are deep ruby in color, with a more pronounced taste than regular Zinfandel, variously described as "mushroom," "bramble," "wild raspberry," "blackberry," or "woodsy." While basically good daily wines, they can be served with confidence on Sunday.

3. *Individual Zinfandels*. These are the finest, made by particular wineries in limited quantities. The skin has been left in the juice longer to extract the last flavor and color, the wine has been aged in wood, and the result is a lovely, distinguished wine. It will develop elegance, polish, complexity, and additional flavor with age, and like Cabernet Sauvignon, it will never be inexpensive.

Vintage

Regular or premium Zinfandel is ready to drink when it appears on the market. It is not likely to improve with age, and in large containers it might actually deteriorate. Ordinarily, wine ages more slowly in large containers, but Zinfandel sold in such containers is likely to come from the warmer climes and have less acidity, and should therefore be drunk at once.

Individual Zinfandel, aged to develop style and complexity, should be at least two years old and is likely to develop its full potential only after the fourth or fifth year, and some improve with even more age. We have tasted Zinfandels from the Sonoma Valley that were almost forty years old but still vigorous, with elegance, style, and complexity, and with no sign of feebleness. Individual Zinfandel is the only category worth aging in your cellar. They cost about $5 a bottle, are always vintage-dated, and usually provide on their back labels valuable information about their style and aging characteristics.

Tasting Notes

We spent considerable time tasting the various Zinfandels and found that this category has more pleasant and agreeable wines than any other wine-type. We decided to compare Zinfandel in blind tastings with Beaujolais, Gamay Beaujolais, and Gamay Noir, to test claims that they are similar. We don't think there is any similarity to these wines in taste, though in style some Zinfandels resembled some Beaujolais in freshness and fruit.

We also discovered, not surprisingly, that Zinfandel's depth, flavor, and substance increases with the price of the wine. Here you get what you pay for.

Similar Alternatives

Premium California Burgundies are sometimes similar because a lot of them are blended with Zinfandel. They are less distinctive, however, their character not so clearly defined. Although they differ in taste, some Gamay Beaujolais from California and some Côtes-du-Rhône are similar to regular or premium Zinfandels.

Congenial Food

Regular Zinfandel, the lightest variety, is an all-purpose red wine. Chilled somewhat below room temperature (twenty minutes in the refrigerator or straight from the cellar), it can be served with chicken, egg dishes, veal, stews, cold meats, and hard cheeses. It is an ideal picnic wine.

Premium Zinfandel can handle more flavorful food, including red meat, as well as the blander dishes listed for the regular wine. The expensive bottles should be reserved for red meat, game, and all cheeses, particularly the soft and pungent ones.

Notes to Remember

- Zinfandel is unique in taste, spicy and fruity.
- It is produced only in California, and ranks as the second-best red wine produced there, after Cabernet Sauvignon.
- There are three styles of Zinfandel: regular, for daily drinking; premium, a step up; and individual, the finest.
- Price correlates with quality.
- Individual Zinfandel is the only one worth aging. Drink the other two when you buy them.

Tasting Results

ZINFANDEL

Region/ Country of Origin	Dry/Semi-dry/ Sweet/ Very sweet	Producer	Name of Wine	Price	DISTRIBUTION AVAILABILITY BY CITY		
					General	Limited	None
			Best Wines at Tasting				
Calif.	D	Ridge Vineyards	California Zinfandel Lytton Springs	$6.00	1	2, 3, 4, 7, 8, 9, 12, 14, 20, 23, 24	All others
Calif.	D	Souverain of Rutherford	Napa Valley Mountain Zinfandel	$4.25	All except→		5, 6, 8, 10, 13, 16, 17, 21, 24, 26, 27
Calif.	D	Buena Vista Winery	Sonoma Zinfandel	$3.25	1, 3	4, 9, 11, 23, 26, 27	All others
			Highly Ranked Wines				
Calif.	D	Sebastiani Vineyards	Sonoma Zinfandel	$2.29	All except→	6, 10, 20, 25	All others
Calif.	D	Inglenook	North Coast Counties Vintage Zinfandel	$2.70	1, 2, 3, 4, 9, 11, 12, 13, 15, 22, 26, 28	All others	
Calif.	D	C. Mondavi & Sons	C. K. Mondavi California Zinfandel	$2.23	1, 2, 3, 4	←All except	6, 7, 11, 16, 20, 22, 24, 25, 27, 28

Tasting Results (*continued*)

ZINFANDEL

| | | | | | DISTRIBUTION AVAILABILITY BY CITY | | |
Region/ Country of Origin	Dry/Semi-dry/ Sweet/ Very sweet	Producer	Name of Wine	Price	General	Limited	None
			Other Recommended Wines				
Calif.	D	San Martin Vineyards	California Zinfandel	$2.25	1, 2, 3, 9	←All except→	5, 6
Calif.	D	Fetzer Vineyards	Mendocino Zinfandel (L.A.)	$3.50	1, 2, 3, 4, 9, 11, 15	All others	
Calif.	D	Parducci Wine Cellars	California Zinfandel	$3.73	1, 2, 3, 4, 11, 14	←All except→	5, 6, 10, 19, 26
Calif.	D	Paul Masson Vineyards	California Zinfandel	$2.49	1, 2, 3, 4, 9, 11, 15, 26	All others	
Calif.	D	Christian Brothers	Napa Valley Zinfandel	$3.15	All markets		
Calif.	D	Cresta Blanca Winery	Mendocino Zinfandel	$3.30	1, 3, 4, 9, 18	←All except→	6, 7, 8, 16, 25, 26, 28, 29
Calif.	D	E. & J. Gallo	Zinfandel, California	$1.99	All markets		
Calif.	D	Italian Swiss Colony	Zinfandel, California	$1.75	All markets		
Calif.	D	Louis M. Martini	California Mountain Zinfandel	$3.19	1, 2, 3, 4, 8, 9, 11, 12, 13, 27	All others	
Calif.	D	Roma Winery	California Zinfandel	$1.69	All except→	3, 5	1, 9, 12, 13, 16, 26, 27
Calif.	D	B. Cribari & Sons Winery	Cribari California Zinfandel	$1.59	All except→	6, 18, 28	14, 15, 19, 21, 24, 26, 27

* See pp. 26–27 for city code.

NOTE: **We found the following wines in very limited distribution to be of outstanding quality:** Mountain Vineyards (Château Chevalier), Zinfandel; David Bruce, Zinfandel.

Italian Chianti, California Chianti, and Related Hearty Reds

Italy	*California*	*Argentina and Mexico*
Chianti	Generic: Chianti	Varietal: Barbera
Chianti Classico	Varietal: Barbera	Hearty red wines
Chianti Riserva	Red wines with Italian names	

Chianti is the wine for young lovers, old bocce players, picnics on the grass, and after-ski ragout, and its price and quality vary as much as the people who drink it. The bottle is easily spotted by its attractive raffia cover, which in America, where handwork is so rare, symbolizes the charm and simplicity of old Europe. It is one of our most popular wines. The word "Chianti" brings to mind a reasonably priced red wine, almost always strong, and deliciously unrefined. In actuality, there are many wines labeled Chianti, and you may want to explore its many variations to find your favorite.

The name Chianti has become confused in the wine drinker's mind because producers have used it to market whatever they think might be popular. Italian Chianti takes on the style preferred by its producer, and within the large and diverse regions of its origin the difference goes from rather light, low-tannin wines to Chianti Classico, a wine of considerable distinction, body, and balance. The best have a bouquet suggestive of violets. Then there are bottles from California labeled Chianti, and other red wines with Italian names which often have only nomenclature in common with the Italian wines. California Chianti is generally hearty, tending to be tart and tannic, for those who like red wine with a bite. To figure out which wines in this broad category are the best values, we also tasted such wines as Barbera, Barberone, and similar wines from other countries.

ITALIAN CHIANTI

The immense Chianti region includes much of the ancient grand duchy of Tuscany, of which Florence was the capital. The production runs to over 13 million cases a year, and is regulated by the Denominazione di Origine Controllata, which is modeled after the French Appellation Contrôlée. There are seven subregions, whose wines range from the rather light Chianti dei Colli Senesi to the full-bodied Chianti Classico. (See map, p. 78.)

Several different varieties of grapes are used in Italian Chianti, of which

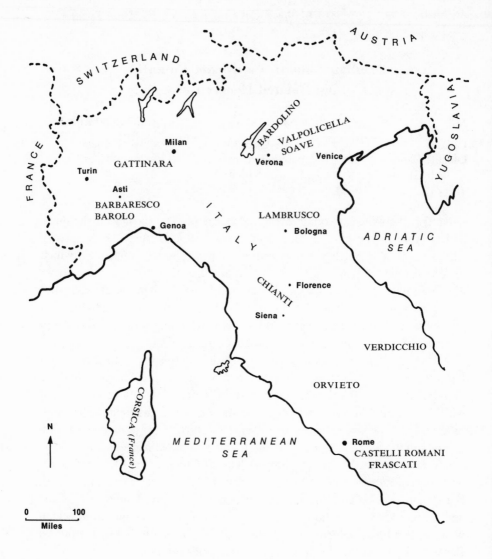

WINE PRODUCING REGIONS OF ITALY

78

the exact proportions are left up to the individual winemaker, within pre-scribed limits. Baron Bettino Ricasoli wrote in the 1850s:

I was convinced by the results of the first experiments, that the wine receives from the Sangioveto grape the most part of its bouquet (to which I particularly aim) and some vigour of sensation; from the Canaiolo it gets the sweetness which moderates the roughness without taking away any bouquet; Malvasia, which could be left out of wines due for long maturation, has a tendency to dilute the products of the first two grapes. It increases the taste and by making it lighter, makes the wine ready for everyday consumption.[2]

The wine still receives most of its bouquet from the Sangioveto grape, and the Canaiolo and Malvasia still play a part, with the addition of Treb-biano Toscano.

Aside from the proportions of different grapes used, there are two basic types of Chianti, which differ markedly in method of preparation, quality, and even traditional bottle style. By far the most prevalent is ordinary Chianti, which is made by the unique *governo* method. About a tenth of the grapes are picked early, dried until they become raisins, pressed late in the year and the juice added to the rest of the already fermented wine. The *governo* treatment produces the necessary second fermentation and gives the wine extra freshness and a slight prickle, or spritz.

Chianti made by the *governo* method is usually bottled in the *fiasco*, the long-necked raffia-covered bottle. Delightfully fresh when young, it is light and inexpensive and the ideal wine for washing down an Italian meal. Rarely a distinguished wine, it deteriorates very rapidly after four or five years. Although the rising cost of the *fiasco* may force Chianti bottlers to turn to a more traditional bottle, for the time being it is also available in a raffia gallon and half-gallon, convenient for daily consumption or for that big party you are planning.

The other type of Italian Chianti is fermented by the standard method and is marketed in the slender, short-necked Bordeaux-style bottle. Most of this type is the Classico, which accounts for about 15 percent of produc-tion, about 2 million cases a year. The Classico ages well, and such bottles permit the horizontal storage necessary for aging. The grapes for Chianti Classico are grown on aristocratic estates, not unlike the Bordeaux châteaux, in a small area between Florence and Siena.

Although the Chianti Classico of each estate has its own character, depending on the soil, location, mixture of grapes, and the wine master, the wines nevertheless resemble each other more consistently than the ordinary

2. Quoted by Lamberto Paronetto in *Chianti* (London, Straker & Sons, 1970).

Chiantis do because each shipper maintains his own uniform style. To make the public more aware of the difference between Chianti and Chianti Classico, growers of the latter have formed an association promoting the use of a neck label bearing a black rooster, but not all the Classico growers use this symbol.

CALIFORNIA CHIANTI

Several California producers use the name Chianti for one of their red wines, but none of them would ever be mistaken for a true Italian Chianti. Pleasant enough in their own way, they are ordinary red table wines. Sometimes they carry Italian names like "Vino Rosso."

BARBERA

A number of California Chiantis contain a proportion of the Barbera grape, which originated in the Piedmont region of northern Italy. There it produces a big, robust wine of deep, almost purple color; an example is Barbera d'Asti. Some wineries in both California and South America market Barbera as a varietal, under the name of the grape.

BARBERONE

This term is used by California producers to describe a particularly robust Barbera, because Barberone means "big Barbera" in Italian. It should be regarded with some skepticism because it has no legal definition and often appears on wine that contains little Barbera at all.

Vintage

The hills of the Chianti region help protect its vineyards, and the mild, consistent weather tends to hold unsuccessful wine years to a minimum. But conditions do vary from year to year, resulting in a smaller rather than an inferior vintage. Reliable shippers do not export the product of a bad year or use it in Chianti that is aged.

Each vintage of Chianti is released annually on March 1. If it is then aged two years, it can be labeled *vecchio*, or old; for three years or more, the designation is *riserva*. All Chianti Classico must be at least two years old. Chianti without a *vecchio* or *riserva* label should be drunk young, like Beaujolais, not more than four years after the date on the bottle.

Vecchio and *riserva*, bought from a dependable shipper and stored correctly, can be considerably older. Twenty-year-old Chianti can have elegance, although such aging tends to impart a thin, harsh quality. To be safe, do not drink *riserva* older than twelve, *vecchio* older than seven, or regular Chianti older than four years.

Regular Chianti, like Beaujolais, can suffer from time lag. These young wines deteriorate markedly when in transit or on the retailer's shelf too long. As a result, the well-known brands that turn over rapidly are better than more obscure competitors, because they are fresher.

Tasting Notes

As we have noted, the panel compared Italian Chiantis with like-named California wines, Barbera, Barberone, and some South American wines that seemed to fit here as well as anywhere. As the style of the wines varied, so did the preferences of individual panel members. Some liked the lighter, fruitier Italian wines. Others liked the deeper, more robust Chiantis. The older Chiantis ranked high with some panelists but were called "tired" by others. As a result, the recommended wines are not all of the same style, but each was sound and well made. Try several to decide which you like the best.

Similar Alternatives

Corbières, a V.D.Q.S. from the Mediterranean slopes in the south of France, a simple hearty red.

Red Côtes de Provence, also a V.D.Q.S. designation, heavier and fuller than Corbières.

Congenial Food

Ruffino, the most popular premium Chianti in the United States, used to advertise the slogan: "If you eat Italian, drink Italian." They were right. Chianti is ideal with spicy dishes, food seasoned with oregano or garlic, the traditional tomato sauces, and Parmesan or Romano cheese. A wine that might be considered harsh and tannic by itself seems soft and silken combined with vigorous Italian food.

Notes to Remember

- There are two different styles of Italian Chianti: the regular, which comes in both a Bordeaux-type bottle and the raffia-covered *fiasco*, and finer wines generally called Classico.
- The regular Chianti is fresh and hearty, and should be consumed young, at slightly colder than room temperature, within four years of the vintage year.
- The Classico lacks the fruit of the regular Chianti, but has more elegance and style.
- California Chiantis are, with California Burgundies and Clarets, the daily reds of America. We prefer Burgundies as daily fare.
- Barbera is a varietal making a rather hearty tannic wine with little charm, but which becomes more pleasant with spicy food. There seemed little difference between California Chianti and varietal Barbera.

Tasting Results

ITALIAN CHIANTI

Region/ Country of Origin	Dry/Semi-dry/ Sweet/ Very sweet	Producer	Name of Wine	Price	DISTRIBUTION AVAILABILITY BY CITY*		
					General	Limited	None
			Best Wines at Tasting				
Italy	D	Ricasoli	Brolio Chianti Classico	$4.55	1, 2, 3, 4, 6, 7, 8, 10, 11, 12, 13, 20	All markets	
Italy	D	Verrazzano	Chianti Classico	$3.99		All others	
Italy	D	Antinori	Santa Cristina Chianti Classico	$3.85		All except→	5, 6, 12, 13, 25, 26
			Highly Ranked Wines				
Italy	D	Ruffino	Chianti	$3.29	All except→	5, 15, 18, 21, 22, 23, 24, 25, 26, 27, 28, 29	12, 13, 14, 19
			Other Recommended Wines				
Italy	D	Antinori	Villa Antinori Chianti Classico	$4.49		All except→	5, 12
Italy	D	Frescobaldi	Castello Di Nipozzano Chianti	$2.99	1, 2, 3, 4, 5, 6, 7, 8, 11	All others	
Italy	D	Melini	Chianti Classico	$3.89		All markets	

* See pp. 26–27 for city code.

Tasting Results

CALIFORNIA CHIANTI AND RELATED HEARTY REDS

Best Wines at Tasting

The panel found no wines in this category.

Highly Ranked Wines

Region/ Country of Origin	Dry/Semi-dry/ Sweet/ Very sweet	Producer	Name of Wine	Price	DISTRIBUTION AVAILABILITY BY CITY*		
					General	Limited	None
Argentina	D	Bodegas y Viñedos López	Rincón Famoso	$2.59	All except→		5, 7, 8, 10, 13, 16, 18, 19, 20, 23, 25, 26, 27, 28, 29
Calif.	SD	G.&D.	Fior di California Barberone (gal.)	$4.99	All except→	2	
Calif.	SD	G.&D.	Fior di California Chianti (gal.)	$4.99	All except→	2	
Calif.	D	Sebastiani Vineyards	North Coast Counties Barbera	$3.00	All except→	6, 10, 20, 25	
Calif.	SD	Roma Wine Co.	Vino D'Uva of California Country Red	$1.35	All except→	3, 5	1, 9, 12, 13, 16, 26, 27
Calif.	D	Louis M. Martini	California Mountain Barbera	$3.19	1, 2, 3	All others	
Calif.	D	Louis M. Martini	California Mountain Chianti	$2.59	1, 2, 3	All others	

Other Recommended Wines

Region	Code	Producer	Wine	Price	Markets	
Argentina	D	Norton	Mendoza Barbera	$2.50	7	2, 11, 13, 14, 15, 20, 25
Calif.	D	E. & J. Gallo	Barbera of California	$1.99	All markets	All others
Calif.	SD	Guild Wine Co.	Tavola Red, California	$1.39	All except→	1, 5, 8, 9, 28
Calif.	D	Italian Swiss Colony	Chianti, California	$1.49	All markets	14, 16, 17, 19, 21, 24, 27
Calif.	D	California Wine Association	Vino Fino California Red Table Wine	$1.29	All except→	14, 15, 16, 21, 28, 29
Calif.	D	Almadén Vineyards	California Chianti	$2.10	All markets	3, 6, 13, 25
Calif.	D	M. LaMont Vineyards	California Barbera	$1.99	1, 2, 4, 9, 10, 11, 16, 20, 22, 23	All others
Calif.	SD	B. Cribari & Sons Winery	Cribari California Vino Rosso Da Pranzo	$1.39	All except→	14, 15, 19, 21, 24, 26, 27

* See pp. 26–27 for city code.

Bardolino and Valpolicella

. . . my own preference is to drink it [Bardolino] young (when it is often a little frizzante) and cool, which is the way that most of it seems to be drunk locally. I have a great fondness for this charming and refreshing wine ever since I found that Max Beerbohm used to take a glass of it every day . . . at what a lesser mortal would have referred to as his teatime.[1]

Italy

Regionals: Bardolino
            Valpolicella

Bardolino, then, could have been responsible for that distortion on the part of Mr. Beerbohm, the great English satirist, when he wrote "sweat started from the brows" of the statues of the Roman emperors at Oxford when they saw his gorgeous Zuleika Dobson.

Bardolino comes from the Verona region of northern Italy that is famous for Romeo and Juliet and, more recently, for the open-air operas presented in its Roman amphitheater. The region produces two other reasonably priced wines of good quality, Valpolicella and Soave. The latter —to our taste, Italy's best white wine—is discussed on pages 147–151. Bardolino and Valpolicella are light, dry reds.

The village of Bardolino is a lakeside resort west of Verona, on the opposite side of the city from the Soave region. Tourists who flock there for the sun and the Verona opera might not even be aware they are on the border of an important wine-producing region. The Bardolino vineyards occupy rolling hills a short distance from Lake Garda, but a smaller sub-region therein called Bardolino Classico produces the best wine. The regular wine and the Classico may be labeled Superiore if they have been aged for a minimum of one year and have attained a slightly higher alcoholic content than the minimum required by law. Higher alcoholic content implies a wine made from riper grapes and therefore a wine with more flavor.

Bardolino comes from relatively unfamiliar grapes, primarily Corvino, secondarily Rondinella, Molinara, and Negrara. They produce a light ruby-red wine, light in body as well as color. We like to say that this wine tastes the way roses ought to taste. It is one of the few dry red wines we know that can be drunk by itself, as Hock and Moselle often are, as an afternoon beverage, ergo Mr. Beerbohm.

Valpolicella is not just a heavier, more full-bodied Bardolino. It is a

1. Cyril Ray, *Wines of Italy* (London, McGraw-Hill, 1966).

finer wine, capable of more nuances of taste and bouquet. Produced just north of Verona, Valpolicella uses the same grapes as Bardolino, but under Italian law it must contain a slightly higher percentage of alcohol and the vineyards must be planted somewhat more sparsely. Both factors have the effect of concentrating the taste of the wine. But Valpolicella differs from Bardolino for other reasons as well: the soil of the region farther from Lake Garda is richer, and its steeper hills give the vines a better exposure to the sun.

The Valpolicella area, like Bardolino, also has a smaller Classico region. And like Bardolino, Valpolicela can be called Superiore if it has been aged a minimum of one year and has a 12 percent alcohol content.

The grapes in both Valpolicella and Bardolino are grown by small farmers. They sell their wine individually or through cooperatives to shippers, who blend and bottle it for the market. Large estates are rare, and we know of no estate-bottling in either region. The two wines are usually sold in the Bordeaux-style bottle, but some shippers use the Chianti *fiasco* with its raffia wrapping to lure consumers who are attracted by quaint packaging.

Vintage

Because Lake Garda moderates extreme temperatures and protects the vines from spring frost, most years for Bardolino and Valpolicella are good years. Italian law permits adding wine from other regions up to 15 percent of the total, so years that have suffered from too much rain or too little sun can be improved by blending in wines from more fortunate vineyards elsewhere.

Both Bardolino and Valpolicella are wines to drink young, Bardolino almost as soon as it is made and certainly before the end of its third year. Valpolicella, especially the Classico, takes a little longer to become ready, being a wine with more flavor. Because freshness is very important, some makers have reduced the time in wooden barrels to preserve the characteristics of young wine. Though some Valpolicellas improve with age, you are safer drinking it young, since freshness and youth are more important than age in this wine.

Tasting Notes

We were somewhat surprised that so popular a category as Bardolino and Valpolicella should have pleased us so little. We tasted them blind, without knowing which was which. Only Peter, guided by the fact that Valpolicella traditionally has more body and Bardolino is a shallower and commoner wine, was able to differentiate correctly between them. They were both rather undistinguished, though the different Valpolicellas were more varied, had more character and more depth. The Bardolinos, on the other hand, all seemed similar. They were pleasant wines, no more and no less. In fact, we felt the Bardolinos, especially considering their price, were particularly lacking in distinction when compared to other red wines we tasted. They would have been more satisfying slightly chilled.

Similar Alternatives

For Bardolino: young Beaujolais or the more commercial varieties of Zinfandel from California.

For Valpolicella: Bordeaux or Bordeaux Supérieur from a good shipper, or Zinfandel from the cooler California counties.

Congenial Food

While these wines can be drunk by themselves, they are ideally suited for delicate dishes, those that a Chianti would overpower. They go well with veal, chicken, cold meats, and hard cheeses such as Swiss, Cheddar, and Provolone. Serve Bardolino slightly chilled, and Valpolicella at room temperature or slightly cooler.

Notes to Remember

- Bardolino and Valpolicella can be disappointing.
- Bardolino is an extremely light wine, so drink it slightly chilled.
- Valpolicella has more substance than Bardolino, and is altogether more satisfying.
- Drink them both young—freshness is more important than age in this category.

BARDOLINO

Region/ Country of Origin	Dry/Semi-dry/ Sweet/ Very sweet	Producer	Name of Wine	Price	DISTRIBUTION AVAILABILITY BY CITY*		
					General	Limited	None
Best Wines at Tasting							
Italy	D	Bertani	Bardolino Classico Superiore	$3.40	2, 8, 11	All others	
Highly Ranked Wines							
The panel found no wines in this category.							
Other Recommended Wines							
Italy	D	Bolla	Bardolino Classico	$3.59	All except→	12, 13, 21, 23	10
Italy	D	Ruffino	Bardolino Classico Superiore	$3.59	2	All others	
Italy	D	Santa Sofia	Bardolino Classico Superiore	$3.25	1, 2, 4, 7 11	All others	
Italy	D	Antinori	Bardolino Classico Superiore	$2.69		All except→	4, 5, 10, 12, 22, 26, 27, 28

* See pp. 26–27 for city code.

Tasting Results

VALPOLICELLA

Region/ Country of Origin	Dry/Semi-dry/ Sweet/ Very sweet	Producer	Name of Wine	Price	DISTRIBUTION AVAILABILITY BY CITY*		
					General	Limited	None
			Best Wines at Tasting				
Italy	D	Bertani	Valpolicella Valpantena	$3.55	2, 5, 7, 8, 11, 14	←All except→	4, 9
			Highly Ranked Wines				
Italy	D	Bolla	Valpolicella Classico	$3.59	All markets		
			Other Recommended Wines				
Italy	D	Masi	Valpolicella Classico Superiore	$3.55	2, 3, 4, 7, 20	←All except→	5, 6, 10, 12, 13, 19, 22, 23, 24, 26, 28, 29
Italy	D	Santa Sofia	Valpolicella Classico Superiore	$3.25	1, 2, 4, 7, 11, 14	All others	
Italy	D	Ruffino	Valpolicella Classico Superiore	$3.59	1, 14	All others	

* See pp. 26–27 for city code.

Two California Varietals: Gamay Beaujolais and Napa Gamay

California

Varietals: Gamay Beaujolais
Napa Gamay

The Gamay Beaujolais and Napa Gamay are two distinct grape varieties, each supposedly producing a different taste in wine. By and large, the wines are pleasant and uncomplicated, but, though meant to be drunk young, they seem to lack fruit. We can describe them best as being in no way as light and fruity as French Beaujolais. They are wines of good substance, and smooth, but lacking clear definition and elegance. They are sold as Gamay Beaujolais, Napa Gamay, and in one case, Gamay Noir.

We tasted these wines together because they are red wines similar in style and illustrate the fact that so often in the wine world the relationship and origin of grape varieties are not clearly known. In this case, the nomenclature alone can be confusing. The grape called Gamay Beaujolais grown in Californa is, according to our information, not the same grape as the Gamay grown in the Beaujolais region of France that produces French Beaujolais. Gamay Beaujolais is actually supposed to be related to the Pinot Noir, which produces a wine that is heavier than Beaujolais. The wine made from the Gamay Beaujolais is actually more akin to the Bourgogne Passe-tout-Grains, an appellation designation in France given to wine made of Gamay and at least 30 percent Pinot Noir. These are wines that have some of the fruit of the Gamay grape but also have body, depth, and balance from the Pinot Noir.

The other Gamay grown in California is the Napa Gamay, often simply called Gamay, and is another distinct grape variety that some claim is the same as the Gamay of the French Beaujolais region. Ampelographers, scientists who define vines, are not quite sure which of the two Gamays resembles the European vine. Regardless of the relationship, however, the soil and weather of California would produce a different wine even if the grape varieties were the same as the Gamay we know in France. Let us not forget that even in France, the Gamay produces an inferior wine in Burgundy proper, whereas in the Beaujolais region it produces a wine of charm and freshness hard to rival.

There are more than three thousand acres of each Gamay planted in the cooler counties of California, which ultimately will produce at least

800,000 cases of Gamay and over 700,000 cases of Gamay Beaujolais. Some of the young wines are blended into Pinot Noir and the better generic Burgundies.

Vintage

Gamay Beaujolais and Napa Gamay, being "uncomplicated" wines, should not differ materially in quality from year to year. By the same token, they should be consumed young, never more than three years from the date on the bottle, if the wine is vintage-dated.

Tasting Notes

We originally tasted the Gamay Beaujolais and the Napa Gamay with French Beaujolais. They had nothing in common. In a separate tasting, the panel judged the California wines straightforward, good, sound reds, the Gamay Beaujolais generally having more substance, the Napa Gamay being a little more shallow. One wine, designated Gamay Beaujolais-Nouveau, an imitation of a French idiosyncrasy, showed more fruit than the rest of the wines, but was not judged superior in any other way.

Similar Alternatives

California premium Burgundy, Beaujolais, Bardolino.

Congenial Food

These wines complement a large variety of roasted meats, fowl, hard cheeses, baked ham, barbecued meats.

Notes to Remember

- Gamay Beaujolais and Napa Gamay are similar in taste, straightforward, uncomplicated red wines, which might profit by being served at slightly cooler than room temperature.
- The younger the wine, the more likely that it will still have some fruit. Shy away from older vintages, and if the wine is not vintage-dated, make sure that it has not been sitting around too long. The more popular brands are likely to be the freshest bottles in your store.

Tasting Results

GAMAY BEAUJOLAIS AND NAPA GAMAY

Region/ Country of Origin	Dry/Semi-dry/ Sweet/ Very sweet	Producer	Name of Wine	Price	DISTRIBUTION AVAILABILITY BY CITY*		
					General	Limited	None
			Best Wines at Tasting				
Calif.	D	Robert Mondavi Winery	Napa Valley Gamay	$3.84	1, 2, 3, 12	←All except→	6, 8, 10, 16, 17, 19, 28
Calif.	D	Fetzer Vineyards	Mendocino Gamay Beaujolais	$3.50	1, 3, 15	All others	
Calif.	D	Monterey Vineyard	Monterey Gamay Beaujolais	$3.40		All markets	
			Highly Ranked Wines				
Calif.	D	Inglenook	Napa Valley Gamay Beaujolais	$3.25	1, 2, 3, 4	All others	
Calif.	D	Christian Brothers	Napa Valley Gamay Noir	$3.15		All markets	
Calif.	D	San Martin Vineyards	California Gamay Beaujolais (L.A.)	$3.00	1, 3, 4	←All except→	5, 6, 10
Calif.	D	Parducci Wine Cellars	Mendocino County Gamay Beaujolais	$3.73	1, 2, 3, 4, 11, 14	←All except→	5, 6, 10, 19, 26
Calif.	D	Almadén Vineyards	California Gamay Beaujolais	$3.10	All except→	10, 16, 17, 22, 23, 25, 29	
			Other Recommended Wines				
Calif.	D	Sebastiani Vineyards	North Coast Counties Gamay Beaujolais	$3.00	1, 3, 4, 9, 14	All others	
Calif.	D	Winemasters' Guild	California Gamay Beaujolais	$2.95		All markets	

* See pp. 26–27 for city code.

93

WHITE WINES

The Chardonnay Grape: French White Burgundies and California Pinot Chardonnay

Burgundy, France

Regionals: White Burgundies

California

Varietals: Pinot Chardonnay
Pinot Blanc

New York State

Varietal: Pinot Chardonnay

The Chardonnay vines produce long bunches of small, translucent golden grapes. They were first grown in the French duchy of Burgundy and derived their name from a village near Mâcon called Chardonnay. This grape variety is the basis for the greatest dry white wines produced in both Burgundy and California. Thus, Burgundy is twice blessed—by growing some of the finest red wines in the world, and by being undisputed king of the dry whites.

As Burgundy's red wines are constantly compared and championed against those of Bordeaux, its whites are challenged by the great Rhines and Moselles of Germany. But the qualities of each are so different that the comparison is irrelevant. While the Burgundies are crisp and bone-dry, the Rhines and Moselles are delicate with a degree of sweetness. The Burgundies are high in alcohol and heady, except for Chablis, while the German wines are light and low in alcohol. Burgundy's production is regrettably small, less than 5 percent of an average German vintage. Whereas red Bordeaux is considered masculine against the feminine softness of red Burgundy, we consider the wines of the Rhine and Moselle feminine versus the whites of Burgundy. The German wines are soft and colorful, charming and complex, but the Burgundies are assertive and all of a piece, lacking the coquettish liveliness of their competitors from the other side of the Rhine. Both are in the truest sense co-equals, the producers of the finest white wines in the world.

FRENCH WHITE BURGUNDIES

The Chardonnay grape produces 3 million cases per year of French white Burgundies from as far north as Chablis to Mâcon and Pouilly-Fuissé in the south (see maps, pp. 52–53). The area encompasses wide differences in climate and topography, producing a great variety of Burgundies. A limited amount of Pinot Blanc is also grown here, and is permitted to be mixed with the Chardonnay in some white Burgundies.

To understand Burgundy, you must know its geography and most important vineyards, all governed by the Appellation Contrôlée system. Each community grows wines with identifiable characteristics. The finer wines are labeled not only with the name of the village but also with the name of the vineyard that produced them. These usually are Premier Cru wines. The best vineyards are designated Grand Cru and carry only the name of the vineyard on the label, except in Chablis.

Four distinct areas in Burgundy produce white wines: Chablis, the Côte de Beaune, the Côte Chalonnaise, and Mâcon. Within these areas the wines take their names from geographic locations: regional (Bourgogne), subregional (e.g., Chablis or Mâcon), communal (e.g., a village such as Meursault or Puligny-Montrachet), or even a specific vineyard within a community (e.g., Puligny-Montrachet les Pucelles).

Very few regionals are exported to the United States and therefore are not important, but subregional and communal names are important because these wines are imported in sufficient quantities to meet our distribution criteria and the geographic information identifies wines of distinct and different character. The important subregionals to know are Chablis and Mâcon. The main communals are Meursault, Puligny-Montrachet, and Chassagne-Montrachet in the Côte de Beaune, and Pouilly-Fuissé in the Mâcon subregion.

We will describe white Burgundy going from north to south.

CHABLIS

One hundred miles southeast of Paris in the northern limit of the Burgundy region is the area of Chablis. The wine-growing area is pretty and hilly, but unfortunately the spring frost and early fall can shorten the growing season. At their best, Chablis are crisp, light, and refreshing wines, with a fleeting elegance and charm. However, the grapes are sometimes barely ripe when harvested, producing wine that is so high in acidity that it never quite loses its green tartness and austerity. Vintage size varies tremendously, as the weather does from year to year, but an average year produces about 365,000 cases. There are four classifications of quality and each has a separate Appellation Contrôlée. Beginning with the best, they are:

Chablis Grand Cru. These wines are heavier in texture than those labeled Chablis, and have great distinction, elegance, and personality. They age well, gaining flavor and balance with time. They come from seven small vineyards with the best drainage and exposure to the sun. The bottle label carries one of the vineyard names: Vaudésir, Les Clos, Grenouilles, Valmur, Blanchot, Les Preuses, or Bougros. (Another Grand Cru Chablis is sold under the property name of Moutonne, which is partly in the Grand Cru vineyards of Vaudésir and Les Preuses.) They produce about 25,000 cases per year, or 7 percent of all Chablis.

Chablis Premier Cru. These wines come from specific Premier Cru vineyards, and the wine is only slightly better than that designated Chablis. The wines usually carry the vineyard name, but sometimes shippers blend the wines of two or more vineyards and identify it simply as Chablis Premier Cru.

Chablis. This wine accounts for nearly half of the total Chablis production. Like Premier Cru, it is greenish-tinged and has a crisp, refreshing, flinty taste. Both wines when young may be too acid in years with insufficient sun, but this has not affected their popularity in the market.

Petit Chablis. The wine is lighter and more common than Chablis, retaining its flavor but having less elegance. It accounts for 15 percent of the crop.

Heading southeast, we come to the main part of Burgundy, the Côte d'Or, the Golden Slope. It is divided into the Côte de Nuits and the Côte de Beaune.

CÔTE DE NUITS

The Côte de Nuits, home of the greatest red wines, produces such a small quantity of outstanding white wines that they are largely curiosities: 800 cases of white Vougeot, 500 cases of white Nuits St. Georges, and 100 cases of white Musigny. The last is a Grand Cru, like its red brother, and can be quite remarkable—big, flavorsome, and expensive.

CÔTE DE BEAUNE

The Côte de Beaune, just south of the Côte de Nuits, produces the great white wines of the region. There are seven Grand Cru vineyards: Bâtard-Montrachet, Bienvenue- Bâtard-Montrachet, Chevalier-Montrachet, Corton, Corton-Charlemagne, Criots-Bâtard-Montrachet, and Montrachet. Their total production rarely reaches 25,000 cases; of this, Corton-Charlemagne accounts for more than half, and Bâtard-Montrachet for 20 percent. All these wines are remarkable and have depth, elegance, and personality that defy description.

Some villages in Burgundy have appropriated the names of nearby famous vineyards, so that lesser vineyards within the village boundaries may profit from the reflected glory. The two best examples are Puligny and Chassagne, which have added the famous name of the Montrachet vineyard to their village names, since the vineyard straddles their communities. Their wines are distinguished but not as exceptional as the Grand Crus. The finer wines in each village come from specific vineyards having the right to the designation Premier Cru, such as Puligny-Montrachet les Pucelles.

Meursault is the other village in the Côte de Beaune whose vineyards produce superior wine. It has no Grand Cru vineyards, but its Premier Cru vineyards, such as Perrières and Charmes, make wines of great distinction, as noble as those of Chassagne-Montrachet and Puligny-Montrachet. Meursault accounts for more than 40 percent of the white wine in the Côte de Beaune, characterized by a nutty, peachy flavor with depth, substance, and strength.

CÔTE CHALONNAISE

The wines of this area, such as Rully and Montagny, are neither well known nor generally available in this country. Though they have less distinction and elegance than the great wines of the Côte de Beaune, they do have charm.

MÂCON

Here, in the southern part of Burgundy, is by far the largest planting of Chardonnay (as many acres as are planted in California), producing more than 1.3 million cases a year. About 70 percent of these carry the name Mâcon, Mâcon Supérieur, or Mâcon-Villages, and the label sometimes bears the name of the village from which the wine comes, such as Mâcon Viré. Similar in style but appearing under a new, politically inspired appellation, St. Véran accounts for another 7 percent of the output. These wines are all crisp, dry, and well balanced, with good varietal characteristics, and among the white Burgundies they are the best value for the money. Because of Mâcon's favorable climate, they are fresh and straightforward, and they do not have the high level of acidity often found in Chablis, though they lack the elegance, lightness, and charm of Chablis made in a ripe year.

The other white wines in the Mâcon area are Pouilly-Fuissé and those of its satellite villages, Pouilly-Loché and Pouilly-Vinzelles. We regard the popularity of Pouilly-Fuissé as out of proportion to its quality; at times these wines have cost twice as much as Mâcon—a case where fashion has created a shortage of supply. Pouilly-Fuissé does have more substance, body, and force than the wines of Mâcon, but we believe that only a price 30 to 40 percent above Mâcon is justified.

The region also produces about 55,000 cases of white Beaujolais, which sells slightly above the price of Mâcon, but shows greater lightness and elegance. This wine is charming and refreshing without being unduly acid.

A warning about the difference between shipper-bottling and estate-bottling is in order here. Burgundy is historically an area of small property holdings in which a single grower may own only a few rows of vines in one or more vineyards. Therefore, there are very few properties that make enough wine under one appellation to sell their wine as estate-bottled. Thus, most white Burgundy is bottled by shippers, who assemble wines from properties having the right to the same appellation, and who are better able to stabilize and bottle them than the small grower. This is particularly true in the case of white wines, which are much harder to stabilize than reds. However, two dozen estates, such as Le Flaive and Marquis de LaGuiche, have built a reputation for superb wine, which is sold in small quantities at, of course, premium prices. Unless the estate has a deserved reputation, such as those listed in the Appendix (p. 248), it is safer to buy from a dependable shipper. You may miss the one-in-a-dozen superb bottle, but you won't be disappointed by faulty treatment.

CHARDONNAY AND AGING METHODS

Before we proceed to California, we should discuss methods of aging, an important factor contributing to different styles of wine made from the Chardonnay grape.

Chardonnay has little identity in its youth, but develops bouquet, complexity, and often distinction during aging. Aging methods vary widely. Chardonnay sold in large commercial volume with little ambition to individuality is usually stored in large glass-lined vats or stainless steel tanks with a minimum of air exposure. The wine is bottled within a year of vintage to preserve its freshness and charm.

Chardonnay with more breeding and style, however, may be kept in small cooperage, oak casks of sixty gallons, for as long as two years to bring out the character of the wine. Often winemakers compromise between these two aging extremes, blending container and cask wines.

With rising concern for quality among California winemakers, aging in wood has become fashionable there, even to the extent of preferring certain kinds of oak. The wine that is put in wood must have the character to profit from wood aging. For example, if you store a fresh young Mâcon Blanc in wood for two years, it oxidizes, becomes tired, and loses its prettiness. However, a short exposure to wood can give it roundness and mellow its crispness. Finer and more expensive wines are partially aged in wood, with the finest aged exclusively in small barrels. If it were stored in large containers, a great Meursault would not develop its nuttiness and power but would remain flat and one-dimensional.

Aging in small wooden barrels is expensive because of the additional equipment and labor needed, and we may reasonably assume that most Chardonnay sold for less than $4 or even $5 a bottle has probably seen little wood.

CALIFORNIA PINOT CHARDONNAY

There are two types of Chardonnay bottlers in California, not unlike the shippers and estates in Burgundy. The large commercial wineries offer a consistent product at a consistent price, from $3 to $4.50 a bottle in the present market. This is not surprising when you consider that there are 7,000 acres of Chardonnay grapes planted in California, which should yield at least 1.7 million cases per year by 1976. There are also small, specialized wineries that make only a few types of wine from their own vineyards or those of carefully selected growers. Their product is equivalent to estate-bottled wines. They are finer, more costly, and vary from year to year depending on conditions.

These two classes of California Chardonnay can be as different as Chablis from Meursault or Mâcon from Puligny-Montrachet. Just as you would expect, wines from the big producers tend to be light, less woody, and less acid, while products from the small wineries, at their best, have more depth, force, and complexity. Choosing between them depends on your preference and the occasion at which the wine is to be served.

Vintage

Like all great grape varieties, Chardonnay gains immeasurably with age. It should not be drunk too young, and its best wines should be aged in the bottle to develop their full potential. Following the maxim "The greater the wine, the longer it takes to develop," we will start with the least important of the Chardonnay wines.

In the California group, price equates with quality. A wine over $4 and those that are vintage-dated should be at least three years old and should continue to improve for at least six years from the vintage date. Any wine under $4 should be ready to drink when purchased.

Among the French wines, the following should be ready to drink when sold:

Mâcon	Petit Chablis
Mâcon-Villages	Chablis
St. Véran	Pouilly-Fuissé and its satellites
Beaujolais Blanc	

These wines should have at least three years total in barrel and bottle:
Chablis Premier Cru
Meursault
Puligny-Montrachet

These should be at least four years old and will improve in the bottle up to six or seven:
All Grand Cru wines
Chablis Grand Cru
Meursault Premier Cru
Chassagne-Montrachet and Puligny-Montrachet Premier Cru

Good white Burgundy years are 1966, 1967, and 1969–72. Lacking in acidity, and therefore not to be kept too long, are 1964 and 1973. Too little sunshine made the 1965 and 1968 vintages acid, lacking fruit.

VINTAGE CHART—WHITE BURGUNDY
CÔTE DE BEAUNE

Vintage Year	Description of Vintage	When to Drink
1974	Uneven, some good wine	1977–1980
1973	Fair	1976–1980
1972	Good, but rather uneven	1976–1980
1971	Good, full-bodied	1976–1981
1970	Excellent, elegant	Until 1979
1969	Very good	Until 1979
1968	Mediocre	Too late
1967	Good	Until 1976
1966	Excellent, strong	Until 1976
1965	Mediocre, some respectable wines	Too late
1964	Good, rather soft	Until 1977
1963	Mediocre	Too late
1962	Nice, pleasant wines	Until 1977

VINTAGE CHART—CHABLIS

Vintage Year	Description of Vintage	When to Drink
1974	Good	1977–1980
1973	Good, but tend to lack acidity	1976–1979
1972	Fair, high acidity	1976–1979
1971	Very good	Until 1980
1970	Very good	Until 1979
1969	Fine	Until 1978
1968	Fair, high acidity	Too late
1967	Good	Until 1977
1966	Excellent	Until 1977
1965	Poor	Too late
1964	Good	Until 1977
1963	Poor	Too late
1962	Good	Too late

Tasting Notes

We tasted about one hundred wines at several different blind sessions, the last of which was limited to eighteen wines at a seated tasting where results could be freely compared. The styles of Chardonnay differed considerably. Those that saw little or no wood were fresh and crisp, and had a good fruity acidity and a lightness and charm all their own. Most of these wines are below $5, and they include a considerable range of French and California wines even in the $3.50 to $4.50 range. These included Chardonnay from the larger premium California wineries as well as French wines labeled Mâcon, Mâcon-Villages, Beaujolais Blanc, Pinot Chardonnay-Mâcon, Petit Chablis, and Chablis. Wines over $5, on the other hand, usually have seen more wood, and some have been in wood a long time. Wood gives the wines broadness, making them heavier and sturdier, but at the expense of fruit. Fashion, according to a California winemaker we respect, forces many wineries to leave their wines in wood so long that many of them sacrifice their charming fruit. Ultimately, the public has to decide if this fashion should continue. Lenin said that people vote with their feet; the wine drinker votes with his palate.

We found two unfortunate faults in our tasting: a smell of sulphur in the French Chardonnays, particularly the more expensive, and the semi-spoiled state called maderization in a number of wines from both France and California.

Sulphur is used as a preservative and stabilizer in wine and a disinfectant for casks and other storage equipment, but it should never be noticeable to the taste. The use of too much sulphur can produce a smell like volcanic vapor or rotten eggs, giving the wine an unpleasant "nose," a slightly prickly sensation. Ordinarily, the smell disappears quickly once the wine is poured and aired.

Maderization occurs in wines that are past their prime. The wine takes on a brownish tinge and an aroma and flavor reminiscent of Madeira, indicating that it is over the hill. We found too many Chardonnays that were maderized, a condition that could reflect unripe grapes, faulty storage, faulty bottling, or wine kept too long in small cooperage.

One of the most difficult wines to buy is a top white Burgundy. We bought ten, each costing over $10, in stores in New York and found most of them disappointing. There is hardly any other wine that suffers so much from bad storage, so it is important to know the shipper or estate and to buy from a store with a good turnover and reputation. The same problem existed with the more expensive California wines. We found a considerable difference in quality in some wines from the same winery in the same year. They could have come from different casks or different bottlings of the same wine. Somehow all the best Chardonnays and white Burgundies share this problem. When the best wines are good, they are superb, but since they develop their full potential after several years, they can suffer in storage. If you buy more than one bottle, you must pretaste the wine.

By and large, these problems do not exist in wines that cost less than $5. We found them to be generally fresher and fruitier than the more expensive ones. French wines under $5 were definitely crisper and more acid than the broader California wines at the same price. The individuality of wines over $5 made comparisons difficult between those from France and those from California. Each had its own personality and style, and personal preference heavily influenced judgment.

Similar Alternatives

Perhaps Sauvignon Blanc, a high-quality white wine from Bordeaux, the upper Loire Valley, and the northern coastal counties of California, where it often is labeled Fumé Blanc.

Congenial Food

The lighter wines, such as Chablis, Mâcon, and California Pinot Chardonnay under $4, are ideal with shellfish, particularly lobster, crab, and shrimp.

The wine is suitable with all fish and white meat not accompanied by a heavy sauce, and it is good by itself as an apéritif. The bigger, heavier wines should accompany foods with more flavor, and seafood and white meat with richer, more flavorsome sauces. They also complement pâté, cold meats, and hard cheeses.

Notes to Remember

- Wines from the Chardonnay grape are called Pinot Chardonnay in California. In the Burgundy area of France, they are named by regional, subregional, village, and vineyard names. The best in this category are spectacular white wines, crisp, dry, and fresh.
- Look for Mâcon as the least expensive good white Burgundy.
- Look for Meursault as the best buy of the fine wines.
- Chardonnay from premium wineries in California and wines from France named Pouilly-Fuissé, Mâcon, and Chablis are the more readily available. They have good varietal character and freshness, but lack the depth and distinction of the great wines.
- The lightest, liveliest white Burgundies come from Chablis. Do not confuse French Chablis with California or New York State Chablis, which are only everyday wines.
- If you want a good wine in this category, be prepared to pay from $3.50 to $5.50. If you want a great wine, be prepared to pay $10 and up. In this category price is commensurate with quality, though selection is tricky.
- A few varietal Pinot Blancs are made in California. They are good wines at their price, but they do not aspire to the greatness of wines made from the Chardonnay.

Tasting Results

FRENCH WHITE BURGUNDIES AND CALIFORNIA PINOT CHARDONNAY

Region/ Country of Origin	Dry/Semi-dry/ Sweet/ Very sweet	Producer	Name of Wine	Price	General	Limited	None
						DISTRIBUTION AVAILABILITY BY CITY*	
Best Wines at Tasting							
France	D	Louis Latour	Pouilly-Fuissé	$5.95	1, 2, 3, 4, 14	All others	
France	D	Joseph Drouhin	Pouilly-Fuissé	$6.99	All except→	6, 11, 15, 16, 17, 18, 19, 22, 23, 25	1, 3, 9, 13, 26, 27, 29
Calif.	D	Parducci Wine Cellars	Mendocino County Chardonnay	$4.99	1, 2, 3, 4, 11, 14	←All except→	5, 6, 10, 19, 25
France	D	A. de Luze	Pouilly-Fuissé	$4.65	1, 2, 8	←All except→	3, 6, 7, 12, 13, 15, 25, 26, 28, 29
France	D	Louis Jadot	Mâcon Blanc-Villages Jadot	$3.98	1, 2, 3	All others	
Calif.	D	Sonoma Vineyards	Sonoma County Chardonnay	$3.99		All except→	6, 12, 24
Calif.	D	Paul Masson Vineyards	California Pinot Blanc	$2.89		All markets	
France	D	Thomas Bassot	Chantefleur Blanc de Blancs	$2.99	2, 4, 11, 19, 24	21, 28	All others
Highly Ranked Wines							
Calif.	D	Wente Bros.	California Pinot Blanc	$3.25		All markets	
Calif.	D	Louis M. Martini	California Mountain Pinot Chardonnay	$3.99	1, 2, 3	All others	
Calif.	SD	Paul Masson Vineyards	California Pinot Chardonnay	$2.99	All except→	6, 13, 16, 17, 19, 20, 22, 23, 24, 25, 28	10

Country		Producer	Wine	Price			
France	D	Louis Jadot	Beaujolais Blanc	$5.29	2, 3	All others	
France	D	Joseph Drouhin	La Forêt Mâcon-Villages	$3.99		All markets	
Calif.	D	Beringer Vineyards	Napa Valley Chardonnay	$5.29		All markets	All others

Other Recommended Wines

Country		Producer	Wine	Price			
Calif.	D	Weibel Champagne Vineyards	California Pinot Chardonnay	$3.95	1, 2, 3, 4	All others	
France	D	Patriarche	Chablis	$4.40	2, 3, 11	1, 4, 5, 7, 12, 14, 18, 27	All others
Calif.	D	Almadén Vineyards	California Pinot Blanc	$3.10	All except→	22, 23, 25, 28, 29	
Calif.	D	Almadén Vineyards	California Pinot Chardonnay	$3.10	All markets		
Calif.	D	Sebastiani Vineyards	North Coast Counties Pinot Chardonnay	$3.50		All markets	
Calif.	D	Wente Bros.	California Pinot Chardonnay	$3.99	All except→	6, 10, 20, 25	
Calif.	D	Souverain of Alexander Valley	Sonoma Chardonnay	$4.75	All except→		5, 6, 8, 10, 13, 16, 17, 21, 24, 26, 27
Calif.	D	Robert Mondavi Winery	Napa Valley Chardonnay	$7.10	1, 3	←All except→	6, 8, 10, 16, 19, 28
Calif.	D	Simi Winery	Alexander Valley Pinot Chardonnay	$4.50		All except→	6, 8, 16, 17, 20, 25, 28
France	D	Sichel	Chablis Special Selection	$4.89		All markets	
France	D	Thomas Bassot	Pinot Chardonnay-Mâcon	$2.99	1, 2, 4, 11, 19, 21, 22	27	All others
France	D	Patriarche	Bourgogne-Aligoté	$3.29	2, 3, 11	1, 4, 5, 7, 10, 12, 14, 18, 27	All others
France	D	A. de Luze	Chablis	$4.00	1, 2, 8, 11	←All except→	6, 7, 12, 13, 15, 25, 26, 27, 28, 29
France	D	Sichel	Pinot Chardonnay-Mâcon	$3.19		All except→	1

Tasting Results (*continued*)

FRENCH WHITE BURGUNDIES AND CALIFORNIA PINOT CHARDONNAY

Region/ Country of Origin	Dry/Semi-dry/ Sweet/ Very sweet	Producer	Name of Wine	Price	DISTRIBUTION AVAILABILITY BY CITY*		
					General	Limited	None
France	D	Joseph Drouhin	Soleil Blanc	$2.99	2, 4, 5, 7, 8, 10	←All except→	1, 9, 13, 23, 26, 27, 29
France	D	Jouvet	Pouilly-Fuissé	$6.45		All markets	
France	D	Cruse	Pouilly-Fuissé	$5.95	1, 2, 4	All others	

* See pp. 26–27 for city code.

NOTE: We found the following wines in very limited distribution to be of outstanding quality: David Bruce, Pinot Chardonnay; Chalone, Pinot Blanc; Freemark Abbey, Pinot Chardonnay; Hanzell, Pinot Chardonnay; Mayacamas, Pinot Chardonnay; Llords & Elwood Winery, Rare Chardonnay; Sterling Vineyard, Napa Valley Pinot Chardonny; Stony Hill, Pinot Chardonnay.

The Riesling Grape, German and Alsatian White Wines, California Johannisberg Riesling, and Gewürztraminer

Germany	*Alsace, France*	*California*
Regionals: Rhine Moselle	Varietals: Riesling Silvaner Gewürztraminer	Varietals: Johannisberg Riesling Gewürztraminer

Some of the most extraordinary white wines in the world are produced in Germany. It is there that the Riesling, the champion of grapes, reaches the height of perfection, producing wines in the Moselle and Rhine valleys so luscious and rich and yet so different that you would never know that they were from the same grape. When planted in different environments, its versatility reveals a whole range of exquisite tastes. All German wines have some degree of sweetness, from those with a fresh, fruity acidity and only a touch of sweetness, to those that are very sweet but somehow still not cloying, with enough styles in between to please any palate except a truly dry one.

The soil and climate in Germany force the Riesling to labor as no other grape in the world. The brisk northern weather wrings every essential of taste from the grapes. Like all fruit, they develop the most concentrated flavor when they mature slowly in the face of some adversity.

The German vineyards profit from a long maturing season, neither baked by a hot sun nor forced too fast by high temperatures. Because the vines must struggle for nourishment, they send their roots deep into the soil and tap the minerals. Some of the hillsides are so steep that they are either terraced or the vines grow on a slope that angles at sixty degrees, and the farmers pile chips of slate around the vines to reflect the sun on to the grapes. The grapes ripen slowly, reinforcing their flavor and producing wines with as much as one-third less alcohol than most. The wines are so light and fresh they do not strain an enthusiastic drinker, and Germans themselves usually drink them without food to fully appreciate their flavor.

These wines are sometimes approached warily by Americans who have heard that dry white wines have the most cachet, but we find the German ones yield unforgettable flavor and pleasure. In any case, they are the most popular imported white wines in America.

We have included in this chapter white wines made from the great Riesling grape grown in Germany, France, and America; German wines without the designation Riesling, which we have simply called Rhine wines; and finally Gewürztraminer, a uniquely spicy wine. We have not included American-produced wines with German names such as Sylvaner, Emerald Riesling, Grey Riesling, and Rhine Wine, but put them in their own section, "White Wines in the German Style." Originally we planned to include them in this section, but we discovered they were not comparable and organized them so they could be judged against one another.

GERMAN WHITE WINES

All German wines come in a characteristic bottle shape, tall, slender, and tapered like a stretched-out Burgundy bottle. If it contains Rhine wine, the glass will be brown; if it is Moselle, the glass will be green. Only wines from Franconia still come in their age-old flacon-shaped *Boxbeutel*.

Virtually all the wine exported from Germany is white. Red wine accounts for less than 15 percent of production. Three grape varieties account for 80 percent of all the German white wine. They are the *Riesling*, sometimes called White Riesling (as though there were a black or pink variety), Rhine Riesling, or Johannisberg Riesling, which we will simply call Riesling; the *Silvaner* (spelled Sylvaner in France and America), which like Count Dracula originally came from Transylvania in what is now Rumania; and the *Müller-Thurgau*, a Riesling-Silvaner or Silvaner-Riesling cross whose uncertain lineage reflects the doubts of the botanist who created it.

Other grape varieties are planted in small quantities and used only for blending, but when a grape variety appears on a German label the wine must contain at least 75 percent of that grape. This requirement will be increased to 85 percent in 1976.

While the Riesling makes very different wines in different districts of Germany, varying with soil and climate, the other two grapes are more consistent. Silvaner makes a soft wine that matures quickly, with good fruit and bouquet and comparatively low acidity. Müller-Thurgau combines the softness of Silvaner with the flowery bouquet of the Riesling. Generally its wines are lighter than those made from the Riesling and Silvaner, and they mature and fade faster.

Despite some claims to the contrary, Riesling is a big producer per acre in Germany, though it ripens later than the other two varieties. Müller-Thurgau ripens the earliest of the three, a big advantage in this cool wine-growing area where grapes struggle to reach ripeness.

About 70 million cases of wine are produced each year in Germany's eleven wine-growing districts, of which only five export wines in any quantity to America. Three of these are along the Rhine, one along a tributary, the

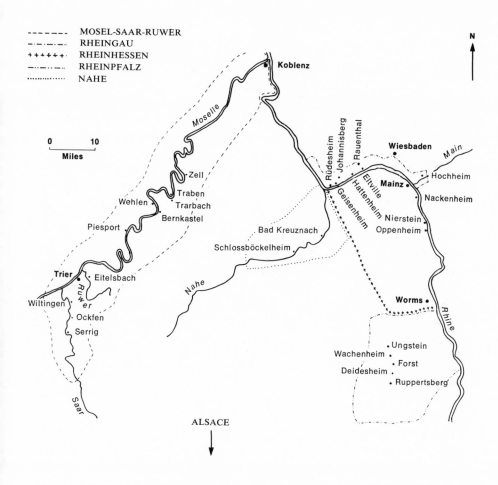

WINE PRODUCING REGIONS OF GERMANY

Nahe, and the last along the Moselle and its tributaries, the Saar and the Ruwer. The other districts, of which Franconia, Baden, and Württemberg are the most important, practically do not export at all. Beginning at the south and working north, let's look briefly at the main districts that send their wines to the United States (see map, p. 109).

RHEINPFALZ

The Rheinpfalz is also known as the Rhenish Palatinate, Germany's largest wine-producing area, stretching north from the French Alsatian border along the Rhine for about fifty miles. Most of the area is planted with Müller-Thurgau and Silvaner grapes, but its finest wines come from the central part of the district, which is planted with the Riesling. These wines are called by the names of the villages from which they come, Ruppertsberg, Deidesheim, Forst, and Wachenheim. The Rheinpfalz wines are full-bodied and rich. Though at times they have an earthy consistency, in great years they compete successfully with Germany's best.

RHEINHESSEN

North of the Rheinpfalz and bounded by the Rhine on the east and north, this fertile area with a comparatively mild climate is the second-largest German wine district. It produces a wide variety of wines, some that are soft and juicy, others that imitate the elegance and style of those from the Rheingau. The principal city is Mainz, but the wine capital is Nierstein, whose wines rank among Germany's greatest.

The Silvaner is the main grape variety here, closely followed by the Müller-Thurgau. In the best vineyards of the area where the Riesling grape predominates, the wines often resemble in elegance and breed some of the finest wines of the Rheingau.

RHEINGAU

This is one of the smallest wine-growing districts, and the most famous. The Rheingau lies north of the Rhine on its twenty-mile western bend below Wiesbaden, and the resulting southern exposure of the vineyards makes it what many experts call the greatest white-wine district in the world. The Rheingau is the only district with many large estates, still owned by the descendants of noblemen who were encouraged to plant grapes there by

Charlemagne. Its noblest wines are made from the Riesling grape in the villages of Johannisberg, Rüdesheim, Hochheim, and Hattenheim. At their best they combine steely elegance with lush fruit.

NAHE

This tributary joins the Rhine just as it turns north again at the western corner of the Rheingau. The small valley district grows wine that is a happy medium between Moselles and Rheingaus. More sturdy than the Moselles, they yet preserve some of the delicacy and softness of that region. Less steely than the Rheingaus, they resemble that region in their grace. This is particularly true of the better wines that are made exclusively from the Riesling grape.

MOSEL-SAAR-RUWER

This district north of the Nahe consists of the valley of the Moselle River and two small tributaries, the Saar and Ruwer. The vineyards are farther north than any commercial ones in the world, at about the latitude of Winnipeg. The steep hillsides and unfertile, slaty soil produce unique Riesling wines with an incredible delicacy, bouquet, flavor, and softness, perfectly balanced by a pleasant acidity, crispness, and a slight sparkle called spritz.

Germany is a country of small wine growers, 90,000 of them, owning an average of two and a half acres of vineyards. Only a little more than 700 own more than twenty acres. Being enterprising, some 20,000 of these growers make and bottle their own wine and market it in a country where almost everyone has his favorite "small estate." The others have their wine made and marketed by the most modern and efficient cooperatives in the world, which make wines every bit as fine as some of the world-famous estates along the Rhine and Moselle. The shippers buy from the growers, estates, and cooperatives, and blend and bottle the wine under the dozen or so geographic designations that make up the largest part of German wine exports. The shippers also select and sell bottled wines from the different estates. These vary greatly from year to year, and many are sold at mammoth auctions preceded by days of careful tastings.

Like the more familiar French labels, the German label carries a great deal of important information about geographic origin, quality, and, in some cases, grape variety. Most of the German wines sold in America carry geographic place names on the label, in this order: the region, *Gebiet* in Ger-

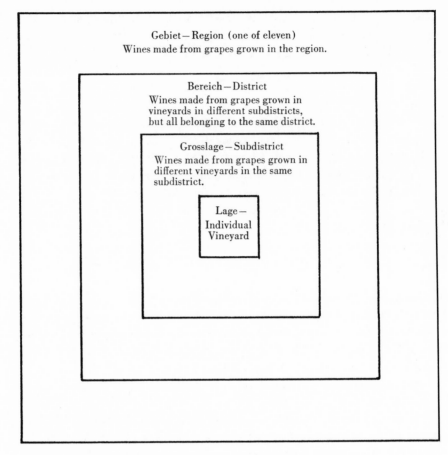

Relationship of geographical place names that appear on a
German wine label

man, one of eleven into which German vineyards are divided; the district,
called *Bereich,* into which the regions are divided; the subdistrict, called
Grosslage, into which districts are divided; and finally, the name of an individual vineyard, called *Lage,* into which subdistricts are divided. The name
of the *Bereich, Grosslage,* or *Lage* is either preceded or followed by the local
village name, e.g., Bereich Nierstein. The label will also always identify the
region, e.g., Rheinhessen.

The label also indicates the level of quality of the wine. German
wines, unlike all other wines in the world, are not only ranked by geography,
but also by the degree of sweetness of the grapes from which they are made.
This is entirely determined by the amount of natural sugar in the grape
juice, which varies with the climate and the time of the harvest. Growers

practice selective picking, which means they pick the grapes at varying stages of ripeness according to the wine they hope to produce. Sometimes they even pick the individual grapes. By leaving some grapes on the vine longer, the wine will have a more concentrated flavor.

All German white wines are divided into three basic quality designations, the highest having four grades. In ascending order of quality, they are:

Tafelwein ("table wine"). This must be made from specified grape varieties and contain a minimum amount of natural grape sugar. It can carry the name of only one Tafelwein district on its label: Mosel, Rhein, Main, Neckar, or Oberrhein.

Qualitätswein ("Quality Wine"). This must be grown in a specified district from authorized grapes, with enough natural sugar to attain a designated minimum alcoholic content, which varies from district to district. The full German name is "Qualitätswein bestimmter Anbaugebiete," which is mercifully reduced to Q.b.A. on the label or simply Qualitätswein. For this category, German law permits the addition of a certain amount of sugar before fermentation to increase alcoholic content. All these wines must pass chemical analysis and win approval from a tasting panel. On their label they carry the letters A.P., short for Amtliche Prüfungsnummer, or official approval number, followed by a ten-digit code and the year of approval.

Qualitätswein mit Prädikat ("Quality Wine with Special Attributes"). This is grown in the same areas and made from the same grape varieties as Q.b.A. wine but from riper grapes, and the addition of sugar is not permitted, which results in a wine with more flavor. Within this designation, there are four grades of quality based on the increasing amount of natural sugar. One of the following grades will always appear on the label along with the Qualitätswein mit Prädikat designation and the A.P. number:

- *Kabinett*. This is usually the driest wine category.
- *Spätlese*. This means "late-harvested" wine. It is more concentrated and usually somewhat sweeter than Q.b.A. or Kabinett because it has more natural sugar.
- *Auslese*. This means "selectively harvested" wine. The grapes are picked only after they have reached a high degree of ripeness. As a result, the wine has even more sugar than Kabinett or Spätlese, and is definitely sweet.
- *Beerenauslese* and *Trockenbeerenauslese*. The first of these is a dessert wine made from selectively picked grapes that are very ripe, and the second is an even sweeter, luscious dessert wine made from selectively picked grapes that were overripe and blessed with the mold we call the "noble

rot." There is a related exotic wine called Eiswein, made from fully ripe grapes that had been frozen by an unexpected frost. All these wines are esoteric, rare nectars of the gods, and will cost accordingly.

American consumers are sometimes confused by the fact that the higher the quality of a German wine, the sweeter it is. Grapes that are picked late have less juice and more sugar, and late picking, particularly if it is selective, costs more. If you want a drier German wine, buy a Q.b.A. or a Kabinett. The Q.b.A., although technically lower on the quality scale, often has more balance and body.

Only about a dozen German wines are sold in any quantity in the United States. The following wines, usually appearing under shippers' labels, account for 80 percent of the German wine imported to this country:

From the Moselle: Moselblümchen, Zeller Schwarze Katz, Piesporter Michelsberg, Piesporter Goldtröpfchen, Bereich Bernkastel, Kröver Nacktarsch, and Zeltinger Münzlay.

From the Rheingau: Bereich Johannisberg, Bereich Hochheim.

From the Rheinhessen: Bereich Nierstein and Oppenheimer Krötenbrunnen.

From the Nahe: Bereich Schloss Böckelheim.

By far the largest amount of German Rhine wine sold abroad carries the collective name Liebfraumilch, a Q.b.A. designation for wine blended from the three Rhine districts and the Nahe. There are tens of thousands of different German wine labels, reflecting gradations of quality and geography, but consumers can simplify the problem by choosing one of the many Liebfraumilch. Within this large category there are considerable variations in quality and price, so it is wise to pick a wine from a reliable shipper. Among the more popular Liebfraumilch brand names in this country are Blue Nun, Hanns Christof, Glockenspiel, and Wedding Veil.

If you are interested in more details about the better-known German vineyards and estates whose wines you may see occasionally, we have provided a listing of them by region and village in the Appendix, pages 241–247.

ALSACE

Although the Riesling grape is grown in many countries besides Germany, only two of them, France and the United States, produce wine available here. From Alsace come wines that are less flowery and delicate than the German Rieslings. They are invariably dry and more alcoholic than the German wines, and their particular breed of the grape variety gives them a graceful polish.

CALIFORNIA

Riesling wines produced in California and called Johannisberg Riesling, have a heavier, fuller quality than those of France and Germany. Because of the warmer climate and richer soil, they lack the delicate flavor of the German wines, but they are among the best white wines of California. In both Alsace and California, small quantities of the sweeter, late-picked (Spätlese) wines are made, but they rarely approach the balance and lusciousness of the German originals.

Some Riesling is also grown in the state of Washington, where the wine comes closer to the German original than does the California product.

GEWÜRZTRAMINER

The Gewürztraminer, though grown in Germany, is more famous in Alsace and California. The wines are so distinctive in taste that they cannot be compared with other white wines of the same price range. The German word *Gewürz* means "spice," and the Traminer grape produces spicy wines. This strong spiciness is the wine's most pronounced characteristic and makes it useful for blending. It is a distinguished varietal for those of us who like it. Others, however, find its taste too strong.

Vintage

Vintage information is important for German wines because the styles vary every year and some wines are worth keeping longer than others (see Vintage Chart on p. 116). Qualitätswein gains a measure of stability from the fact that up to 25 percent of the wine can be blended from a year other than that on the label. Alsatian, Washington State, and California Riesling as well as Alsatian and California Gewürztraminer all improve in the bottle. We would advise not drinking the wines until they are three years old. If they have been stored properly, you could drink them safely for another three years. We have tasted Alsatian Gewürztraminers that were fifteen years old and were beautifully harmonious. If anything, the overpowering perfume of youth makes way for balance and polish in maturity.

Tasting Notes

We organized these wines into four groups: Moselles; wines made in Germany, France, and America from the Riesling grape; German wines without

Vintage Chart—German Wines*

Vintage Year	Description of Vintage	Moselle When to Drink	Rhine Wine When to Drink
1974	Average quality with good, fruity acidity	Until 1978	Until 1980
1973	Well-balanced, fruity wines, good for early drinking	Until 1976	Until 1980
1972	Stylish vintage, firm acidity preserving Rhine wines a long time	Until 1976	Until 1980
<u>1971</u>	One of the great vintages of the century. Great charm, balance, and concentration. Spätlese, Auslese, Beerenauslese, and Trockenbeerenauslese will live long	Until 1977	Top wines until 1990, others until 1980
1970	Good vintage, with light and elegant wines	Until 1976	Until 1976
1969	Good vintage, firm acidity with a touch of greenness	Until 1976	Until 1977
<u>1967</u>	General vintage average, Auslese, Beerenauslese, and Trockenbeerenauslese among greatest of this century and long-lived	Too late	Top wines until 1985, others until 1976
1966	Very good vintage, light and fruity wines, good Spätlese and Auslese	Too late	Until 1976
1964	Good vintage, lacking acidity and therefore rather heavy, only Spätlese and Auslese from Rhine and Moselle still good	Top wines until 1976, others too late	Until 1978
1959	Great vintage, too alcoholic, only great Auslese, Beerenauslese, and Trockenbeernauslese will live much longer	Until 1979	Until 1979

* Underlined vintages should be put away for aging, but only in Spätlese, Auslese, Beerenauslese, and Trockenbeerenauslese quality.

the designation Riesling, which we have simply called Rhine wines; and the Gewürztraminers that had any substantial distribution in America. It should be pointed out that this category suffers from the same problem as red Burgundy, a fragmented market. There are many wines as good as the ones we recommend, but which do not reach America or are sold in such limited quantities that you will have to search them out in your market area with the help of the Best Vineyards and Estates listings in the Appendix (pp. 241–247). Here are the results of our tastings.

MOSELLE

We found many delightful Moselles. Though none had the great flower we associate with the best, they all had liveliness and a slight effervescence. They also proved our contention that Moselles must be fresh; comparative quality of vintages is not as important as the youth of the wine.

RHINE WINES

This was the most satisfactory tasting category, and even our French-oriented tasters found them exceptional in character and appeal. We were surprised at the high standard of quality of the Liebfraumilchs that are in wide distribution. Of the other Rhine wines, only wines from Nierstein met our distribution criteria. They did not differ materially from the Liebfraumilchs, and they can be regarded as a good substitute.

RIESLING

The German wines were easily identified by their elegance, though Rieslings from California, at their best, showed great style. They are higher in alcohol and fuller in body, but as they lack the high acidity of the German wines, they seemed less fresh and fruity. We found one other interesting phenomenon: Rieslings with a slight bit of residual sugar show better balance than totally dry ones.

GEWÜRZTRAMINER

Of the eight we tasted, we can recommend five, with only Almadén and Hugel winning our total approval. They were both outstanding, with Hugel possibly having the edge in refinement, not being quite as perfumed as the Almadén. The others were all very "gewürzig," and possibly too highly flavored to enjoy without food. They would all make excellent companions to that famous Alsatian sauerkraut, pork, and sausage meal called choucroûte garnie.

Similar Alternatives

Alsatian and California Sylvaner; Hungarian white wines shipped in Rhine wine bottles.

Congenial Food

Moselles are best with cold meats, poached fish, and fowl, or just by themselves, being our favorite apéritif. Rhine wines, especially Liebfraumilch, are all-purpose wines, good with red meat, but ideal with fowl, pork, smoked ham, and seafood with cream sauces. The same applies to the Riesling wines. Gewürztraminer takes to hearty food, balancing red meat and game.

Notes to Remember

- German Rieslings, most of them from Johannisberg (a village along the Rhine), have more elegance than Johannisberg Riesling from California. The California wines are broader and less crisp, but are considered one of the best white varietals from California. Both are expensive, but worth it.
- Of the Rhine wines, Liebfraumilch, Nierstein, and Oppenheim are the most satisfactory all-purpose white wines. Fruit, body, and freshness make them America's favorite imported white wines. They keep well, get better with age up to seven years, and are good value.
- Moselles are the lightest white wines, full of charm. Drink them young, no more than three years old. Names to remember are Bernkastel, Zell, Zeller Schwarze Katz, Zeltingen, Piesporter, Kröver Nacktarsch, Moselblümchen, and Piesporter Goldtröpfchen.
- Gewürztraminer is a spicy wine, not to everyone's taste, but to us one of the great white wines with enough pizazz to stand up even to sauerkraut and hearty beef stew.
- For the drier German wines, look on the label for the designation Qualitätswein or Kabinett.
- The more expensive a German wine, the sweeter it is. They increase in sweetness from Spätlese, Auslese, Beerenauslese to Trockenbeerenauslese. The last two are great dessert wines. If you buy these, you should consult the Appendix ("The Best Vineyards and Estates of the German Wine Regions") and Vintage Chart.

Tasting Results

RIESLING

Region/ Country of Origin	Dry/Semi-dry/ Sweet/ Very sweet	Producer	Name of Wine	Price	DISTRIBUTION AVAILABILITY BY CITY*		
					General	Limited	None
			Best Wines at Tasting				
Germany	SD	Sichel	Bereich Johannisberg Riesling	$4.95		All markets	
Germany	SD	Deinhard	Bereich Johannisberg Riesling	$4.89		All markets	
Germany	SD	Anheuser & Fehrs	Anheuser Johannisberger	$5.55		All markets	
			Highly Ranked Wines				
Germany	SD	Wasum	Schloss Fürstenberger Riesling	$3.89		All markets	
Germany	SD	Weinexport Hattenheim	Madrigal Johannisberg Riesling	$3.89		All markets	
Calif.	SD	Charles Krug Winery	Napa Valley Johannisberg Riesling	$4.03	1, 3	All others	
Calif.	SD	Souverain of Alexander Valley	Johannisberg Riesling, Sonoma (L.A.)	$4.50	All except→		5, 6, 8, 10, 13, 16, 17, 21, 24, 26, 27
Calif.	SD	Monterey Vineyard	Monterey Johannisberg Riesling	$4.30		All markets	

119

Tasting Results (continued)

RIESLING

| | Dry/Semi-dry/ | | | | DISTRIBUTION AVAILABILITY BY CITY* | | |
Region/ Country of Origin	Sweet/ Very sweet	Producer	Name of Wine	Price	General	Limited	None
Other Recommended Wines							
Calif.	D	Inglenook	Napa Valley Johannisberg Riesling	$4.75	1, 3	All others	
Calif.	SD	Llords & Elwood Winery	Castle Magic Johannisberg Riesling, California (L.A.)	$4.25		1, 3, 7, 9, 12, 15, 21, 23, 26, 27, 29	All others
Calif.	D	Almadén Vineyards	California Johannisberg Riesling	$3.10	All except→	13, 22, 23, 25, 29	
Calif.	D	Christian Brothers	Napa Valley Johannisberg Riesling	$2.59		All markets	
Washington	SD	Ste. Michelle Vintners	Washington State Johannisberg Riesling	$3.49		All except→	2, 3, 6
Calif.	D	Weibel Champagne Vineyards	California Johannisberg Riesling	$3.95	1, 2, 3, 4	All others	

* See pp. 26-27 for city code.

NOTE: We found the following wine in limited distribution to be of outstanding quality: Chappellet, Johannisberg Riesling.

Tasting Results

MOSELLE

Region/ Country of Origin	Dry/Semi-dry/ Sweet/ Very sweet	Producer	Name of Wine	Price	DISTRIBUTION AVAILABILITY BY CITY*		
					General	Limited	None
			Best Wines at Tasting				
Germany	SD	Sichel	Bereich Bernkastel	$3.89		All markets	
Germany	SD	Anheuser & Fehrs	Anheuser Bernkastel	$4.65		All markets	
Germany	SD	Deinhard	Bereich Bernkastel Green Label	$4.25		All markets	
Germany	SD	Tytell	Bereich Bernkastel	$2.79		All except→	1, 6, 9, 14, 17, 22, 23, 24, 26
			Highly Ranked Wines				
Germany	SD	Anheuser & Fehrs	Piesporter Michelsberg	$5.55		All markets	
Germany	SD	Tytell	Zeller Schwarze Katz	$2.69	2	←All except→	26
Germany	SD	Leonard Kreusch	Bernkasteler Kurfürstlay Riesling	$2.49		All markets	
			Other Recommended Wines				
Germany	SD	Sichel	Zeller Schwarze Katz	$3.89		All markets	
Germany	SD	Tytell	Moselblümchen	$2.49		All except→	6, 26
Germany	SD	Leonard Kreusch	Kröver Nacktarsch	$2.59	All except→	3, 6, 25, 26, 27, 29	
Germany	D	Weinexport Hattenheim	Madrigal Bernkastel Riesling	$3.98	1, 2, 3	All others	
Germany	SD	Leonard Kreusch	Piesporter Goldtröpfchen Kabinett	$2.89		All except→	6, 9, 10, 12, 13, 17, 19, 22, 23, 26, 27, 29
Germany	SD	Weinexport Hattenheim	Madrigal Zeller Schwarze Katz	$3.79	2, 3	All others	

* See pp. 26–27 for city code.

121

Tasting Results

RHINE WINES

Region/ Country of Origin	Dry/Semi-dry/ Sweet/ Very sweet	Producer	Name of Wine	Price	DISTRIBUTION AVAILABILITY BY CITY*		
					General	Limited	None
Best Wines at Tasting							
Germany	SD	(Jacquin Selection)	Little Rhine Bear Liebfraumilch	$1.99		2, 4, 7	All others
Germany	D	Export Union	Wedding Veil Liebfraumilch	$3.79	2, 4, 7, 8, 11, 14, 18, 21, 24		All others
Germany	SD	Sichel	Blue Nun Liebfraumilch	$3.89	All markets		
Germany	SD	Julius Kayser	Glockenspiel Liebfraumilch	$2.99		All markets	
Highly Ranked Wines							
Germany	SD	Anheuser & Fehrs	Anheuser Liebfraumilch	$3.99	1, 2, 4	All others	
Germany	SD	Leonard Kreusch	Niersteiner Gutes Domtal	$2.35	All except→	1, 9, 26, 27	
Germany	SD	Tytell	Liebfraumilch	$2.39	All except→	8, 9, 14, 16, 19, 21, 22, 23	26
Germany	SD	Leonard Kreusch	Liebfraumilch	$2.29		All markets	
Other Recommended Wines							
Germany	D	Weinexport Hattenheim	Madrigal Liebfraumilch	$3.79	2, 3, 4	All others	
Germany	SD	Sichel	Bereich Nierstein	$3.89		All markets	
Germany	SD	Langenbach	Rheinkeller Liebfraumilch	$2.90		All except→	6, 7, 8, 9, 12, 16, 17, 21, 22, 23, 25, 26, 27, 28
Germany	SD	Deinhard	Hanns Christof Liebfraumilch	$4.25		All markets	
Germany	SD	L. Guntrum	Niersteiner Hölle Kabinett	$3.99		All except→	4, 5, 7, 8, 12, 13, 16, 17, 18, 19, 21, 22, 23, 25, 26, 27, 28

* See pp. 26–27 for city code.

Tasting Results
GEWÜRZTRAMINER

Region/ Country of Origin	Dry/Semi-dry/ Sweet/ Very sweet	Producer	Name of Wine	Price	DISTRIBUTION AVAILABILITY BY CITY* General	Limited	None
			Best Wines at Tasting				
Calif.	SD	Almadén Vineyards	California Gewürztraminer	$3.10	All except→	5, 6, 8, 10, 12, 13, 17, 18, 22, 23, 25, 26, 28, 29	
France	SD	Hugel	Gewürztraminer	$4.69	2, 4, 5, 8, 14, 20, 24	All others	
			Highly Ranked Wines				
Calif.	D	Mirassou Vineyards	Monterey Gewürztraminer	$4.50	All except→	1, 2, 3, 4, 7, 9, 11, 12, 14, 19, 21, 22, 29	
Calif.	D	Charles Krug Winery	Napa Valley Gewürz Traminer	$4.03		All markets	
			Other Recommended Wines				
Calif.	D	Louis M. Martini	California Mountain Gewürz Traminer	$3.99		All markets	

* See pp. 26–27 for city code.

123

White Bordeaux, the Sauvignon Blanc and Sémillon Grapes

Bordeaux, France

Regionals: Graves
               Entre-Deux-Mers
               Bordeaux Blanc
Varietal: Sauvignon Blanc

Loire Valley, France

Regional: Pouilly-Fumé

California and Washington State

Varietals: Sauvignon Blanc
             Sémillon
             Fumé Blanc

At one time the Bordeaux wines made from Sauvignon Blanc and Sémillon grapes were golden and full-bodied and had great elegance and flavor. They also frequently had a degree of sweetness. More recently, the Bordeaux winemakers have started to make drier, lighter, fresher wines. It is still possible, however, to find wines made in the old style, a style we frankly prefer.

The most popular white Bordeaux comes from Graves, a region just south of the city of Bordeaux (see map, p. 33). Most Graves are blended by shippers to a uniform house style from young wine bought from growers. Some are bottled by châteaux, some of which also make red wines.

As everywhere else in France, the production of these wines is governed by the Appellation Contrôlée system. The wines are labeled Graves or Graves Supérieures, the latter appellation requiring a higher degree of alcohol, though there is little difference in taste between the two. Since each shipper blends what he thinks the public wants, the styles of Graves from different shippers lack uniformity. Some are completely dry, while others have a degree of sweetness, and some are light, while others have more body and varietal taste. The old-style Graves, a broad, golden wine with great elegance, was fermented and aged in oak hogsheads that hold up to 300 bottles each. Now Graves is almost always fermented in large vats, and rarely sees oak. Less exposure to wood gives the wine a fresher taste but deprives it of some of the body, fragrance, depth, and distinction it once had. There is so little difference in quality between the shippers' and chateau-bottled wines that the more expensive château Graves are not worth the difference in price.

One dry white Bordeaux of good value is from Entre-Deux-Mers, a large district to the east of Graves. The wines are usually dry, clean, and pleasant, but lack distinction. The better ones, inexpensive, dry, white wines, represent good value.

The small Sauternes district, just south and east of Graves, produces wines under its own name and that of Barsac, a township in the district, where winemakers have a choice between the two names. The wines of Sauternes and Barsac are among the world's greatest naturally sweet white wines. They are rich and luscious, but since so few are exported to this country we have not included them in our tastings. In the nineteenth century they were as highly regarded as the great red wines of Bordeaux, and the wines made by the twenty-four best châteaux of the region were ranked in the historic Classification of 1855. Not surprisingly, they are expensive to make, since they are made from selectively picked shriveled grapes, producing little wine. They are blended from Sauvignon and Sémillon grapes, with a small addition of Muscadelle. They owe their outstanding lusciousness to the rare mold called "noble rot."

(Sauterne, without an s, produced in the United States, is a dry white generic with no resemblance to the great sweet white wines of Bordeaux. It is one of the three American-produced white generics—the others are Chablis (see pp. 136–141) and Rhine (pp. 142–146).

Another popular French wine made from the Sauvignon Blanc is Pouilly-Fumé, grown around the town of Pouilly-sur-Loire in the upper reaches of the river. Here the Sauvignon Blanc is known as Blanc Fumé, because of the distinct smoky taste of its wine, which has made it famous. Pouilly-Fumé has become very popular in the United States in the past fifteen years, but production is limited to less than 40,000 cases a year, forcing the price up to an unjustified level. Do not confuse Pouilly-Fumé with Pouilly-Fuissé, a white Burgundy made from the Chardonnay grape a hundred miles away.

In California's northern coastal counties, the Sauvignon Blanc produces a distinguished and highly aromatic wine. Several wineries market it under the name Blanc Fumé, or Fumé Blanc, though it does not have the smokiness of its cousin from the Loire. Most Sauvignon Blanc produced in the United States is dry, though there are those with a degree of sweetness. They are labeled Sweet or Haut.

In Bordeaux, the Sémillon grape is normally blended with the Sauvignon Blanc, but in California it is used separately to make a varietal wine that is lush, flowery, and full-bodied. Because of the high productivity of the grape, it is also reasonably priced. These wines range from dry, labeled Dry Sémillon or simply Sémillon, to sweet, labeled Sweet, Haut, or Château Sémillon.

Vintage

White Bordeaux almost always carry a vintage, which is an important factor in selecting these wines, because quality varies significantly from year to year. Graves improves in the bottle, and will keep for at least five years. Good years for white Bordeaux do not correlate with good years for red; in fact, the best dry white Bordeaux often result from years that do not have enough sun to make fine red wine.

The best years for Pouilly-Fumé usually correspond to those of the other Loire wines. After an off-and-on sequence in the 1960s, the region produced six consecutive good vintages, from 1969 through 1974. Bad years are infrequent because the Sauvignon Blanc ripens early.

The varietal Sauvignon Blanc and Sémillon wines produced in this country frequently carry vintages. The Sauvignon Blanc is bottled young to preserve its freshness and fruitiness, and can be drunk beginning a year or so after the vintage. The Sémillon, particularly the sweeter styles, benefits from a little more time in the bottle, gaining depth, lusciousness, and bouquet.

VINTAGE CHART—WHITE GRAVES

Vintage Year	Description of Vintage	When to Drink
1974	Fair	Until 1977
1973	Medium quality	Until 1976
1972	Uneven, some good wines	Until 1976
1971	Good	Until 1977
1970	Fine wines	Until 1977
1969	Good	Until 1977
1968	Poor	Never
1967	Some fine wines	Until 1976

VINTAGE CHART—SAUTERNES/BARSAC

Vintage Year	Description of Vintage	When to Drink
1974	Only a few fair wines	From 1977
1973	Mediocre	1976–1980
1972	Uneven, mediocre	1976–1980
1971	Some very fine wines, elegant	1975–1990
1970	Fine wines	Until 1985
1969	Pleasant, light	Until 1980
1968	Poor	Never
1967	Fine wines	Until 1985
1966	Good	Until 1980
1965	Poor	Never
1964	Bad	Never
1963	Poor	Never
1962	Good, elegant	Until 1978

Tasting Notes

The Graves, dry or semi-dry, showed more character and balance than the other wines we tasted. The Sauvignon Blanc, lighter and fresher, might have been overpowered by the bigger Graves, but we preferred it to the Sémillon. Most California Sauvignons were dry and well balanced, and had good flavor. We believe that this varietal has a good future.

Similar Alternatives

Try California Chenin Blanc varietals.

Congenial Food

Graves, Sauvignon Blanc, and Sémillon are agreeable with fish in cream sauce, veal, pork, cold meats, and hard cheeses. They are also good picnic wines. Because it is dry without being excessively acid, the Sauvignon is excellent as an apéritif.

Sauternes, either as an apéritif by itself or with Paté de Fois Gras, canard à l'orange, Roquefort, and any dessert except one with coffee or chocolate flavor, is particularly good with citrus fruit or such flavored desserts.

Notes to Remember

- The Sauvignon Blanc makes some of the best white varietal wines in California, sold as Sauvignon Blanc and Fumé Blanc. The names are interchangeable. The Sauvignon Blanc in the Loire Valley makes Pouilly-Fumé, an excellent but overpriced wine.
- Graves is a superior French white wine, which can be either dry or semi-dry. It is made from the Sauvignon and Sémillon grapes. The same grapes make Bordeaux Blanc and Entre-Deux-Mers, decent everyday white wines.
- Sémillon is a grape variety which in California makes a full-bodied, luscious, deep-golden wine. Usually dry when called Sémillon, it is sweet if called Haut, Sweet, or Château Sémillon.
- Consult the Vintage Chart for Graves and Sauternes. Vintage is unimportant for Pouilly-Fumé, Entre-Deux-Mers, and Sauvignon Blanc from Bordeaux.
- Drink the California Sauvignon Blanc young; the Sémillon benefits from a little age.

Tasting Results

WHITE BORDEAUX, THE SAUVIGNON BLANC AND SÉMILLON GRAPES

Region/ Country of Origin	Dry/Semi-dry/ Sweet/ Very sweet	Producer	Name of Wine	Price	DISTRIBUTION AVAILABILITY BY CITY*		
					General	Limited	None
			Best Wines at Tasting				
France	D	Sichel	Graves Supérieures	$2.95		All except→	1
Calif.	SD	Sonoma Vineyards	Sonoma County Sauvignon Blanc	$2.99		All except→	5, 12, 25
			Highly Ranked Wines				
France	D	Alexis Lichine	Graves	$2.69		All markets	
Calif.	D	Almadén Vineyards	California Sauvignon Blanc	$3.10	1, 2, 3, 4, 7, 14, 21	All others	
			Other Recommended Wines				
Calif.	D	Wente Bros.	California Dry Sémillon	$2.95		All markets	
Israel	SD	Carmel Wine Company	Israel Sémillon	$2.59		All except→	6, 12, 13, 14, 23, 24, 26, 27, 29
France	D	Sichel	Blanc de Blancs Sauvignon Sec	$3.09		All markets	
Calif.	D	Robert Mondavi Winery	Napa Valley Fumé Blanc	$5.09	1, 2, 3, 12	←All except	6, 8, 10, 16, 17, 19, 28
Calif.	D	Almadén Vineyards	California Blanc Fumé	$3.10	1, 2, 3, 4, 7	All others	
Argentina	D	Bodegas y Viñedos López	Château Vieux	$3.19		All markets	
France	D	Dulong	Ecu Royal French Country White	$1.99		All markets	

Calif.	D	Almadén Vineyards	California Dry Sémillon Sauterne	$2.45		All markets
Calif.	D	San Martin Vineyards	Sémillon Sauterne	$2.10		All markets
France	D	Ginestet	Graves Extra	$3.29		All markets
France	D	La Bergèrie	Mouton Cadet	$3.99		All markets
France	D	Calvet	Réserve Blanc	$1.99	2, 3, 4, 7, 20	←All except→	5, 6, 10, 12, 13, 19, 22, 23, 24, 26, 28,29
France	D	Ackerman-Laurance	Ackerman Sauvignon	$2.89		2, 4, 5, 7, 10, 11, 12, 13, 14, 20, 24, 28	All others
Calif.	D	Oakville Vineyards	Napa Valley Sauvignon Blanc	$4.69		All except→	5, 6, 8, 10, 16, 17, 18, 19, 22, 27, 28, 29

* See pp. 26–27 for city code.

NOTE: We found the following wines in limited distribution to be of outstanding quality: Spring Mountain Vineyards, Sauvignon Blanc; Concannon Vineyard, Sauvignon Blanc.

California Chenin Blanc and Wines
of the Lower Loire Valley

California	*Loire Valley, France*
Varietal: Chenin Blanc	Regionals: Vouvray
	Muscadet

No white wine tells the phenomenal success story of California varietal wines better than Chenin Blanc. For many years the grape had been used for blending, and only since the late 1950s has it stepped out of the chorus and turned into a star. Chenin Blanc wines have a strong varietal character, fruity "nose," intensity of flavor, and freshness. Because most of its flower and fruit is at the beginning of the palate, the wine rarely shows length and depth; as a rather shallow wine, it should be quaffed rather than savored. Pleasant and refreshing, thirst-quenching and yet pretty, it deserves its increasing popularity.

The Chenin Blanc is second only to French Colombard as the most widely grown white grape in California. The vine is highly productive and bears early enough to escape the risks of harmful cold or rain at harvest time. In addition to making a wide variety of different styles of white wines, it is a principal component of California champagne.

Wines made predominantly from the Chenin Blanc grape also appear under two aliases, Pineau de la Loire and White Pinot, neither having any relationship to the grape varieties Pinot Blanc or (Pinot) Chardonnay. Several wineries make both a dry and a slightly sweet wine from this grape and market them under two of the three pseudonyms. Unfortunately, there is no consistent pattern of nomenclature, and it is impossible to identify one from the other by the label. To add to the difficulty, the dry and semidry versions, if from the same winery, often appear in the shorter, relatively squat Burgundy bottle.

Our taste favors the Chenin Blancs whose degree of sweetness hides their lack of depth. Some of the drier wines, without the balance of adequate sweetness, come up short and leave the palate a little dissatisfied. The most balanced come from small wineries restricted in production where wines are matured in wood, but they are usually quite expensive.

In France, where the Chenin Blanc grape originated, it is used to make the finest wines of the Loire Valley. The best-known is Vouvray, which is both full-bodied and fruity, and is grown around the town of the same name in Touraine, in the center of the "château country." Vouvray rarely appears under an estate label but is usually bottled and marketed by

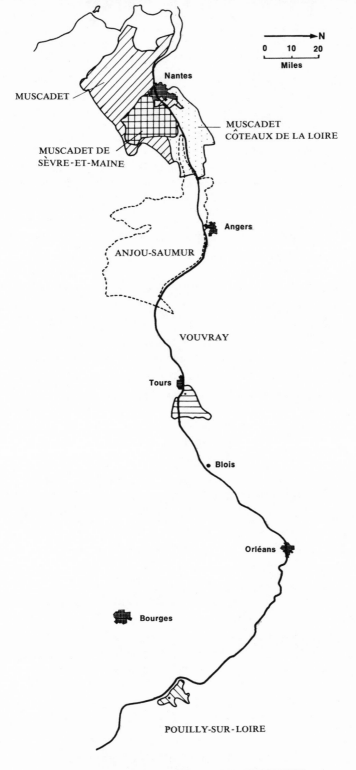

MUSCADET

Nantes

MUSCADET
CÔTEAUX DE LA LOIRE

MUSCADET DE
SÈVRE-ET-MAINE

Angers

ANJOU-SAUMUR

VOUVRAY

Tours

Blois

Orléans

Bourges

POUILLY-SUR-LOIRE

WINE PRODUCING REGIONS OF THE LOIRE VALLEY

131

shippers, who depend on their name on the label to sell it, rather than the name of a specific vineyard. A good Vouvray lasts many years. The local growers store their wine in caves dug into the chalky hillsides, which maintain a perfect temperature for aging wine.

Muscadet is another popular wine from the lower Loire near its mouth on the Atlantic. Muscadet is not a regional as some people believe, but a varietal, named for a grape that is also known as Melon de Bourgogne. As has also happened in Italy, the grape has succeeded in giving its name to the region where it grows.

Although it does not often rise above the level of a good *vin de pays*, ("wine of the country," local wine), Muscadet can be delightfully light and fresh, with a crispness that makes it ideal with seafood. Some people, however, find it too dry and acid. The best Muscadet comes from southeast of Nantes and is called Muscadet de Sèvre-et-Maine. The rest, from two adjacent regions, is called Muscadet Côteaux de la Loire and simply Muscadet.

The Loire, France's longest river, has many excellent vineyards along its banks, but we have discussed only two of its wines because others, such as Saumur, Côteaux du Layon, and Montlouis, are not yet available in sufficient quantity in America to include in this book.

Vintage

Vintage is not important for California Chenin Blanc, since its early-ripening grapes are as likely to produce a good wine one year as another. It should be drunk not more than three years after the date on the bottle. Exceptions may be found in the northern counties in the small individual wineries, such as Chappellet, that make Chenin Blanc with more character and which develops with age. The name of the maker and a price over $4 will help you spot these longer-lasting wines.

Recent good vintage years for Vouvray are 1970 through 1974. Muscadet, like Beaujolais, needs to be drunk young and, above all, fresh, no more than two years after the vintage, or three in the case of ripe wines like 1972 and 1973. The 1974 Muscadets are lighter, more acid, and probably more suitable for Paris bistros than for shipment to this country.

Tasting Notes

We found a good number of pleasant and satisfying wines, both French and California, made from the Chenin Blanc, with no marked difference in quality between the two countries. Probably because of their youth, our favorites proved to be the California wines. Tasted singly, they are delightful, but their shallowness and lack of distinction soon tire the palate when a whole range is tasted.

The Muscadets were pleasant, one-dimensional dry white wines. Peter admits to a personal dislike for this wine; he finds it too acid without offsetting body or other redeeming qualities. If you are one of those who really like acid wines, feel free to attribute this dissent on Muscadet to his somewhat Germanic palate.

Similar Alternatives

If you like Chenin Blanc and Vouvray, you might try Emerald Riesling. If your preference is for Muscadet and you're willing to stretch your imagination a little, try Sauvignon Blanc or Blanc Fumé.

Congenial Food

Drink Chenin Blanc and Vouvray with white meat, pork, boiled red meat, and any sort of cold meats. It is an ideal picnic wine and a very good cocktail wine, much better and only pennies more expensive than most of the generic California Chablis that is offered at so many cocktail parties today.

Serve Muscadet in place of a cocktail. As for food, it is really ideal only with oysters, clams, shrimp, and other seafood.

Notes to Remember

- Chenin Blanc varietals are among the most pleasant wines from California. They are a more satisfactory cocktail white wine than California Chablis or Sauterne.
- California Chenin Blancs are variously sold as Chenin Blanc, Pineau de la Loire, and White Pinot. They may be dry or have a degree of sweetness.
- Vouvray, a wine from the Loire Valley, is made from Chenin Blanc and is similar to the California wines.
- In all the wines in this chapter, look for freshness and youth. Three years should be the maximum age, particularly for wines under $4.

Tasting Results

CALIFORNIA CHENIN BLANC AND WINES OF THE LOWER LOIRE VALLEY

| | | | | | DISTRIBUTION AVAILABILITY BY CITY* | | |
Region/ Country of Origin	Dry/Semi-dry/ Sweet/ Very sweet	Producer	Name of Wine	Price	General	Limited	None
			Best Wines at Tasting				
Calif.	SD	Christian Brothers	Napa Valley Chenin Blanc	$3.15		All markets	
Calif.	SD	Charles Krug Winery	Napa Valley Chenin Blanc	$3.00	1, 2, 3, 4, 9, 11, 12, 13, 23	All others	
Calif.	SD	Robert Mondavi Winery	Napa Valley Chenin Blanc	$3.59	1, 2, 3, 12	←All except→	6, 8, 10, 16, 17, 19, 28
Calif.	D	Parducci Wine Cellars	Mendocino County Chenin Blanc	$3.25	1, 2, 3, 4, 11, 14	←All except→	5, 6, 10, 19, 26
			Highly Ranked Wines				
Calif.	D	Souverain of Rutherford	Napa Valley Dry Chenin Blanc	$3.75	All except→		5, 6, 8, 10, 13, 13, 16, 17, 21, 24, 26, 27
Calif.	SD	J. Pedroncelli Winery	Sonoma County Chenin Blanc	$2.90	1, 3	4, 7, 9, 10, 12, 13, 14, 15, 22, 23, 24	All others
Calif.	D	Monterey Vineyard	Monterey Chenin Blanc	$3.10		All markets	

Other Recommended Wines

		Producer	Wine	Price	Markets	
Calif.	SD	Almadén Vineyards	California Chenin Blanc	$2.45	All except→	12, 13, 17, 19, 22, 23, 25, 29
France	D	Chanson	Muscadet de Sèvre-et-Maine	$3.15		All markets
Calif.	D	Christian Brothers	Napa Valley Pineau de la Loire	$3.99		All markets
France	SD	Ackerman-Laurance	Ackerman Vouvray	$3.79	5	←All except→	6, 16, 18, 19, 21, 22, 23, 25, 26, 27, 29
Calif.	SD	California Wine Association	Fino Eleven Cellars California Chenin Blanc	$2.85		All except→	14, 15, 16, 17, 21, 27, 28, 29
Calif.	D	Souverain of Alexander Valley	North Coast Dry Chenin Blanc	$2.95	All except→	5, 6, 8, 10, 13, 16, 17, 21, 24, 26, 27
Calif.	D	Winemasters' Guild	California Chenin Blanc	$2.29		All except→	5, 6, 8, 10, 15, 16, 17, 19, 21, 22, 24, 25, 26, 27, 28, 29

* See pp. 26–27 for city code.

NOTE: We found the following wines in very limited distribution to be of outstanding quality: Charlone, Chenin Blanc; Chappellet, Chenin Blanc.

The Everyday White Wines:
Non-French Chablis and Sauterne

United States

Generics: Chablis
          Sauterne

American-produced Chablis and Sauterne are by far the best-selling white wines of this country. They are light, pleasant, and uncomplicated—perfect for drinking at the table on a daily basis when price is an object. Both names are taken from the French wines of the same name but are in no other way related. True Chablis is the light, flinty wine grown around the French village of that name. Sauternes, with an *s*, is the luscious sweet wine from the Sauternes area of France, just south of Bordeaux. The French products are much finer, more substantial wines, made from different grapes and in an altogether different class from our straightforward American product. The American wine producers merely picked up the names some decades ago to give their products a recognized name.

Chablis and Sauterne are two of the American generic white wines (the third is Rhine, discussed in the next section, pp. 142–146). Chablis, a regional name in France, has become a generic name in America. In France it remains strictly geographic; the name only appears on the labels of wine grown on the 4,700 acres of vineyards that surround the town of Chablis, southeast of Paris. By law, French Chablis must be made from the Chardonnay grape, with production per acre limited and a minimum alcoholic level guaranteed.

But outside France the name Chablis on a bottle of wine means very little. In the rest of the world and particularly in the United States, Chablis signifies a general type of wine, white and reasonably dry. Its style is determined by the individual producer, who may or may not choose to give it some character. It is made from a blend of undistinguished and plentiful grape varieties. Since generic wines have no legal definition in this country, the grapes in Chablis can be grown anywhere and be of any variety. Thus, the Chablis you buy at the supermarket could come from a grape as pedestrian as the Thompson seedless or as distinguished as the Chardonnay. It is a safe bet, however, that since the maker decided to label it Chablis, he did not use a grape that would have brought a higher price if bottled under its own name as a varietal. Probably, your Chablis is a blend of such grapes as the Chenin Blanc and the French Colombard, which are productive enough, yet make a good wine that can be sold at a modest price.

Don't be put off by the fact that a wine is blended. A blended wine is not adulterated—quite the opposite—nor is it of lower quality. Most wines benefit from skillful blending. A wine that lacks acidity can be blended with one that has too much, an expensive wine can add some elegance to an inexpensive one, the effect of adverse weather conditions on one year's grape crop can be blended out.

Several California wineries have abandoned the name Chablis and now identify the same wine by the varietal name of the grape that makes up more than half the blend, usually French Colombard or Folle Blanche. This welcome trend toward varietal names gives the consumer a better idea of what he is buying. Although French Colombard is the most extensively planted white-wine grape in California, its name is not widely known, and it remains to be seen whether such a label will attract as many customers as the familiar Chablis.

Nearly every winery in the United States makes a Chablis and a Sauterne, usually its least expensive white table wines. Some wineries make them both in very similar styles, bottling the product under two different names to promote larger sales. When they are different, Sauterne is usually a little less acid than Chablis. American Sauterne can be made from any variety of white-wine grape. Although most of it is dry or semidry, some wineries produce a sweeter version that is generally labeled Haut Sauterne or Château Sauterne. Again, do not confuse these labels with the French Sauternes, which is a sweet white wine of much higher quality.

Chablis and Sauterne are sold by the gallon and half-gallon as well as by the quart and fifth.

Vintage

American Chablis and Sauterne are rarely labeled by vintage because these wines are blended to ensure consistent products from year to year and do not require any additional aging after they are sold. In fact, if they are kept too long they will begin to go downhill.

Tasting Notes

Since almost every winery in America sells a Chablis and a Sauterne, this was an enormous category. In our tastings, we also included other white wines we thought would fit this wine style. They were from France and other countries, characterized by nondescript names and Burgundy-style bottles (the bottle of Chablis' more expensive namesake). We preferred three wines. Two were E. & J. Gallo's Sauterne and Paul Masson's Chablis, both fresh, the Gallo Sauterne a little more elegant, the Masson a little heavier. The other was broader and fuller: Sonoma Vineyards' French Colombard, an aromatic wine, showed the good effects of aging. The other wines listed in the chart were pleasant daily wines. We suspect that in some cases the same wines were being used by California wineries for their Chablis and Sauterne. The American consumer is well served by these inexpensive wines, though over a period of time they would be boring as a daily diet. For a few dimes more you can get a varietal, like a Sauvignon Blanc, also called Fumé Blanc, or a California Chenin Blanc, and receive much more pleasure.

Similar Alternatives

White Graves for a few cents more. American Rhine wine in the same price category.

Congenial Food

American Chablis and Sauterne are pleasant with fowl, fish, white meat, cold dishes, salads, and picnic fare. They are extensively served as an apéritif, and usually ice is added. If you take our advice and drink Sauvignon Blanc instead, you can save the ice.

Notes to Remember

- These are the American white *vins ordinaires*, with prices to match.
- American Chablis and Sauterne carry generic labels and in no way resemble the French wines they were named after.
- If you can afford to buy a varietal, do. The small difference in price buys you a more diversified and pleasurable wine experience.
- Drink them as young as possible—freshness is important.

Tasting Results

Non-French Chablis and Sauterne

Region/ Country of Origin	Dry/Semi-dry/ Sweet/ Very sweet	Producer	Name of Wine	Price	DISTRIBUTION AVAILABILITY BY CITY*		
					General	Limited	None
			Best Wines at Tasting				
Calif.	D	Sonoma Vineyards	Sonoma County French Colombard	$2.79	1, 3, 4	←All except→	6, 24
New York	D	Bully Hill Vineyards	Aurora Blanc	$3.36		All except→	6, 12, 13, 15, 18, 26, 27
Calif.	D	Paul Masson Vineyards	California Chablis	$2.15	All markets		
Calif.	D	E. & J. Gallo	Sauterne of California	$1.59	All markets		
			Highly Ranked Wines				
Calif.	D	Mirassou Vineyards	Monterey White Burgundy	$3.89	All except→	1, 2, 3, 4, 7, 9, 11, 14, 19, 21, 22, 28	
Calif.	D	C. Mondavi & Sons	C. K. Mondavi Chablis	$1.59	1, 2, 3, 4,	←All except→	6, 7, 11, 16, 20, 21, 23, 24, 26, 27
Calif.	D	Christian Brothers	California Sauterne	$2.59		All markets	
Calif.	D	San Martin Vineyards	California Petite Chablis	$2.10	1, 2, 3, 11	←All except→	5, 6, 10
Calif.	D	Cresta Blanca Winery	California French Colombard	$2.55	All except→	10, 14, 17, 20, 22, 26	6, 7, 8, 16, 19, 24, 25, 27, 28
Calif.	D	J. Pedroncelli Winery	Sonoma County Chablis	$2.39	1, 3	2, 4, 7, 9, 10, 12, 13, 14, 15, 22, 23, 24	All others
Calif.	D	Parducci Wine Cellars	Mendocino County Chablis	$3.15	1, 2, 3, 4, 11, 14	←All except→	5, 10, 19, 26
Calif.	D	Italian Swiss Colony	California Gold Chablis	$1.59	All markets		

Tasting Results (continued)

NON-FRENCH CHABLIS AND SAUTERNE

Other Recommended Wines

Region/ Country of Origin	Dry/Semi-dry/ Sweet/ Very sweet	Producer	Name of Wine	Price	DISTRIBUTION AVAILABILITY BY CITY*		
					General	Limited	None
Calif.	D	California Wine Association	L. & J. California Chablis	$1.29		All except→	11, 15, 16, 19, 20, 21, 27, 28
Calif.	D	California Wine Association	L. & J. California Sauterne	$1.29		All except→	11, 15, 16, 19, 20, 21, 27, 28
Calif.	D	California Wine Association	Guasti California Chablis	$1.29		1, 2, 3, 4, 5, 7, 9, 12, 13	All others
Calif.	D	San Martin Vineyards	California Mountain Chablis	$2.10	1, 2, 3, 7, 9, 11, 14, 15, 19, 23	←All except→	5, 6, 10
Calif.	D	Simi Winery	North Coast Chablis	$2.45		All except→	6, 8, 16, 17, 20, 25, 28
Calif.	D	Almadén Vineyards	California Mountain White Sauterne	$2.10	All markets		
Calif.	D	Sebastiani Vineyards	North Coast Counties Mountain Chablis	$1.65	All except→	6, 10, 20, 25	
Calif.	D	Almadén Vineyards	California Chablis	$2.10	All markets		
Calif.	D	Heitz Cellar	Napa Valley Chablis	$3.19		All except→	5, 6, 8, 10, 18, 19, 25, 26, 27, 28
Calif.	D	Inglenook	North Coast Counties Vintage Chablis	$2.59	All except→	5, 7, 10, 14, 16, 17, 18, 19, 20, 23, 25, 26, 28	

State	Type	Winery / Brand	Price			
Calif.	D	California Wine Association — Fino Eleven Cellars California Chablis	$2.09		All except→	14, 15, 16, 17, 21, 27, 28, 29
Calif.	D	Wente Bros. — California Chablis	$2.35		All markets	
Calif.	D	M. LaMont Vineyards — California French Colombard	$1.99	1, 2, 3, 4, 10, 11, 13, 18, 20, 22, 23	6, 9, 25	All others
Calif.	D	Louis M. Martini — California Mountain Chablis	$2.59	1, 2, 3	All others	
Calif.	D	Souverain of Alexander Valley — North Coast Chablis	$2.40	All except→		5, 6, 8, 10, 13, 16, 17, 21, 24, 26, 27
Calif.	D	California Growers Winery — California Chablis	(L.A.) $0.99	1, 3	12, 13, 23	All others
Calif.	SD	B. Cribari & Sons Winery — Cribari California Vino Bianco Da Pranzo	$1.39	All except→	18, 28	14, 15, 19, 21, 24, 26, 27
Calif.	D	Concannon Vineyard — California Chablis	$2.50	1, 2	←All except→	6, 10, 18, 19, 27, 28
Calif.	D	Los Hermanos California Vineyards — Mountain Chablis	(½ gal.) $3.70		All markets	
Calif.	D	California Wine Association — Vino Fino California White Wine	$1.29		All except→	11, 15, 16, 19, 20, 21, 27, 28
Calif.	D.	Monterey Vineyard — Del Mar Ranch White Monterey Wine	$2.90		All markets	

* See pp. 26–27 for city code.

White Wines in the German Style

California

Generic: Rhine Wine
Varietals: Sylvaner (Riesling)
          Emerald Riesling
          Grey Riesling

Alsace, France

Varietal: Sylvaner

Austria, Yugoslavia, Argentina

Some American blends, although named for European wines of traditional elegance and distinction, are only common table wines. They're not imposters in price or taste, but simply products labeled with splendid but wildly incongruous names. Just as American wine producers appropriated the names Sauterne and Chablis from France and put them on blends very different from the original, they took "Rhine wine" from Germany in much the same fashion. In fact, there is very little difference in taste or quality between any of these three under their American labels, and we suspect that some wineries even use the same blend.

A generic name theoretically describes the style of the wine, but few of the American products labeled Rhine wine even suggest the characteristics of their namesakes, which are light and fresh white wines, filled with fruit and flavor, balance and elegance. This is not to deny that the American Rhine wines have merit, but they are different, grown on different soil and made from different grapes. While the genuine Rhine wines are grown in specific vineyards from specified grape varieties (Riesling, Sylvaner, etc.), American Rhine wine can be made from any grape grown anywhere in this country. As a result, the American wines vary tremendously in character and quality, from dry to semisweet. Ultimately, we can only describe this diverse category as white table wine.

True Riesling is made in Germany from one of the world's noblest grapes, the Riesling, sometimes called White or Johannisberg Riesling (see pp. 107–123). American producers are permitted to label as Riesling wine produced from three entirely different grapes, the Sylvaner, Emerald Riesling, and Grey Riesling, as well as genuine Riesling.

Although it is not a Riesling, the Sylvaner is used in France and Germany for making Rhine wine, and it is also one of the principal grapes in Liebfraumilch. It is unfortunate that American wine made from the Sylvaner can be labeled Riesling, because the Sylvaner is a fine grape in its own right and deserves to carry its own name. When it is planted in California, the Sylvaner produces a fresh wine quite different from Sylvaner grown in Germany. It is golden in color, with little bouquet but good fruit and balance. California Sylvaner reaches a higher level of ripeness, at the expense of acidity, than in Germany, and is consequently broader with less fruit than its German counterpart.

Sylvaner is also grown in the Alsace region of France, along the Rhine just north of Switzerland. Here the wines have more style than the ones from California, but less body. They are always dry. Alsatian Sylvaners are sold as a varietal and, under French law, must consist entirely of that grape variety.

An American grape, the Emerald Riesling, is a cross of the Riesling and the Muscadelle. Its clean fresh taste and low price have made it very popular, and it should be drunk very young because it ages quickly. Often labeled simply Riesling, it is not as substantial as Sylvaner.

Unlike Emerald Riesling, the Grey Riesling is not even related to the true Riesling grape. It is made from the Chauché Gris, which produces a mild, soft, bland wine. The best Grey Riesling is grown in the Livermore Valley, southeast of San Francisco, but it does not merit the distinguished name it carries. Green Hungarian, a grape of uncertain origins, also produces a bland, inoffensive wine.

Vintage

For these American versions using German names, vintage is unimportant. Most of them are sold without a year on the label. Dates should be taken as an indication of age rather than quality. All these wines should be drunk young, no more than three years old, or two in the case of Emerald Riesling.

Tasting Notes

Like American Sauterne and Chablis, this proved to be a category of pleasant, undistinguished, everyday white wines with only an Austrian wine of uncertain origin, a California Grey Riesling from Sonoma County, and a California Emerald Riesling from Santa Clara titillating our rather bored taste buds.

Similar Alternatives

Consider American Chablis and Sauterne, but do try the white varietals, Sauvignon Blanc, Chenin Blanc, and Sémillon.

Congenial Food

Fowl, white meat, cold dishes, picnic foods, light fare.

Notes to Remember

- American Rhine wine, a generic label, like American Chablis and Sauterne, in no way resembles the European wine it was named after. If you can afford to buy a varietal, do.
- Try the California Sylvaner varietal, often labeled Riesling, before the Emerald Riesling, but don't expect a lot from either.
- Drink them as young as possible—freshness is important.

Tasting Results

White Wines in the German Style

Region/ Country of Origin	Dry/Semi-dry/ Sweet/ Very sweet	Producer	Name of Wine	Price	DISTRIBUTION AVAILABILITY BY CITY*		
					General	Limited	None
Best Wines at Tasting							
Austria	D	Lenz Moser	Tytell Lipizzaner	$2.76		All except→	1, 6, 11, 14, 17, 23, 24, 26, 28, 29
Calif.	SD	San Martin Vineyards	Santa Clara Valley Emerald Riesling	$2.10		All markets	
Calif.	SD	Sonoma Vineyards	Sonoma County Grey Riesling	$2.99		All markets	
Highly Ranked Wines							
Calif.	D	Paul Masson Vineyards	California Riesling	$2.39		All markets	
Calif.	SD	Italian Swiss Colony	Rhine, California	$1.59	All markets		
Calif.	D	Sebastiani Vineyards	North Coast Counties Green Hungarian	$2.29			
Calif.	D	Parducci Wine Cellars	Mendocino County Sylvaner Riesling	$3.73		All markets	
Calif.	D	Almadén Vineyards	California Mountain Grey Riesling	$1.85	All markets		

Tasting Results (continued)

WHITE WINES IN THE GERMAN STYLE

Region/ Country of Origin	Dry/Semi-dry/ Sweet/ Very sweet	Producer	Name of Wine	Price	DISTRIBUTION AVAILABILITY BY CITY*		
					General	Limited	None
Other Recommended Wines							
Calif.	SD	E. & J. Gallo	Prime Vineyard Rhine Garten, California	$1.39		All markets	
Calif.	D	Beringer Vineyards	North Coast Grey Riesling	$2.99		All markets	All others
Calif.	D	California Wine Association	Guasti California Rhine	$1.29		1, 2, 3, 4, 5, 7, 9, 12, 13	
Calif.	SD	Almadén Vineyards	California Mountain Rhine	$1.85	All markets		
Argentina	D	Valmont	Valmont Riesling Kleinburg	$2.99		All markets	5, 6, 10
Calif.	D	San Martin Vineyards	California Sylvaner Riesling (L.A.)	$2.50		All except→	
Yugoslavia	D	Adriatica	Rizling from Fruška Gora	$2.59		All markets	
Calif.	D	Louis M. Martini	California Mountain Riesling (Sylvaner)	$3.19		All markets	
Calif.	D	Cresta Blanca Winery	California Grey Riesling	$2.55		All markets	
Calif.	D	Souverain of Alexander Valley	Mendocino County Grey Riesling	$2.99		All markets	
New York	SD	Gold Seal	New York State Rhine	$2.00	2, 4, 7, 10, 18	←All except→	1, 3, 6, 9, 12, 13, 23, 26, 27, 29
Calif.	D	Christian Brothers	Napa Valley Riesling	$3.15	All markets		
Calif.	D	Wente Bros.	California Grey Riesling	$2.95	All markets		
Calif.	SD	Paul Masson Vineyards	Emerald Dry	$2.25	All markets		
Calif.	SD	Mirassou Vineyards	Monterey Riesling	$3.59	All except→	1, 2, 3, 4, 7, 9, 11, 12, 14, 19, 21, 22, 29	

* See pp. 26–27 for city code.

White Wines of Italy, Spain, and Portugal

Italy	*Spain*	*Portugal*
Regionals: Soave	Regionals: Rioja	Regional: Vinho Verde
Frascati	Panadés	
Orvieto		
Varietal: Verdicchio		

We have grouped the white wines of Italy, Spain, and Portugal together because, though they are fresh, fragrant, and satisfying when made well, they grow in hot, sunny areas that share certain winemaking problems. Fine white wine is harder to make in southern climes than it is farther north. A distinguished white wine is usually low in alcohol, with a pleasant, fruity acidity that gives it freshness and life. Grapes that are baked under the sun produce wine that is high in alcohol, low in acidity, and is often broad without an offsetting fruity charm. In addition, the makers of these southern wines age them too long before bottling and shipping, and slow movement through the distribution channels does nothing to improve them. They can lose their freshness, become oxydized and dull, and show regrettably little of the charm they must have had when they left home.

ITALY

SOAVE

The best of the few Italian white wines that reach this country is Soave, a firm, well-balanced wine of some freshness and fragrance. Soave is grown in a hilly area east of Verona, the best coming from a smaller subregion identified as Classico. The sun is not too harsh there, and the soil is well suited to white-wine grapes, so Soave gains the acidity lacking in some of the other southern white wines we discuss here.

Soave is made from several grape varieties, principally Garganega and Trebbiano. There are only a few volume producers of this wine, and they usually supplement their own vineyard harvest by buying from smaller growers. These producers, such as Bolla and Ruffino, are large modern wineries that utilize the most advanced winemaking techniques.

FRASCATI

Another popular Italian white wine is Frascati, from the town of the same name in the Castelli Romani district just south of Rome. Made in large part from Trebbiano and Malvasia grapes, it can be dry (*secco*), semi-dry, (*amabile*), or sweet (*cannellino*). The dry version is shipped to this country. Grown in a hot climate, Frascati is picked green to preserve the acidity necessary for good balance. Unfortunately, it does not travel well.

ORVIETO

From the town of Orvieto in Umbria, north of Rome, comes the light, delicate, semi-sweet wine of that name. Like Frascati, Orvieto is primarily made from the Trebbiano and Malvasia grapes and comes in *secco* or *amabile* versions, with the semidry also called *abboccato*. The dry version, blended with more Trebbiano to meet the current style trend, lacks the distinction of the old-fashioned semi-sweet Orvieto.

VERDICCHIO

Verdicchio is a varietal, made from the grape of that name and up to 20 percent Trebbiano and Malvasia, and its taste goes from full-flavored to bitter. Verdicchio is grown in the Apennine foothills near the Adriatic coast, and its Classico section occupies most of the vineyard area. Though Verdicchio can be enjoyable with Italian food, when tasted alone it lacks fruit and flavor.

SPAIN

Spanish white wines do not occupy a large place in the American market, partly because they were sold here for many years under generic names like Spanish Chablis and Spanish Sauterne and did not develop any identity of their own. This labeling practice is no longer permitted, and Spanish wine relies largely on its low price rather than identifiable reputation to attract its customers.

There are two white-wine–producing regions in Spain that export to the United States: Rioja, in the Ebro Valley southwest of the Pyrenees, and Panadés, south of Barcelona on the Catalonian coast. Rioja, which is justly famous for its distinguished red wines, produces dry and semi-sweet whites as well. The dry is a pleasant but not distinguished wine, pale gold in color, aged in wood and sold in Burgundy-shape bottles to resemble true Chablis. The semisweet wines are pleasant when well chilled, their sweetness making up for a lack of character. They are usually sold in Rhine-wine bottles.

The Panadés wines are normally dry and pale golden in color, and the best of them have a little more fruit and less acidity than the wines from Rioja. Although they lack the distinction and varietal character of wines made from the Chardonnay, they are not unworthy substitutes, and they are cheaper because they are less distinguished.

PORTUGAL

The Portuguese ship one white wine abroad in significant quantity, Vinho Verde (literally, "green wine"). Green is not a reference to the color of the wine—actually it can be either white, red, or rosé—but to the fact that the grapes are picked when they are not fully ripe, in order to get less sugar and more acid. The result is an extremely dry wine, perhaps too dry for many people.

Vinho Verde can be produced only in a legally established region between the Douro and Minho rivers in northern Portugal, and is authentic only if it carries the Selo de Origem of the Comissão de Viticultura de Região dos Vinhos Verdes. The vines there are trained high off the ground, on trees and arbors, to lessen the effect of the hot Portuguese sun and make maximum use of the land, because the farmers grow other crops under the arbors.

Light in alcohol, Vinho Verde tends to have a slight prickle because it is bottled only four or five months after the vintage, when the wine still retains some carbon dioxide. In the past, wine with bubbles that was imported to the United States was subject to the high tax levied on fine French champagne, and the Portuguese shipped Vinho Verde here without the traditional sparkle. Now the law treats wine with a light sparkle the same as still table wines, so Vinho Verde is available here with its characteristic effervescence. Many Vinhos Verdes are made by the large, successful shippers of Portuguese rosé, so the white wines have good distribution in the United States.

Vintage

Unlike their French and German counterparts, these Italian and Iberian wines vary little from vintage to vintage, because the southern climate makes poor years relatively rare. They should all be drunk young, no more than three years old. Frascati ought to be drunk within a year, which is nearly impossible here. The more popular wines turn over faster and thus are more likely to be fresh.

Tasting Notes

The three best wines in this category were all Soaves, the best of them the largest-selling Soave in the United States. Their freshness and youth confirmed our theory that wines from southern climes should be drunk young.

As a control, we put into this tasting some of the best wines from the American Chablis category, to see how the panel would find these widely sold wines in comparison to Italian and Iberian whites. Though the panel agreed that Soave had more taste and distinction than Chablis by Paul Masson and Concannon, they infinitely preferred these American Chablis to all other wines tasted in this category, which included Spanish whites of various origins, Frascati, Verdicchio, and Portuguese whites. Basically these wines cannot be faulted as everyday whites, but certainly bear out our contention that excessive sun does not create distinctive white wines.

We tasted separately a number of white wines with a degree of sweetness and found Riunite from Sicily and Brillante from Spain attractive, their attractiveness no doubt being due to no small extent to their freshness. Being popular wines, they were young and pleasant enough for everyday use. However, they proved dull and boring tasted against wines with a degree of sweetness from France and Germany.

Similar Alternatives

American Chablis and Sauterne.

Congenial Food

Italian and Iberian white wines go well with seafood, chicken, veal, cold dishes, and picnic fare.

Notes to Remember

- In this category, Soave is the best wine.
- You should drink all wines in this category as young as possible, and never older than three years.
- The more popular the wine, the fresher it is likely to be. Success means better wines on the shelf.
- If you want an inexpensive semidry white, try Brillante or Riunite.
- Except for Soave, Brillante, and Riunite, you are just as well served with a Chablis from a premium California winery—generally under $3.

Tasting Results

WHITE WINES OF ITALY, SPAIN, AND PORTUGAL

Region/ Country of Origin	Dry/Semi-dry/ Sweet/ Very sweet	Producer	Name of Wine	Price	DISTRIBUTION AVAILABILITY BY CITY*		
					General	Limited	None
			Best Wines at Tasting				
Italy	D	Bolla	Soave Classico	$3.59	All except→	12, 13, 16, 17, 18, 23, 25, 26, 28, 29	
			Highly Ranked Wines				
Italy	D	Masi	Soave Classico Superiore	$3.55	2, 3, 4, 7, 20	1, 11, 14, 15, 16, 17, 18, 21, 25, 27	All others
Italy	D	Ruffino	Soave Classico Superiore	$3.59		All markets	
			Other Recommended Wines				
Italy	D	Fazi Battaglia	Titulus Verdicchio	$3.50	1, 2, 4, 6, 7, 8	All others	
Italy	D	Bertani	Soave	$3.40	1, 2, 5, 7, 8, 11	All others	
Portugal	D	Mateus	Branco	$3.19	All markets		
Italy	D	Antinori	Est! Est! Est!	$3.20		All markets	
Italy	D	Antinori	Bianco della Costa Toscana	$3.89		All markets	
Italy	D	Santa Sofia	Soave Classico Superiore	$3.25	1, 2, 3, 4, 7, 11, 14	All others	
Spain	D	René Barbier	Blanco Seco	$2.29	1, 2, 4, 8, 14	All others	
Italy	SD	Riunite	Bianco	$2.29		All markets	
Portugal	SD	Lancers	Vinho Branco	$4.25	All except→	17, 18, 23, 24, 25, 27, 28	9
Spain	SD	Bodegas Bilbainas	Brillante Blanco	$3.29	2	←All except→	5, 6, 8, 17, 21, 22, 26, 27

* See pp. 26–27 for rating code.

ROSÉS

California

Varietals: Grenache Rosé
           Gamay Rosé
           Cabernet Sauvignon Rosé
Generic: Rosé

France

Regionals: Anjou Rosé
            Tavel Rosé
            Côtes de Provence Rosé

All Other Countries

Generic: Rosé

Rosé wine is a total joy for those who like it and a thing to be avoided for those who disapprove. It is a case of disapproval rather than mere dislike, because a rosé is considered to be something of a stepchild by wine experts. It is neither white nor red, but somewhere in between. For not the first time in history, though, the stepchild is having the laugh on the aristocrats, because rosé now accounts for about 20 percent of American wine consumption. For many Americans, rosé is a first step in the wine-drinking experience.

Rosé takes its name from the French word for pink. The traditionally accepted way to make a rosé is to leave the dark skins of red grapes in the juice for about the first twenty-four hours of the fermentation cycle, just long enough to color the wine pink. If the juice were drained off immediately, a white wine would result; if it were left longer, the wine would become red, as some American rosés are.

Rosé can be made by mixing red and white wine, but it is not as fresh and fruity as wine made by the traditional method. Once a rosé is taken off the grape skins, it is treated like a white wine for the rest of the vinification process. Sometimes it is given a degree of sweetness by arresting the fermentation before all the sugar has been converted into alcohol. Rosé can be made from any red grape with white juice, but the most successful are Grenache, Cabernet Franc, Cabernet Sauvignon, Gamay, Zinfandel, and Carignan.

Rosé has no geographic home; almost every wine-growing area produces some. It is never a great wine and only rarely a fine one, but that does not mean that some rosés are not very much better than others. Higher quality usually results from a grape variety that is particularly well suited to the place of origin, or from successful blending of wines made from several grape varieties.

The rosés made in the United States are sold under two designations. By far the largest is the pink wine labeled Rosé or Vin Rosé. These wines can be made from any suitable grape variety, but are usually a blend of several. In California the Carignan grape is a popular base, because it is productive and gives good color. American rosés are made for every taste, from dry to sweet, and many wineries produce both a dry and semi-sweet version.

Popular belief is that a rosé's quality is better if it is made predominantly from a single grape and marketed under a varietal name, such as Grenache Rosé. Most of the varietal rosé wines come from California, and the grape varieties used are Grenache, Gamay, Cabernet, and Zinfandel. Gamay, Cabernet, and Zinfandel rosés are usually dry, while Grenache rosé is produced in both a dry and semidry version. We have found no particular difference in quality between wines labeled simply Vin Rosé and the ones bearing a varietal label.

Tavel is generally accepted as the best rosé made in France. It is made principally from the Grenache grape in the vicinity of Tavel, a village across the Rhone River from Châteauneuf-du-Pape. The wine is orange-pink and full-bodied as rosés go, and yet dry and delicate with finesse. Much of the 600,000-gallon production comes from the district's cooperative cellar, but there are also estate-bottled Tavels, some of which are widely distributed in the United States.

Several other good rosés are made in southern France. Lirac, just north of Tavel, produces one similar to that of its famous neighbor but less expensive. Southeast of this area is the immense Côtes de Provence along the Mediterranean coast between Marseilles and Nice. There rosés are made from a variety of grapes and, though dry, tend to be more alcoholic and fatter. These wines are popular in France. A somewhat lighter version is blended for foreign markets.

Of the successful rosés produced in the Loire Valley, the most famous come from Anjou. The wine called Rosé d'Anjou is made from an assortment of grapes (Groslot, Gamay, Cot, Noble, Pineau d'Aunis) and is full, mellow, and lightly perfumed. Normally of better quality is Cabernet Rosé d'Anjou (also called Anjou Rosé de Cabernet), which is made from Cabernet Franc and Cabernet Sauvignon grapes. It is fruitier and fresher, with more bouquet, and, not surprisingly, is more expensive. Generally, the Cabernet is drier than Rosé d'Anjou.

Since World War II, rosés from Portugal have dominated the import market in the United States, primarily those sold under the Mateus and Lancer labels. Their popularity is a result of skillful promotion, attractive packaging and pricing, and blends that appeal to the American taste. The main rosé area in Portugal is the Douro River in the north, but the wine can come from anywhere in the country because there are no legally designated production regions. There are also no requirements as to which grape must be used, making Portugal's wine supply very elastic, expanding to meet increasing demand without sacrificing competitive price.

Vintage

Any vintage found on a bottle of rosé is an indication of age, not quality. Rosé does not differ from year to year. As a rule, drink rosé young, not more than three years old. The better Tavels might last another year or so.

Tasting Notes

Our panel, professionals and knowledgeable consumers, approached the rosé tasting with condescension and prejudice bordering on hostility. They had assumed over the years that rosé was a kind of pink soda pop, and wanted to get the tasting over quickly and move on to more interesting wines.

But the rosés proved to be of enormous interest. There was a wide variety of different wine styles, which made them both difficult and challenging to taste. One of our most important conclusions, as the tasting results show, was that the price of a rosé definitely does not correlate with its quality.

The wines were all pleasant, and some of them were quite outstanding, with individual character giving them an identity of their own. We concluded that there is a sounder basis for the wide popularity of rosé in this country than we had believed. The wine is easy to drink because it is not very complicated, and seems well suited to a consuming public that does not demand the finesse, elegance, and complexity that professionals value in the finer wines.

Similar Alternatives

None.

Congenial Food

These wines are great with all fast foods; McDonald's of the Golden Arches, Howard Johnson's, and Kentucky Fried Chicken are in, caviar is out. Ideal for summer lunches and suppers, picnics and snacks, but not for dessert.

Notes to Remember

- American rosés are good value. Give them a try.
- There is little relationship between price and quality.
- American rosés vary tremendously in sweetness. Many wineries produce both a dry and semisweet version.
- Drink rosé young, not more than three years old.

Tasting Results

Rosés, Dry

Region/ Country of Origin	Dry/Semi-dry/ Sweet/ Very sweet	Producer	Name of Wine	Price	DISTRIBUTION AVAILABILITY BY CITY*		
					General	Limited	None
			Best Wines at Tasting				
Calif.	D	Italian Swiss Colony	California Grenache Rosé	$1.49	All markets		
			Highly Ranked Wines				
Calif.	D	Inglenook	Napa Valley Gamay Rosé	$2.99	1, 2, 3, 4	All others	
Calif.	D	Louis M. Martini	California Mountain Vin Rosé	$2.39	1, 2, 3, 4, 5, 6, 7, 9, 23, 27, 29	All others	
Calif.	D	Christian Brothers	California Vin Rosé	$2.59	All markets		
Calif.	D	Robert Mondavi Winery	Napa Valley Gamay Rosé	$3.36	1, 2, 3, 12	←All except→	6, 8, 10, 16, 17, 19, 28
Calif.	D	Sonoma Vineyards	Sonoma County Grenache Rosé	$2.79		All markets	

156

Other Recommended Wines

Calif.	D	California Wine Association	Fino Eleven Cellars California Vin Rosé	$2.09		All except→	14, 15, 16, 20, 26, 27, 28, 29
Calif.	D	Almadén Vineyards	California Grenache Rosé	$2.10	All markets	All except→	1
France	D	Sichel	Rosé de Provence	$2.93		All others	
France	D	Cruse	Grenache Rosé	$3.45	1, 2	All markets	
Spain	D	Paternina	Rosado	$1.98		All others	
France	D	Cruse	Tavel	$4.55	1, 2, 4	All markets	
France	D	Chapoutier	Tavel La Marcelle	$4.99		All markets	
New York	D	Taylor Wine Company	New York State Rosé	$2.15	All except→	1, 3, 5, 9, 12, 13, 23, 26, 27, 28, 29	
New York	D	Widmer Vineyards	Naples Valley Isabella Rosé	$2.49	2, 4, 6, 7, 10, 11, 14, 18, 20, 25	1, 5, 8, 16, 17, 22, 28	All others
Calif.	D	Paul Masson Vineyards	California Vin Rosé Sec	$2.15	All markets		
New York	D	Gold Seal	Catawba Pink	$1.89		All markets	
Calif.	D	Sebastiani Vineyards	North Coast Counties Vin Rosé	$2.15	All except→	6, 10, 20, 25	
Calif.	D	Italian Swiss Colony	Pink Chablis of California	$1.59		All markets	
Calif.	D	Brookside Vineyard Company	California Vino Rosado (L.A.)	$1.65	1, 3, 29	All markets	
Calif.	D	Roma Winery	California Pink Chablis	$1.59		All markets	All others

* See pp. 26–27 for city code.

157

Tasting Results

Rosés, Other Than Dry

Region/ Country of Origin	Dry/Semi-dry/ Sweet/ Very sweet	Producer	Name of Wine	Price	DISTRIBUTION AVAILABILITY BY CITY*		
					General	Limited	None
			Best Wines at Tasting				
Calif.	SD	Roma Winery	California Vin Rosé	$1.59	All except→	3, 5, 6, 27	1, 9, 12, 13, 15, 26
Calif.	SD	Christian Brothers	California Napa Rosé	$2.59	All markets		
			Highly Ranked Wines				
Calif.	SD	E. & J. Gallo	Prime Vineyard Vin Rosé of California	$1.39	All markets		
Calif.	SD	Franzia	Vin Rosé of California	$1.29	All markets		
			Other Recommended Wines				
Israel	SD	Carmel Wine Company	Israel Grenache Rosé	$2.25		1, 2, 3, 4, 7, 8, 10, 11, 15, 18, 19, 20, 22	
Portugal	SD	Publicker Distillers (importer)	Trovador Rosé	$1.99	1, 2, 4, 6, 10, 14, 21, 22, 24	←All except→	8, 15, 19, 20, 26, 27, 28, 29

Origin	Code	Winery	Wine	Price	Markets	Markets	Markets
Calif.	SD	San Martin Vineyards	California Mountain Vin Rosé	$2.10	1, 2, 3, 9, 11, 14, 15	←All except→	4, 5, 6, 10
Washington State	SD	Ste. Michelle Vintners	Washington State Grenache Rosé	$2.49		All except→ 4, 7, 10, 16, 17, 18, 19	6, 23
Michigan	SD	Warner Vineyards	Cask Michigan Mountain Rosé Wine	$1.75	5, 11		All others
New York	SD	Great Western	New York State Rosé	$2.19	2, 4, 5, 6, 8, 10, 11, 18, 20, 25	1, 14, 16, 17, 19, 21, 22, 24, 27, 29	All others
New York	SD	Taylor Wine Company	New York State Lake Country Pink	$2.15	All except→	1, 3, 9, 12, 13, 23, 25, 26, 27, 28, 29	
Portugal	SD	C. Da Silva	Isabel Rosé	$2.79	All except→	11, 19, 21, 23	
Calif.	SD	Almadén Vineyards	California Mountain Nectar Vin Rosé	$2.10	All markets	All markets	
France	SD	Moc-Baril	Rosé d'Anjou	$2.98	1, 2, 3, 4, 5, 10	All others	
New York	SD	Widmer's Wine Cellars	New York State Naples Valley Pink	$2.09	2, 4, 6, 7, 10, 11, 14, 18, 20, 25	1, 5, 8, 16, 17, 22, 28	All others
France	SD	Sichel	Amourosé	$3.19	10, 14	All others	
France	SD	Chanson	Rosé des Anges (Anjou)	$2.50		All markets	
Spain	VS	Bodegas Bilbainas	Brillante Vino Rosado	$3.29	2, 16	←All except→	
Calif.	SD	B. Cribari & Sons Winery	Cribari California Vino Fiamma Da Pranzo	$1.39	All except→	18, 28	14, 15, 21, 24, 26, 27

* See pp. 26–27 for city code.

OTHER NORTH AMERICAN WINES

U.S. Wines Produced East of the Rockies and Canadian-Produced Wines

Although most of the wine drunk in the United States comes from Europe or California, there is significant wine production elsewhere in this country, primarily in New York, Michigan, and Ohio, and it accounts for 18 percent of all wine sold in America. In Canada, too, a sizable industry has developed.

UNITED STATES

The native American wines differ principally from their European and California cousins because they are made from grapes that are indigenous to North America. As we have seen, the basic European grape is a member of the species *Vitis vinifera*, which was successfully transplanted in California to create the thriving industry there. Among the outstanding vinifera grapes are Cabernet Sauvignon, Pinot Noir, Chardonnay, and Riesling; they produce wines of subtler taste and character than the American grapes. It is possible to grow vinifera in states other than California, but it is very difficult. The European vines are vulnerable to harsh winter weather, particularly to severe frosts that penetrate the ground and freeze the sap in their roots. In addition, unlike the American grape varieties, vinifera tends to ripen late and is thus unable to enjoy a long-enough growing season, except in California and parts of Washington State.

There are some methods of solving the problem of grapes that are less than fully ripened. When white wine is being made, sugar can be added to produce alcohol and water can be added to reduce acidity. But ripeness is essential for red wines. It gives them color, balance, and body.

Our native species, such as *Vitis labrusca*, *Vitis riparia*, and *Vitis rupestris*, grow in the eastern United States and Canada. They were originally discovered growing wild on the Atlantic coast, in such profusion, in fact, that the Vikings called the country Vinland. They are hardy vines, resistant to the harsh winter climate of the Northeast, and their grapes have a pronounced taste and unique character. They produce wines that are very pungent and have the grapy flavor, almost like the juice or jelly made from Concord grapes, that wine tasters call "foxy." Generally, these wines are more successful when they have a degree of sweetness. People who are introduced to wine drinking through these native American products often develop a strong preference for this taste, but sometimes it is too pronounced for wine drinkers who are used to the European vinifera products, whether grown here or abroad.

To bridge this gap, hybrids of the European and American species have been developed, combining some of the native vines' hardiness with the more delicate taste of the vinifera. The French as well as the Americans have experimented extensively with these vines, although the laws in France restrict the use of such grapes to non-appellation wine or *vin ordinaire*.

These hybrids have been the most encouraging development for the American wine industry outside California, but, unfortunately, breeding a successful hybrid is very long, painstaking work. Hundreds or even thousands of combinations must be grown and tasted to produce one with the strengths of its parents but without their weaknesses.

Each of these new grape hybrids is assigned a number during its development; only the few successful ones are ultimately given names of their own. It takes several years after the initial crossing to produce the first grapes, then some twenty years to determine whether the vine is resistant to cold and to check the ultimate taste of the grape, which changes as the vine matures. It is work for patient men.

Such long labors have been rewarded, and there are now a number of hybrids that combine resistance to cold weather with taste and bouquet reminiscent of their European ancestors. The native American grapes have to be hot-pressed to extract color, but red hybrids do not. Among the most successful red hybrids are Baco Noir, Chancellor, de Chaunac, Chelois, and Maréchal Foch; the whites include Aurora, Seyval, and Verdelet.

These eastern U.S. wines often have a less pronounced taste because they can be blended up to 25 percent with California wines from the vinifera stock, moderating the strong character of the native grapes. Winemakers can blend more than 25 percent California if they choose, but the final product must then be labeled "American" rather than "New York" or "Michigan," etc.

CANADA

In Canada, some of the French settlers in the seventeenth century tried unsuccessfully to plant *Vitis vinifera*. Early in the 1800s commercial wineries were established in Ontario, and by 1900 wine production had become an important part of the Canadian economy. Then Prohibition, adopted on a province-by-province basis, raised new difficulties. In Ontario, wine remained legal but could only be obtained at the winery in minimum lots of five gallons or a case. Quebec resisted Prohibition with French tenacity and never did outlaw wine or beer.

While Prohibition did little to improve the quality of Canadian wine, it brought a dramatic increase in its quantity. When wine produced within the province became the only legal alcoholic beverage in Ontario, the rush to open new wineries was on. Prohibition went into effect nationally in the United States in 1920, and this further stimulated Canadian wine production; shipments ostensibly bound for Cuba, Nassau, or Mexico found their way into the United States with amazing regularity.

By 1927, six years earlier than their American cousins, Canadians had had their fill of the "Noble Experiment" and exchanged Prohibition for government control. The sale of alcoholic beverages was legalized, but only at government-monopoly stores operated by each of the ten provinces and two territories. A board of commissioners was established in each province to manage the retail stores and to decide, among other things, which wines on the world market would be available to Canadian consumers.

As a result, the quality and number of wines that can be bought varies from province to province. Among the factors affecting the selection are consumer preferences as reflected in sales volume, the urban or rural character of the province, and the popularity of locally produced wines. Ontario operates a special "rare wine" store for wines of small production for which there is limited demand. In Quebec, the Liquor Control Board itself buys inexpensive wine outside the province and bottles and sells it inside.

Most Canadian vineyards are in Ontario, on the Niagara peninsula between Lake Ontario and Lake Erie. The two lakes moderate extremes of temperature in the area, making the climate milder than the New York State wine district only a hundred miles to the east. There are now about 22,000 acres under cultivation there. The other important wine-growing region is the Okanagan Valley in British Columbia, where production has increased tremendously in recent years. Growers there hope to duplicate the success with the vinifera that has been achieved south of the border in the state of Washington.

A considerable volume of Canadian wines is also "produced," in a manner of speaking, in other provinces. They import it from California and Europe, sometimes in concentrated form, and bottle it locally, thus qualifying for special consideration from the provincial liquor-control authorities. In addition, at a very rough guess, about half the wine drunk in Canada is home-made, taking it outside the scope of this book.

The Canadian wine market used to be dominated by fortified wines like port and sherry, which are about 50 percent higher in alcohol and normally not drunk with food. Today there is more interest in the lighter table wines that are designed to accompany meals, and this has encouraged wineries to pay more attention to their quality.

In a related, encouraging trend, production and marketing of individual hybrid wines are increasing rapidly. One of the most successful hybrid grapes is the de Chaunac, named for Adhemar de Chaunac, for many years the winemaker for T. G. Bright and Company.

Most of the wine made in Canada, however, is still made from native American grape varieties and is sold under generic names, like Claret or Sauterne, or under the brand name of the producer. Sale of varietal wines has only recently become important, and there are no laws as yet establishing what proportion of the variety on the label must be in the bottle, as there are in France and the United States.

Rapidly growing demand continues to increase Canadian wine production, and consumer interest in better wines has encouraged the wineries to make more progress in the quality of table wines in the last twenty years than had been achieved in the previous three hundred.

Vintage

Vintage is not important for either Canadian or U.S. wines coming from east of the Rockies. Most of the wines are not even vintage-dated, so the problem does not arise.

Tasting Notes

We limited ourselves to wines from the native American grapes or hybrids. Because of the very limited plantings of vinifera in this country outside California, we tasted those wines with the comparable California and European wines.

The best red wines showed the tremendous strides of the New York wine industry in using French-American hybrids. The wines made from hybrids were preferred by the panel, though the members felt there were fewer pleasant red wines than white ones from east of the Rockies. We also found that in wines made largely from native American grapes a degree of sweetness was desirable, which was not the case with hybrids.

When tasting the Canadian-produced wines, we were favorably surprised by what we tasted, particularly by the quality of the red wines. No doubt hybrids have refined the taste of these wines, and the Canadian consumer can find a pleasant red wine for around $1.50. Some finer hybrids and even European varietals are now being made in small amounts, which will ultimately give the consumer a selection of locally grown wines of which he should be proud. The whites and rosés were pleasant enough daily wines, but many of them were found too sweet by the tasting panel.

Similar Alternatives

None.

Congenial Food

Since this chapter discusses both white and red wines, you will find a wine for every dish; we suggest you consult the Food and Wine Chart, pages 212–214.

Tasting Results

U.S. WINES PRODUCED EAST OF THE ROCKIES—RED WINES

Region/ Country of Origin	Dry/Semi-dry/ Sweet/ Very sweet	Producer	Name of Wine	Price	DISTRIBUTION AVAILABILITY BY CITY*		
					General	Limited	None
			Best Wines at Tasting				
New York	D	Bully Hill Vineyards	Bully Hill Red	$3.36		All except→	6, 12, 13, 15, 18, 26, 27
New York	D	Benmarl Vineyards	Hudson River Region Baco Noir	$3.25		2, 4, 7, 11, 29	All others
New York	D	Boordy	Red Wine	$2.19		2, 4, 7, 11, 20, 25	All others
New York	D	Widmer's Wine Cellars	Naples Valley Foch	$2.49	20	←All except→	3, 9, 12, 13, 15, 19, 21, 23, 24, 26, 27, 29
			Highly Ranked Wines				
New York	D	Great Western	New York State Chelois	$2.35	2, 20	←All except→	1, 3, 6, 9, 12, 13, 14, 15, 22, 23, 26, 27, 29
Michigan	D	Warner Vineyards	Cask Michigan Mountain Red Wine	$1.75	5	4, 7, 10, 16, 17, 18, 19	All others
New York	D	Taylor Wine Company	New York State Burgundy	$2.15	All except→	1, 3, 9, 12, 13, 23, 26	
			Other Recommended Wines				
New York	D	Bully Hill Vineyards	Chancellor Noir	$3.36		All except→	6, 12, 13, 15, 18, 26, 27
New York	D	Taylor Wine Company	New York State Claret	$2.15	2, 4	All others	
New York	D	Great Western	New York State Burgundy	$2.19	2, 5, 6, 7, 20	←All except→	3, 9, 12, 13, 15, 23, 26, 27
New York	SD	Widmer's Wine Cellars	New York State Naples Valley Red	$2.09	2, 4, 6, 7, 10, 11, 14, 18, 20, 25	1, 5, 8, 16, 17, 22, 28	All others
New York	SD	Taylor Wine Company	New York State Lake Country Red	$2.15	All except→	3, 9, 12, 13, 23, 26, 27	

* See pp. 26–27 for city code.

Tasting Results

U.S. Wines Produced East of the Rockies—Dry White Wines

Region/ Country of Origin	Dry/Semi-dry/ Sweet/ Very sweet	Producer	Name of Wine	Price	DISTRIBUTION AVAILABILITY BY CITY*		
					General	Limited	None
			Best Wines at Tasting				
New York	D	Bully Hill Vineyards	Aurora Blanc	$3.36		All except→	6, 12, 13, 15, 18, 26, 27
New York	D	Taylor Wine Company	New York State Rhine Wine	$2.15	All except→	1, 3, 5, 9, 12, 13, 23, 26, 27, 28, 29	1, 3, 9, 12, 13, 23, 26, 27
New York	D	Gold Seal	Charles Fournier Chablis Nature	$2.35	2, 4, 7, 8, 11, 16, 20, 25, 28	←All except→	1, 3, 9, 12, 13, 23, 26, 27
			Highly Ranked Wines				
New York	D	Widmer's Wine Cellars	Naples Valley Vergennes	$2.49	20	←All except→	3, 9, 12, 13, 15, 19, 21, 23, 24, 26, 27, 29
			Other Recommended Wines				
Michigan	D	St. Julian Wine Company	Continental Michigan Rhine	$2.19	4, 5	10, 18, 19, 22	All others
New York	D	Great Western	New York State Chablis	$2.19	2, 4, 5, 6, 7, 20	←All except→	1, 3, 9, 12, 13, 23, 26, 27
New York	D	Widmer's Wine Cellars	Naples Valley Delaware	$2.49	20	←All except→	3, 9, 12, 13, 15, 19, 23, 24, 26, 27, 29
New York	D	Brotherhood Corporation	New York State Chablis	$2.19	2	All others	
New York	D	Bully Hill Vineyards	Seyval Blanc	$3.36		All except→	6, 12, 13, 15, 18, 26, 27

* See pp. 26–27 for city code.

166

Tasting Results

U.S. Wines Produced East of the Rockies—Sweet White Wines

Region/ Country of Origin	Dry/Semi-dry/ Sweet Very sweet	Producer	Name of Wine	Price	DISTRIBUTION AVAILABILITY BY CITY*		
					General	Limited	None
Best Wines at Tasting							
New York	VS	Gold Seal	Catawba White	$1.89	All except→	24, 29	1, 2, 3, 12, 13, 23, 26, 27
New York	SD	Taylor Wine Company	New York State Lake Country White	$2.15	All except→	1, 3, 9, 12, 13, 23, 26, 27	
New York	SD	Great Western	New York State Dutchess Rhine Wine	$2.35	2, 20	←All except→	3, 9, 12, 13, 14, 15, 23, 26, 27
Highly Ranked Wines							
New York	SD	Widmer's Wine Cellars	New York State Sauterne	$2.09	2, 4, 6, 7, 10, 11, 14, 18, 20, 25	←All except→	3, 9, 12, 13, 15, 19, 21, 23, 24, 26, 27
Michigan	SD	St. Julian Wine Company	Continental Michigan Sauterne	$2.00	4, 5	10, 18, 19, 22	All others

Tasting Results (continued)

U.S. Wines Produced East of the Rockies—Sweet White Wines

Region/ Country of Origin	Dry/Semi-dry/ Sweet Very sweet	Producer	Name of Wine	Price	DISTRIBUTION AVAILABILITY BY CITY*		
					General	Limited	None
			Other Recommended Wines				
Michigan	SD	St. Julian Wine Company	LaSalle Club Michigan Mello White	$2.00	5		All others
New York	SD	Widmer's Wine Cellars	New York State Haute Sauterne	$2.09	All except→	1, 5, 8, 16, 17, 22, 28	3, 9, 12, 13, 15, 19, 21, 23, 24, 26, 27, 29
New York	SD	Taylor Wine Company	New York State Sauterne	$2.15	All except→	1, 3, 9, 12, 13, 23, 26, 27	
Michigan	SD	St. Julian Wine Company	LaSalle Club Kastel Rhine	$2.00	5	4	All others
New York	VS	Manischewitz Wine Company	Cream White Concord	$2.09	All except→		26
Ohio	SD	Meier's Wine Cellars	Isle St. George Sauternes	$2.29	4, 5, 6, 10, 14, 15, 21, 22	←All except→	3, 9, 12, 13, 23, 25, 26, 27, 29
Ohio	VS	Meier's Wine Cellars	Isle St. George Haut Sauternes	$2.29	4, 5, 10, 14, 24	←All except→	3, 6, 7, 9, 12, 13, 20, 23, 25, 26, 27, 29
Michigan	SD	Warner Vineyard	Michigan Vineyard White	$2.59	5	3, 7, 10, 11, 16, 17, 18, 19	All others

* See pp. 26–27 for city code.

Tasting Results

CANADIAN-PRODUCED RED WINES

Region/ Country of Origin	Dry/Semi-dry/ Sweet/ Very sweet	Producer	Name of Wine	Price as of January 1975

The following wines were available in Ontario as well as other Canadian markets as of January 1975.

Best Wines at Tasting

Canada	D	Bright's Wines	President's Canadian Burgundy	$1.95
Canada	D	Château Cartier	Canadian Burgundy	$1.95
Canada	D	Château Gai	Maréchal Foch	$2.09
Canada	D	Château Cartier	Canadian Claret	$1.59

Highly Ranked Wines

Canada	D	Castle Ste. Michelle	Château Rouge	$1.77
Canada	SD	Secrestat	Chambord	$2.00
Canada	D	Bright's Wines	Baco Noir	$2.50
Canada	D	Château Cartier	Gamay Beaujolais	$2.82
Canada	D	Château Gai	Pinot Noir	$4.73

Other Recommended Wines

Canada	D	Calona	San Pietro Paisano	$2.00
Canada	D	Barnes	Canadian Claret	$1.59
		Bright's Wines	Manor St. David's Canadian Claret	$1.55
Canada	D	Andrés	Similkameen	$2.20
Canada	D	Andrés	Canadian Claret	$1.55
Canada	D	Turner	Bon Appetit	$1.59
Canada	SD	Bright's Wines	Blue Seibel	$1.86
Canada	D	Jordan	Côte Ste. Catherine	$2.40
Canada	D	Andrés	Richelieu Vin de Chaunac	$2.40
Canada	D	Château Gai	Seibel	$1.82
Canada	D	Bright's Wines	de Chaunac	$2.40
Canada	D	Andrés	Vino Buono	$1.82
Canada	D	Jordan	Valley Red	$1.77

Tasting Results

CANADIAN-PRODUCED WHITE WINES

Region/ Country of Origin	Dry/Semi-dry/ Sweet/ Very sweet	Producer	Name of Wine	Price as of January 1975

The following wines were available in Ontario as well as other Canadian markets as of January 1975.

Best Wines at Tasting

Canada	D	Château Gai	Pinot Chardonnay	$3.45
Canada	D	Bright's Wines	Aurora White Table Wine	$4.09

Highly Ranked Wines

Canada	D	Château Gai	White Table Wine	$2.00
Canada	VS	Jordan	Sauternes Canadien	$1.55
Canada	D	Château Cartier	Johannisberg Riesling	$2.45

Other Recommended Wines

Canada	D	Andrés	Vino Bianco	$1.82
Canada	D	Andrés	Regency Extra Dry Vin Blanc	$1.68
Canada	D	Bright's Wines	Pinot Chardonnay	$2.70
Canada	D	Bright's Wines	President White Table Wine	$1.95
Canada	SD	Normandie	White Table Wine	$1.82
Canada	SD	Turner	Heritage White Table Wine	$1.50
Canada	SD	Château Cartier	Vin d'Or	$1.73
Canada	SD	Barnes	Lake Niagara White	$1.95
Canada	VS	Bright's Wines	Manor St. David's Canadian Sauterne	$1.55
Canada	SD	Château Gai	Canadian Sauternes	$1.55

Tasting Results

CANADIAN-PRODUCED ROSÉ

Region/ Country of Origin	Dry/Semi-dry/ Sweet/ Very sweet	Producer	Name of Wine	Price as of January 1975

The following wines were available in Ontario as well as other Canadian markets as of January 1975.

Best Wines at Tasting

The panel found no wines in this category.

Highly Ranked Wines

Canada	SD	Barnes	Lake Roselle	$1.95
Canada	SD	Bright's Wines	DuBarry Medium-Dry Still Rosé	$1.73

Other Recommended Wines

Canada	D	Barnes	Ontario Country Rosé	$1.86
Canada	SD	Andrés	Still Rosé	$1.55
Canada	D	Jordan	Santa Maria	$2.36
Canada	VS	Château Cartier	Jolly Friar Rosé	$1.45
Canada	VS	Château Gai	Rosé	$1.73
Canada	VS	Barnes	Medium-Dry Still Rosé	$1.77
Canada	VS	Château Cartier	Vin Rosé	$1.68

Purchase Recommendations by Price Categories

The Tasting Results charts of the wine-type sections
are summarized on the following pages by *price* under
red, white, and rosé wine headings.

Red Wines up to $1.99

Rating*	Region/ Country of Origin	Dry/Semi-dry/ Sweet/ Very sweet	Producer	Name of Wine	Price
			French Red Bordeaux, Bordeaux-style Wines, and California Cabernet Sauvignon		
H.R.	France	D	Dulong	Ecu Royal Claret Reserve	$1.99
H.R.	France	D	Leonard Kreusch	Le Chat Noir Rouge Velouté (½ gal.)	$3.99
	California	D	M. LaMont Vineyards	California Ruby Cabernet	$1.99
	California	D	Almadén Vineyards	California Mountain Red Claret	$1.85
	France	D	Calvet	Calvet Réserve	$1.99
			Zinfandel		
	California	D	E. & J. Gallo	Zinfandel, California	$1.99
	California	D	Italian Swiss Colony	Zinfandel, California	$1.75
	California	D	Roma Winery	California Zinfandel	$1.69
	California	D	B. Cribari & Sons Winery	Cribari California Zinfandel	$1.59

172

Italian Chianti, California Chianti, and Related Hearty Reds

H.R.	California	G. & D.	SD	Fior di California Barberone (gal.)	$4.99
H.R.	California	G. & D.	SD	Fior di California Chianti (gal.)	$4.99
H.R.	California	Roma Wine Co.	SD	Vino D'Uva of California Country Red	$1.35
	California	E. & J. Gallo	D	Barbera of California	$1.99
	California	Guild Wine Co.	SD	Tavola Red, California	$1.39
	California	Italian Swiss Colony	D	Chianti, California	$1.49
	California	California Wine Association	D	Vino Fino California Red Table Wine	$1.29
	California	M. LaMont Vineyards	D	California Barbera	$1.99
	California	B. Cribari & Sons Winery	SD	Cribari California Vino Rosso Da Pranzo	$1.39

French Red Burgundies, Burgundy-style Wines, and California Pinot Noir

H.R.	California	San Martin Vineyards	D	California Mountain Burgundy	$1.59
H.R.	California	E. & J. Gallo	D	Burgundy of California	$1.59
H.R.	California	Sebastiani Vineyards	D	Northern California Mountain Burgundy	$1.65
H.R.	California	California Growers Winery	D	California Burgundy (L.A.)	$0.99
H.R.	California	Pastene	D	Red Burgundy, California	$1.33
	California	G. & D.	D	Fior di California Burgundy Scelto	$1.39
	California	Italian Swiss Colony	D	Burgundy, California	$1.59
	California	B. Cribari & Sons Winery	D	Cribari California Burgundy	$1.39
	California	Pastene	SD	Mellow Burgundy, California	$1.33
	California	E. & J. Gallo	D	Hearty Burgundy of California	$1.69
	California	M. LaMont Vineyards	D	California Burgundy	$1.89

U.S. Wines Produced East of the Rockies

H.R.	Michigan	Warner Vineyards	D	Cask Michigan Mountain Red Wine	$1.75

* See p. 26 for rating code.

173

Red Wines $2 to $2.49

Rating*	Region/ Country of Origin	Dry/Semi-dry/ Sweet/ Very sweet	Producer	Name of Wine	Price
			French Red Bordeaux, Bordeaux-style Wines, and California Cabernet Sauvignon		
B.A.T.	California	D	Paul Masson Vineyards	Rubion	$2.25
H.R.	California	D	Charles Krug Winery	Napa Valley Claret	$2.48
	California	D	California Wine Association	Fino Eleven Cellars California Claret	$2.09
H.R.	France	D	A. de Luze	Club Claret	$2.29
			Zinfandel		
H.R.	California	D	C. Mondavi & Sons	C. K. Mondavi California Zinfandel	$2.23
H.R.	California	D	Sebastiani Vineyards	Sonoma Zinfandel	$2.29
	California	D	San Martin Vineyards	California Zinfandel	$2.25
	California	D	Paul Masson Vineyards	California Zinfandel	$2.49
			Italian Chianti, California Chianti, and Related Hearty Reds		
	California	D	Almadén Vineyards	California Chianti	$2.10

French Red Burgundies, Burgundy-style Wines, and California Pinot Noir

B.A.T.	California	Napa Valley Burgundy	$2.48
H.R.	California	California Burgundy	$2.15
H.R.	California	Baroque	$2.25
H.R.	California	Sonoma County Burgundy	$2.39
	California	California Mountain Red Wine	$2.39
	Israel	Avdat Red Wine	$2.29

Charles Krug Winery
Paul Masson Vineyards
Paul Masson Vineyards
J. Pedroncelli Winery
Louis M. Martini
Carmel Wine Company

U.S. Wines Produced East of the Rockies

B.A.T.	New York	Red Wine	$2.19
B.A.T.	New York	Naples Valley Foch	$2.49
H.R.	New York	New York State Chelois	$2.35
H.R.	New York	New York State Burgundy	$2.15
	New York	New York State Claret	$2.15
	New York	New York State Burgundy	$2.19
SD	New York	New York State Naples Valley Red	$2.09
SD	New York	New York State Lake Country Red	$2.15

Boordy
Widmer's Wine Cellars
Great Western
Taylor Wine Co.
Taylor Wine Co.
Great Western
Widmer's Wine Cellars
Taylor Wine Co.

* See p. 26 for rating code.

175

Red Wines $2.50 to $2.99

Rating*	Region/ Country of Origin	Dry/Semi-dry/ Sweet/ Very sweet	Producer	Name of Wine	Price
				French Red Bordeaux, Bordeaux-style Wines, and California Cabernet Sauvignon	
H.R.	Yugoslavia	D	Adriatica	Cabernet from Istria	$2.59
	Argentina	D	Norton	Mendoza Malbec	$2.50
	Chile	D	Viña Undurraga	Cabernet	$2.69
	California	D	Paul Masson Vineyards	California Cabernet Sauvignon	$2.99
	Argentina	D	Schenley (importer)	Valmont Cabernet Sauvignon	$2.99
	France	D	Alexis Lichine	Cabernet Sauvignon	$2.69
	Argentina	D	Trumpeter	Cabernet-Malbec	$2.99
	France	D	Barton & Guestier	Médoc	$2.99
				Zinfandel	
H.R.	California	D	Inglenook	North Coast Counties Vintage Zinfandel	$2.70
				Bardolino and Valpolicella	
	Italy	D	Antinori	Bardolino Classico Superiore	$2.69
				Italian Chianti, California Chianti, and Related Hearty Reds	
H.R.	Argentina	D	Bodegas y Viñedos López	Rincón Famoso	$2.59
H.R.	California	D	Louis M. Martini	California Mountain Chianti	$2.59
	Italy	D	Frescobaldi	Castello Di Nipozzano Chianti	$2.99
	Argentina	D	Norton	Mendoza Barbera	$2.50

Beaujolais

B.A.T.	France	D	Chanson	Beaujolais	$2.95
H.R.	France	D	Reine Pédauque	Beaujolais	$2.99
H.R.	France	D	Excelsior (importer)	Château des Tours, Brouilly	$2.99

Gamay Beaujolais and Gamay Noir

	California	D	Winemasters' Guild	California Gamay Beaujolais	$2.95

French Red Burgundies, Burgundy-style Wines, and California Pinot Noir

B.A.T.	California	D	Beaulieu Vineyard	Napa Valley Burgundy	$2.99
H.R.	California	D	Paul Masson Vineyards	California Pinot Noir	$2.89
H.R.	France	D	Sichel	Côtes-du-Rhône	$2.89
H.R.	Portugal	D	Grão Vasco	Dão	$2.99
	California	D	Sonoma Vineyards	California Petit Sirah	$2.99
	France	D	Thomas Bassot	Pinot Noir Réserve des 3 Glorieuses	$2.99
	California	D	Louis M. Martini	California Mountain Burgundy	$2.59
	California	D	Christian Brothers	California Burgundy	$2.59
	California	D	F. Korbel & Bros.	California Burgundy	$2.50
	France	D	Chanson	Côtes du Rhône	$2.59
	France	D	Delas Frères	Côtes-du-Rhône	$2.99
	California	D	Souverain of Alexander Valley	North Coast Burgundy	$2.95

* See p. 26 for rating code.

Red Wines $3 to $3.49

Rating*	Region/ Country of Origin	Dry/Semi-dry/ Sweet/ Very sweet	Producer	Name of Wine	Price
				French Red Bordeaux, Bordeaux-style Wines, and California Cabernet Sauvignon	
B.A.T.	France	D	A. Delor	Cabernet Sauvignon	$3.49
B.A.T.	France	D	Austin, Nichols (importer)	Château Guiraud-Cheval-Blanc (A.C. Côtes de Bourg)	$3.25
B.A.T.	France	D	Prats	Médoc	$3.39
H.R.	France	D	Cruse	Bordeaux Roc Rouge	$3.49
	California	D	California Wine Association	Fino Eleven Cellars California Cabernet Sauvignon	$3.35
	California	D	Almadén Vineyards	California Cabernet Sauvignon	$3.10
	France	D	Barton & Guestier	Prince Noir	$3.49
	France	D	Alexis Lichine	Médoc	$3.29
	France	D	Tytell	St. Emilion	$3.49
				Zinfandel	
B.A.T.	California	D	Buena Vista Winery	Sonoma Zinfandel	$3.25
	California	D	Christian Brothers	Napa Valley Zinfandel	$3.15
	California	D	Cresta Blanca Winery	Mendocino Zinfandel	$3.30
	California	D	Louis M. Martini	California Mountain Zinfandel	$3.19
				Bardolino and Valpolicella	
B.A.T.	Italy	D	Bertani	Bardolino Classico Superiore	$3.40
	Italy	D	Santa Sofia	Bardolino Classico Superiore	$3.25
	Italy	D	Santa Sofia	Valpolicella Classico Superiore	$3.25

Italian Chianti, California Chianti, and Related Hearty Reds

H.R.	Italy	D	Chianti	$3.29
H.R.	California	D	North Coast Counties Barbera	$3.00
H.R.	California	D	California Mountain Barbera	$3.19

Beaujolais

B.A.T.	France	D	Beaujolais	$3.25
	France	D	Beaujolais St. Louis	$3.29

Gamay Beaujolais and Gamay Noir

B.A.T.	California	D	Monterey Gamay-Beaujolais	$3.40
H.R.	California	D	Napa Valley Gamay Beaujolais	$3.25
H.R.	California	D	Napa Valley Gamay Noir	$3.15
H.R.	California	D	California Gamay Beaujolais (L.A.)	$3.00
H.R.	California	D	California Gamay Beaujolais	$3.10
H.R.	California	D	North Coast Counties Gamay Beaujolais	$3.00

French Red Burgundies, Burgundy-style Wines, and California Pinot Noir

H.R.	California	D	North Coast Carignane	$3.00
	California	D	Mendocino Carmine Carignane	$3.25
	California	D	California Petit Sirah	$3.30
	California	D	California Pinot Noir	$3.10
	California	D	Mendocino County Burgundy	$3.15
	France	D	Domaine de St. Georges, Côtes-du-Rhône	$3.50

U.S. Wines Produced East of the Rockies

B.A.T.	New York	D	Bully Hill Red	$3.36
B.A.T.	New York	D	Hudson River Region Baco Noir	$3.25
	New York	D	Chancellor Noir	$3.36

The wineries/shippers listed in the center column (reading down):
Ruffino; Sebastiani Vineyards; Louis M. Martini; Sichel; Barton & Guestier; Monterey Vineyard; Inglenook; Christian Brothers; San Martin Vineyards; Almadén Vineyards; Sebastiani Vineyards; Simi Winery; Fetzer Vineyards; Cresta Blanca Winery; Almadén Vineyards; Parducci Wine Cellars; Calvet; Bully Hill Vineyards; Benmarl Vineyards; Bully Hill Vineyards.

* See p. 26 for rating code.

179

Red Wines $3.50 to $3.99

Rating*	Region/ Country of Origin	Dry/Semi-dry/ Sweet/ Very sweet	Producer	Name of Wine	Price
			French Red Bordeaux, Bordeaux-style Wines, and California Cabernet Sauvignon		
B.A.T.	California	D	F. Korbel & Bros.	California Cabernet Sauvignon	$3.95
H.R.	California	D	Louis M. Martini	California Mountain Cabernet Sauvignon	$3.99
H.R.	France	D	Sichel	My Cousin's Claret (A.C. Bordeaux)	$3.69
H.R.	France	D	Dourthe Frères	Grande Marque Bordeaux (A.C. Bordeaux)	$3.79
	France	D	Pierre Cartier	Cartier St. Emilion	$3.59
	France	D	Prats	St. Emilion	$3.59
	California	D	Christian Brothers	Napa Valley Cabernet Sauvignon	$3.65
	California	D	Weibel Champagne Vineyards	California Cabernet Sauvignon	$3.95
	California	D	Widmer Vineyards	Sonoma Cabernet Sauvignon	$3.50
	France	D	La Bergerie	Mouton Cadet (A.C. Bordeaux)	$3.99
	California	D	Cresta Blanca Winery	California Cabernet Sauvignon	$3.90
	California	D	Sonoma Vineyards	Sonoma County Cabernet Sauvignon	$3.99
	France	D	Ginestet	Bordeaux Vieux	$3.98
	Spain	D	Marqués de Riscal	Rioja	$3.98
	France	D	Tytell	Médoc	$3.59
	France	D	A. Delor	La Cour Pavillon Médoc	$3.99

Zinfandel

	California	D	Fetzer Vineyards	Mendocino Zinfandel	(L.A.) $3.50
	California	D	Parducci Wine Cellars	California Zinfandel	$3.73

Bardolino and Valpolicella

B.A.T.	Italy	D	Bertani	Valpolicella Valpantena	$3.55
H.R.	Italy	D	Bolla	Valpolicella Classico	$3.59
	Italy	D	Ruffino	Bardolino Classico Superiore	$3.59
	Italy	D	Bolla	Bardolino Classico	$3.59
	Italy	D	Masi	Valpolicella Classico Superiore	$3.55
	Italy	D	Ruffino	Valpolicella Classico Superiore	$3.59

Italian Chianti, California Chianti, and Related Hearty Reds

B.A.T.	Italy	D	Verrazzano	Chianti Classico	$3.99
B.A.T.	Italy	D	Antinori	Santa Cristina Chianti Classico	$3.85
	Italy	D	Melini	Chianti Classico	$3.89

Beaujolais

B.A.T.	France	D	Louis Jadot	Beaujolais-Villages Jadot	$3.98
B.A.T.	France	D	Chanson	Beaujolais-Villages St. Vincent	$3.79
B.A.T.	France	D	Browne Vintners (importer)	Château de la Chaize, Brouilly	$3.99
B.A.T.	France	D	Schenley (importer)	Château de Buffavent, Beaujolais Superieur	$3.99
H.R.	France	D	Louis Latour	Beaujolais Supérieur	$3.95
H.R.	France	D	Jaboulet-Vercherre	Beaujolais Garelle	$3.69
	France	D	Joseph Drouhin	Beaujolais-Villages	$3.99
	France	D	Pasquier Desvignes	Marquisat Beaujolais-Villages	$3.99
	France	D	Cruse	Beaujolais	$3.55
	France	D	Bouchard Père et Fils	Beaujolais Supérieur	$3.99

181

Red Wines $3.50 to $3.99 (continued)

Rating*	Region/ Country of Origin	Dry/Semi-dry/ Sweet/ Very sweet	Producer	Name of Wine	Price
			Gamay Beaujolais and Gamay Noir		
B.A.T.	California	D	Robert Mondavi Winery	Napa Valley Gamay	$3.84
B.A.T.	California	D	Fetzer Vineyards	Mendocino Gamay Beaujolais	$3.50
H.R.	California	D	Parducci Wine Cellars	Mendocino County Gamay Beaujolais	$3.73
			French Red Burgundies, Burgundy-style Wines, and California Pinot Noir		
B.A.T.	California	D	Christian Brothers	Napa Valley Pinot Saint George	$3.99
H.R.	California	D	Weibel Champagne Vineyards	California Pinot Noir	$3.95
H.R.	California	D	Louis M. Martini	California Mountain Pinot Noir	$3.99
	California	D	Sonoma Vineyards	Sonoma County Pinot Noir	$3.99
	California	D	Christian Brothers	Napa Valley Pinot Noir	$3.65
	California	D	Wente Bros.	California Pinot Noir	$3.79
	California	D	San Martin Vineyards	California Pinot Noir (L.A.)	$3.50

* See p. 26 for rating code.

182

Red Wines $4 to $4.49

Rating*	Region/ Country of Origin	Dry/Semi-dry/ Sweet/ Very sweet	Producer	Name of Wine	Price
French Red Bordeaux, Bordeaux-style Wines, and California Cabernet Sauvignon					
	France	D	Sichel	St. Emilion	$4.10
	France	D	Cordier	Médoc	$4.00
Zinfandel					
B.A.T.	California	D	Souverain of Rutherford	Napa Valley Mountain Zinfandel	$4.25
Italian Chianti, California Chianti, and Related Hearty Reds					
	Italy	D	Antinori	Villa Antinori Chianti Classico	$4.49
Beaujolais					
H.R.	France	D	Piat	Château de Saint-Amour	$4.49
French Red Burgundies, Burgundy-style Wines, and California Pinot Noir					
	California	D	Parducci Wine Cellars	Mendocino County Petit Sirah	$4.29

* See p. 26 for rating code.

183

Red Wines $4.50 to $4.99

Rating*	Region/ Country of Origin	Dry/Semi-dry/ Sweet/ Very sweet	Producer	Name of Wine	Price
			French Red Bordeaux, Bordeaux-style Wines, and California Cabernet Sauvignon		
	California	D	Parducci Wine Cellars	Mendocino County Cabernet Sauvignon	$4.99
	California	D	Beaulieu Vineyard	Napa Valley Cabernet Sauvignon	$4.75
	California	D	Simi Winery	Alexander Valley Cabernet Sauvignon	$4.95
	France	D	Cruse	St. Emilion "La Garderie"	$4.79
	California	D	Pedrizzetti	Cabernet Sauvignon	$4.79
	California	D	Beringer Vineyards	Napa Valley Cabernet Sauvignon	$4.79
			Italian Chianti, California Chianti, and Related Hearty Reds		
B.A.T.	Italy	D	Ricasoli	Brolio Chianti Classico	$4.55
			French Red Burgundies, Burgundy-style Wines, and California Pinot Noir		
B.A.T.	California	D	Beaulieu Vineyard	Beaumont Napa Valley Pinot Noir	$4.68
	California	D	Llords & Elwood Winery	Velvet Hill Pinot Noir, California (L.A.)	$4.50
	California	D	Simi Winery	North Coast Pinot Noir	$4.70
	California	D	Parducci Wine Cellars	Mendocino County Pinot Noir	$4.99
	France	D	Sichel	Châteauneuf-du-Pape	$4.89

* See p. 26 for rating code.

Red Wines $5 to $5.49

Rating*	Region/ Country of Origin	Dry/Semi-dry/ Sweet/ Very sweet	Producer	Name of Wine	Price
			French Red Bordeaux, Bordeaux-style Wines, and California Cabernet Sauvignon		
H.R.	France	D	Austin, Nichols (importer)	Château Simard (A.C. St. Emilion)	$5.49
	Spain	D	Paternina	Gran Riserva (Rioja)	$5.35
			French Red Burgundies, Burgundy-style Wines, and California Pinot Noir		
H.R.	California	D	Souverain of Rutherford	Napa Valley Petit Sirah	$5.00
	California	D	Mirassou Vineyards	Monterey Pinot Noir	$5.49
	France	D	Cruse	Châteauneuf-du-Pape	$5.19

* See p. 26 for rating code.

Red Wines $5.50 to $5.99

Rating*	Region/ Country of Origin	Dry/Semi-dry/ Sweet/ Very sweet	Producer	Name of Wine	Price
			French Red Bordeaux, Bordeaux-style Wines, and California Cabernet Sauvignon		
	France	D	Dubroca	St. Emilion	$5.75
			French Red Burgundies, Burgundy-style Wines, and California Pinot Noir		
B.A.T.	France	D	Delas Frères	Châteauneuf-du-Pape Saint Esprit	$5.99
	France	D	Chapoutier	Châteauneuf-du-Pape La Marcelle	$5.99

* See p. 26 for rating code.

Red Wines $6 and Over

Rating*	Region/ Country of Origin	Dry/Semi-dry/ Sweet/ Very sweet	Producer	Name of Wine	Price
			French Red Bordeaux, Bordeaux-style Wines, and California Cabernet Sauvignon		
B.A.T.	California	D	Robert Mondavi Winery	Napa Valley Cabernet Sauvignon	$6.59
B.A.T.	California	D	Souverain of Rutherford	Napa Valley Cabernet Sauvignon	$7.92
H.R.	California	D	Freemark Abbey	Napa Valley Cabernet Sauvignon	$8.93
			Zinfandel		
B.A.T.	California	D	Ridge Vineyards	California Zinfandel Lytton Springs	$6.00
			French Red Burgundies, Burgundy-style Wines, and California Pinot Noir		
B.A.T.	France	D	Chanson	Châteauneuf-du Pape Saint Vincent	$6.45
	California	D	Souverain of Rutherford	Napa Valley Pinot Noir	$6.00

* See p. 26 for rating code.

White Wines up to $1.99

Rating*	Region/ Country of Origin	Dry/Semi-dry/ Sweet/ Very sweet	Producer	Name of Wine	Price
			Non-French Chablis and Sauterne		
B.A.T.	California	D	E. & J. Gallo	Sauterne of California	$1.59
H.R.	California	D	C. Mondavi & Sons	C. K. Mondavi Chablis	$1.59
H.R.	California	D	Italian Swiss Colony	California Gold Chablis	$1.59
	California	D	California Wine Association	L. & J. California Chablis	$1.29
	California	D	California Wine Association	L. & J. California Sauterne	$1.29
	California	D	California Wine Association	Guasti California Chablis	$1.29
	California	D	Sebastiani Vineyards	North Coast Counties Mountain Chablis	$1.65
	California	D	M. LaMont Vineyards	California French Colombard	$1.99
	California	D	California Growers Winery	California Chablis (L.A.)	$0.99
	California	SD	B. Cribari & Sons Winery	Cribari California Vino Bianco Da Pranzo	$1.39
	California	D	California Wine Association	Vino Fino California White Wine	$1.29
	California	D	Los Hermanos California Vineyards	Mountain Chablis (½ gal.)	$3.70

White Wines in the German Style

H.R.	California	SD	Italian Swiss Colony	Rhine, California	$1.59
H.R.	California	D	Almadén Vineyards	California Mountain Grey Riesling	$1.85
	California	SD	E. & J. Gallo	Prime Vineyard Rhine Garten, California	$1.39
	California	D	California Wine Association	Guasti California Rhine	$1.29
	California	SD	Almadén Vineyards	California Mountain Rhine	$1.85

Dry White Bordeaux, the Sauvignon Blanc and Sémillon Grapes

	France	D	Dulong	Ecu Royal French Country White	$1.99
	France	D	Calvet	Réserve Blanc	$1.99

German and Alsatian White Wines and California Johannisberg Riesling

B.A.T.	Germany	SD	(Jacquin Selection)	Little Rhine Bear Liebfraumilch	$1.99

U.S. Wines Produced East of the Rockies

B.A.T.	New York	VS	Gold Seal	Catawba White	$1.89

* See p. 26 for rating code.

White Wines $2 to $2.49

Rating*	Region/ Country of Origin	Dry/Semi-dry/ Sweet/ Very Sweet	Producer	Name of Wine	Price
			Non-French Chablis and Sauterne		
B.A.T.	California	D	Paul Masson Vineyards	California Chablis	$2.15
H.R.	California	D	J. Pedroncelli Winery	Sonoma County Chablis	$2.39
H.R.	California	D	San Martin Vineyards	California Petite Chablis	$2.10
	California	D	Simi Winery	North Coast Chablis	$2.45
	California	D	Almadén Vineyards	California Mountain White Sauterne	$2.10
	California	D	San Martin Vineyards	California Mountain Chablis	$2.10
	California	D	Almadén Vineyards	California Chablis	$2.10
	California	D	California Wine Association	Fino Eleven Cellars California Chablis	$2.09
	California	D	Wente Bros.	California Chablis	$2.35
	California	D	Souverain of Alexander Valley	North Coast Chablis	$2.40
			White Wines of Italy, Spain, and Portugal		
	Spain	D	René Barbier	Blanco Seco	$2.29
	Italy	SD	Riunite	Bianco	$2.29

White Wines in the German Style

B.A.T.	California	D	San Martin Vineyards	Santa Clara Valley Emerald Riesling	$2.10
H.R.	California	D	Sebastiani Vineyards	North Coast Counties Green Hungarian	$2.29
H.R.	California	D	Paul Masson Vineyards	California Riesling	$2.39
	California	SD	Paul Masson Vineyards	Emerald Dry	$2.25
	New York	SD	Gold Seal	New York State Rhine	$2.00
H.R.	New York	SD	Widmer's Wine Cellars	New York State Sauterne	$2.09

Dry White Bordeaux, the Sauvignon Blanc and Sémillon Grapes

	California	D	Almadén Vineyards	California Dry Sémillon Sauterne	$2.45
	California	D	San Martin Vineyards	California Sémillon Sauterne	$2.10

California Chenin Blanc and Wines of the Lower Loire Valley

	California	SD	Almadén Vineyards	California Chenin Blanc	$2.45
	California	D	Winemasters' Guild	California Chenin Blanc	$2.29

German and Alsatian White Wines and California Johannisberg Riesling

H.R.	Germany	SD	Leonard Kreusch	Niersteiner Gutes Domtal	$2.35
H.R.	Germany	SD	Leonard Kreusch	Liebfraumilch	$2.29

White Wines $2 to $2.49 (continued)

Rating*	Region/ Country of Origin	Dry/Semi-dry/ Sweet/ Very Sweet	Producer	Name of Wine	Price
H.R.	Germany	SD	Tytell	Liebfraumilch	$2.39
H.R.	Germany	SD	Leonard Kreusch	Bernkasteler Kurfürstlay Riesling	$2.49
	Germany	SD	Tytell	Moselblümchen	$2.49

U.S. Wines Produced East of the Rockies

Rating*	Region/ Country of Origin	Dry/Semi-dry/ Sweet/ Very Sweet	Producer	Name of Wine	Price
B.A.T.	New York	D	Taylor Wine Co.	New York State Rhine	$2.15
B.A.T.	New York	D	Gold Seal	Charles Fournier Chablis Nature	$2.35
B.A.T.	New York	SD	Taylor Wine Co.	New York State Lake Country White Wine	$2.15
B.A.T.	New York	SD	Great Western	New York State Dutchess Rhine Wine	$2.35
H.R.	New York	D	Widmer's Wine Cellars	Naples Valley Vergennes	$2.49
H.R.	Michigan	SD	St. Julian Wine Company	Continental Michigan Sauterne	$2.00
	Michigan	SD	St. Julian Wine Company	LaSalle Club Michigan Mellow White	$2.00
	New York	D	Great Western	New York State Chablis	$2.19
	New York	D	Widmer's Wine Cellars	Naples Valley Delaware	$2.49

U.S. Wines Produced East of the Rockies

New York	Brotherhood Corporation	D	New York State Chablis	$2.19
New York	Taylor Wine Co.	SD	New York State Sauterne	$2.15
New York	Widmer's Wine Cellars	SD	New York State Haut Sauterne	$2.09
New York	Manischewitz Wine Co.	VS	Cream White Concord	$2.09
Michigan	St. Julian Wine Company	SD	LaSalle Club Kastel Rhine	$2.00
Ohio	Meier's Wine Cellars	SD	Isle St. George Sauternes	$2.29
Ohio	Meier's Wine Cellars	VS	Isle St. George Haut Sauternes	$2.29
Michigan	St. Julian Wine Co.	D	Continental Michigan Rhine	$2.19

* See p. 26 for rating code.

193

White Wines $2.50 to $2.99

Rating*	Region/ Country of Origin	Dry/Semi-dry/ Sweet/ Very sweet	Producer	Name of Wine	Price
French White Burgundies and California Chardonnay					
B.A.T.	California	D	Paul Masson Vineyards	California Pinot Blanc	$2.89
B.A.T.	France	D	Thomas Bassot	Chantefleur Blanc de Blancs	$2.99
H.R.	California	D	Paul Masson Vineyards	California Pinot Chardonnay	$2.99
	France	D	Thomas Bassot	Pinot Chardonnay-Mâcon	$2.99
	France	D	Joseph Drouhin	Soleil Blanc	$2.99
Non-French Chablis and Sauterne					
B.A.T.	California	D	Sonoma Vineyards	Sonoma County French Colombard	$2.79
H.R.	California	D	Christian Brothers	California Sauterne	$2.59
H.R.	California	D	Cresta Blanca Winery	California French Colombard	$2.55
	California	D	Inglenook	North Coast Counties Vintage Chablis	$2.59
	California	D	Concannon	California Chablis	$2.50
	California	D	Louis M. Martini	California Mountain Chablis	$2.59
	California	D	Monterey Vineyard	Del Mar Ranch White Monterey Wine	$2.90
White Wines in the German Style					
B.A.T.	California	D	Sonoma Vineyards	Sonoma County Grey Riesling	$2.99
B.A.T	Austria	D	Lenz Moser	Tytell Lipizzaner	$2.76
	California	D	Beringer Vineyards	North Coast Grey Riesling	$2.99
	California	D	San Martin Vineyards	California Sylvaner Riesling (L.A.)	$2.50
	Yugoslavia	D	Adriatica	Rizling from Fruška Gora	$2.59
	California	D	Cresta Blanca Winery	California Grey Riesling	$2.55

	California	D	Souverain of Alexander Valley	Mendocino County Grey Riesling	$2.99
	California	D	Wente Bros.	California Grey Riesling	$2.95

Dry White Bordeaux, the Sauvignon Blanc and Sémillon Grapes

B.A.T.	France	D	Sichel	Graves Supérieures	$2.95
B.A.T.	California	SD	Sonoma Vineyards	Sonoma County Sauvignon Blanc	$2.99
H.R.	France	D	Alexis Lichine	Graves	$2.69
	California	D	Wente Bros.	California Dry Sémillon	$2.95
	Israel	SD	Carmel Wine Co.	Israel Sémillon	$2.59
	France	D	Ackerman-Laurance	Ackerman Sauvignon	$2.89

California Chenin Blanc and Wines of the Lower Loire Valley

	California	SD	J. Pedroncelli Winery	Sonoma County Chenin Blanc	$2.90
	California	SD	California Wine Association	Fino Eleven Cellars California Chenin Blanc	$2.85
	California	D	Souverain of Alexander Valley	North Coast Dry Chenin Blanc	$2.95

German and Alsatian White Wines and California Johannisberg Riesling

B.A.T.	Germany	SD	Julius Kayser	Glockenspiel Liebfraumilch	$2.99
B.A.T.	Germany	SD	Tytell	Bereich Bernkastel	$2.79
H.R.	Germany	SD	Tytell	Zeller Schwarze Katz	$2.69
	Germany	SD	Leonard Kreusch	Kröver Nacktarsch	$2.59
	California	D	Christian Brothers	Napa Valley Johannisberg Riesling	$2.59
	Germany	SD	Leonard Kreusch	Piesporter Goldtröpfchen Kabinett	$2.89

U.S. Wines Produced East of the Rockies

	Michigan	SD	Warner Vineyard	Michigan Vineyard White	$2.59

White Wines $3 to $3.49

Rating*	Region/ Country of Origin	Dry/Semi-dry/ Sweet Very Sweet	Producer	Name of Wine	Price
			French White Burgundy and California Chardonnay		
H.R.	California	D	Wente Bros.	California Pinot Blanc	$3.25
	California	D	Almadén Vineyards	California Pinot Blanc	$3.10
	California	D	Almadén Vineyards	California Pinot Chardonnay	$3.10
	France	D	Patriarche	Bourgogne-Aligoté	$3.29
	France	D	Sichel	Pinot Chardonnay-Mâcon	$3.19
			Non-French Chablis and Sauterne		
H.R.	California	D	Parducci Wine Cellars	Mendocino County Chablis	$3.15
	California	D	Heitz Cellar	Napa Valley Chablis	$3.19
			White Wines of Italy, Spain, and Portugal		
	Italy	D	Bertani	Soave	$3.40
	Portugal	D	Mateus	Branco	$3.19
	Italy	D	Antinori	Est! Est! Est!	$3.20
	Italy	D	Santa Sofia	Soave Classico Superiore	$3.25
	Spain	SD	Bodegas Bilbainas	Brillante Blanco	$3.29
			White Wines in the German Style		
	California	D	Louis M. Martini	California Mountain Riesling (Sylvaner)	$3.19
	California	D	Christian Brothers	Napa Valley Riesling	$3.15

Dry White Bordeaux, the Sauvignon Blanc and Sémillon Grapes

H.R.	California	Almadén Vineyards	California Sauvignon Blanc	$3.10
	France	Sichel	Blanc de Blancs Sauvignon Sec	$3.09
	California	Almadén Vineyards	California Blanc Fumé	$3.10
	France	Ginestet	Graves Extra	$3.29
	Argentina	Bodegas y Viñedos López	Château Vieux	$3.19

California Chenin Blanc and Wines of the Lower Loire Valley

B.A.T.	California	Christian Brothers	Napa Valley Chenin Blanc	$3.15
B.A.T.	California	Charles Krug Winery	Napa Valley Chenin Blanc	$3.00
B.A.T.	California	Parducci Wine Cellars	Mendocino County Chenin Blanc	$3.25
H.R.	California	Monterey Vineyard	Monterey Chenin Blanc	$3.10
	France	Chanson	Muscadet de Sèvre-et-Maine	$3.15

German and Alsatian White Wines and California Johannisberg Riesling

B.A.T.	California	Almadén Vineyards	California Gewürztraminer	$3.10
	California	Almadén Vineyards	California Johannisberg Riesling	$3.10
	Washington State	Ste. Michelle Vineyards	Washington State Johannisberg Riesling	$3.49

U.S. Wines Produced East of the Rockies

B.A.T.	New York	Bully Hill Vineyards	Aurora Blanc	$3.36
	New York	Bully Hill Vineyards	Seyval Blanc	$3.36

* See p. 26 for rating code.

197

Rating*	Region/ Country of Origin	Dry/Semi-dry/ Sweet/ Very sweet	Producer	Name of Wine	Price
French White Burgundies and California Chardonnay					
B.A.T.	France	D	Louis Jadot	Mâcon Blanc-Villages Jadot	$3.98
B.A.T.	California	D	Sonoma Vineyards	Sonoma County Chardonnay	$3.99
H.R.	California	D	Louis M. Martini	California Mountain Pinot Chardonnay	$3.99
H.R.	France	D	Joseph Drouhin	La Foret Mâcon-Villages	$3.99
	California	D	Weibel Champagne Vineyards	California Pinot Chardonnay	$3.95
	California	D	Sebastiani Vineyards	North Coast Counties Pinot Chardonnay	$3.50
	California	D	Wente Bros.	California Pinot Chardonnay	$3.99
Non-French Chablis and Sauterne					
H.R.	California	D	Mirassou Vineyards	Monterey White Burgundy	$3.89
White Wines of Italy, Spain, and Portugal					
B.A.T.	Italy	D	Bolla	Soave Classico	$3.59
H.R.	Italy	D	Ruffino	Soave Classico Superiore	$3.59
H.R.	Italy	D	Masi	Soave Classico Superiore	$3.55
	Italy	D	Fazi Battaglia	Titulus Verdicchio	$3.50
	Italy	D	Antinori	Bianco della Costa Toscana	$3.89
White Wines in the German Style					
H.R.	California	D	Parducci Wine Cellars	Mendocino County Sylvaner Riesling	$3.73
	California	SD	Mirassou Vineyards	Monterey Riesling	$3.59

Dry White Bordeaux, the Sauvignon Blanc and Sémillon Grapes

	France	D	La Bergèrie	Mouton Cadet	$3.99

California Chenin Blanc and Wines of the Lower Loire Valley

B.A.T.	California	SD	Robert Mondavi Winery	Napa Valley Chenin Blanc	$3.59
H.R.	California	D	Souverain of Rutherford	Napa Valley Dry Chenin Blanc	$3.75
	France	SD	Ackerman-Laurance	Ackerman Vouvray	$3.79
	California	D	Christian Brothers	Napa Valley Pineau de la Loire	$3.99

German and Alsatian White Wines and California Johannisberg Riesling

B.A.T.	Germany	D	Export Union	Wedding Veil Liebfraumilch	$3.79
B.A.T.	Germany	SD	Sichel	Blue Nun Liebfraumilch	$3.89
B.A.T.	Germany	SD	Sichel	Bereich Bernkastel	$3.89
H.R.	Germany	SD	Wasum	Schloss Fürstenberger Riesling	$3.89
H.R.	Germany	SD	Weinexport Hattenheim	Madrigal Johannisberg Riesling	$3.89
H.R.	Germany	SD	Anheuser & Fehrs	Anheuser Liebfraumilch	$3.99
	Germany	SD	Sichel	Zeller Schwarze Katz	$3.89
	Germany	D	Weinexport Hattenheim	Madrigal Liebfraumilch	$3.79
	Germany	SD	Sichel	Bereich Nierstein	$3.89
	Germany	SD	L. Guntrum	Niersteiner Hölle Kabinett	$3.99
	Germany	D	Weinexport Hattenheim	Madrigal Bernkastel Riesling	$3.98
	Germany	SD	Weinexport Hattenheim	Madrigal Zeller Schwarze Katz	$3.79
	California	D	Weibel Champagne Vineyards	California Johannisberg Riesling	$3.95
	California	D	Louis M. Martini	California Mountain Gewürz Traminer	$3.99

* See p. 26 for rating code.

White Wines $4 to $4.49

Rating*	Region/ Country of Origin	Dry/Semi-dry/ Sweet/ Very sweet	Producer	Name of Wine	Price
				French White Burgundies and California Chardonnay	
	France	D	Patriarche	Chablis	$4.40
	France	D	A. de Luze	Chablis	$4.00
				White Wines of Italy, Spain, and Portugal	
	Portugal	SD	Lancers	Vinho Branco	$4.25
				German and Alsatian White Wines and California Johannisberg Riesling	
B.A.T.	Germany	SD	Deinhard	Bereich Bernkastel Green Label	$4.25
H.R.	California	SD	Charles Krug Winery	Napa Valley Johannisberg Riesling	$4.03
H.R.	California	SD	Monterey Vineyard	Monterey Johannisberg Riesling	$4.30
H.R.	California	SD	Charles Krug Winery	Napa Valley Gewürz Traminer	$4.03
	Germany	SD	Deinhard	Hanns Christof Liebfraumilch	$4.25
	California	SD	Llords & Elwood	Castle Magic Johannisberg Riesling, California (L.A.)	$4.25

* See p. 26 for rating code.

200

White Wines $4.50 to $4.99

Rating*	Region/ Country of Origin	Dry/Semi-dry/ Sweet/ Very sweet	Producer	Name of Wine	Price
French White Burgundies and California Chardonnay					
B.A.T.	California	D	Parducci Wine Cellars	Mendocino County Chardonnay	$4.99
B.A.T.	France	D	A. de Luze	Pouilly-Fuissé	$4.65
	France	D	Sichel	Chablis Special Selection	$4.89
	California	D	Souverain of Alexander Valley	Sonoma Chardonnay	$4.75
	California	D	Simi Winery	Alexander Valley Pinot Chardonnay	$4.50
Dry White Bordeaux, the Sauvignon Blanc and Sémillon Grapes					
	California	D	Oakville Vineyards	Napa Valley Sauvignon Blanc	$4.69
German and Alsatian White Wines and California Johannisberg Riesling					
B.A.T.	Germany	SD	Anheuser & Fehrs	Anheuser Bernkastel	$4.65
B.A.T.	Germany	SD	Sichel	Bereich Johannisberg Riesling	$4.95
B.A.T.	Germany	SD	Deinhard	Bereich Johannisberg Riesling	$4.89
B.A.T.	France	SD	Hugel	Gewürztraminer	$4.69
H.R.	California	SD	Souverain of Alexander Valley	Johannisberg Riesling, Sonoma (L.A.)	$4.50
H.R.	California	D	Mirassou Vineyards	Monterey Gewürztraminer	$4.50
	California	D	Inglenook	Napa Valley Johannisberg Riesling	$4.75

* See p. 26 for rating code.

201

White Wines $5 to $5.99

Rating*	Region/ Country of Origin	Dry/Semi-dry/ Sweet/ Very sweet	Producer	Name of Wine	Price
			French White Burgundies and California Chardonnay		
B.A.T.	France	D	Louis Latour	Pouilly-Fuissé	$5.95
H.R.	France	D	Louis Jadot	Beaujolais Blanc	$5.29
H.R.	California	D	Beringer Vineyards	Napa Valley Chardonnay	$5.29
	France	D	Cruse	Pouilly-Fuissé	$5.95
			Dry White Bordeaux, the Sauvignon Blanc and Sémillon Grapes		
	California	D	Robert Mondavi Winery	Napa Valley Fumé Blanc	$5.09
			German and Alsatian White Wines and California Johannisberg Riesling		
B.A.T.	Germany	SD	Anheuser & Fehrs	Anheuser Johannisberger	$5.55
H.R.	Germany	SD	Anheuser & Fehrs	Piesporter Michelsberg	$5.55

* See p. 26 for rating code.

White Wines $6 and Over

Rating*	Region/ Country of Origin	Dry/Semi-dry/ Sweet/ Very sweet	Producer	Name of Wine	Price

French White Burgundies and California Chardonnay

B.A.T.	France	D	Joseph Drouhin	Pouilly-Fuissé	$6.99
	Calif.	D	Robert Mondavi Winery	Napa Valley Chardonnay	$7.10
	France	D	Jouvet	Pouilly-Fuissé	$6.45

* See p. 26 for rating code.

203

Rosé Wines (Dry) up to $1.99

Rating*	Region/ Country of Origin	Producer	Name of Wine	Price
B.A.T.	California	Italian Swiss Colony	California Grenache Rosé	$1.49
	Spain	Paternina	Rosado	$1.98
	New York	Gold Seal	Catawba Pink	$1.89
	California	Italian Swiss Colony	Pink Chablis of California	$1.59
	California	Brookside Vineyard Co.	California Vino Rosado (L.A.)	$1.65
	California	Roma Winery	California Pink Chablis	$1.59

$2 to $2.49

Rating*	Region/ Country of Origin	Producer	Name of Wine	Price
H.R.	California	Louis M. Martini	California Mountain Vin Rosé	$2.39
	California	California Wine Association	Fino Eleven Cellars California Vine Rosé	$2.09
	California	Almadén Vineyards	California Grenache Rosé	$2.10
	California	Taylor Wine Co.	New York State Rosé	$2.15
	New York	Widmer Vineyards	Naples Valley Isabella Rosé	$2.49
	New York	Paul Masson Vineyards	California Vin Rosé Sec	$2.15
	California	Sebastiani Vineyards	North Coast Counties Vin Rosé	$2.15

$2.50 to $2.99

Rating*	Region/ Country of Origin	Producer	Name of Wine	Price
H.R.	California	Inglenook	Napa Valley Gamay Rosé	$2.99
H.R.	California	Christian Brothers	California Vin Rosé	$2.59
H.R.	California	Sonoma Vineyards	Sonoma County Grenache Rosé	$2.79
	France	Sichel	Rosé de Provence	$2.93

* See p. 26 for rating code.

$3 to $3.49

Rating*	Region/ Country of Origin	Producer	Name of Wine	Price
H.R.	California	Robert Mondavi Winery	Napa Valley Gamay Rosé	$3.36
	France	Cruse	Grenache Rosé	$3.45

$4.50 to $4.99

Rating*	Region/ Country of Origin	Producer	Name of Wine	Price
	France	Cruse	Tavel	$4.55
	France	Chapoutier	Tavel La Marcelle	$4.99

Rosé Wines (Other Than Dry) up to $1.99

Rating*	Region/ Country of Origin	Dry/ Semi-dry/ Sweet/ Very sweet	Producer	Name of Wine	Price
B.A.T.	California	SD	Roma Winery	California Vin Rosé	$1.59
H.R.	California	SD	E. & J. Gallo	Prime Vineyard Vin Rosé of California	$1.39
H.R.	California	SD	Franzia	Vin Rosé of California	$1.29
	Portugal	SD	Publicker (importer)	Trovador Rosé	$1.99
	Michigan	SD	Warner Vineyards	Cask Michigan Mountain Rosé Wine	$1.75
	California	SD	B. Cribari & Sons Winery	Cribari California Vino Fiamma Da Pranzo	$1.39

* See p. 26 for rating code.

$2 to $2.49

Rating*	Region/ Country of Origin	Dry/ Semi- dry/ Sweet/ Very sweet	Producer	Name of Wine	Price
	Israel	SD	Carmel Wine Co.	Israel Grenache Rosé	$2.25
	Washington State	SD	Ste. Michelle Vintners	Washington State Grenache Rosé	$2.49
	New York	SD	Great Western	New York State Rosé	$2.19
	New York	SD	Taylor Wine Co.	New York State Lake Country Pink	$2.15
	California	SD	Almadén Vineyards	California Mountain Nectar Vin Rosé	$2.10
	New York	SD	Widmer's Wine Cellars	New York State Naples Valley Pink	$2.09
	California	SD	San Martin Vineyards	California Mountain Vin Rosé	$2.10

$2.50 to $2.99

Rating*	Region/ Country of Origin	Dry/ Semi- dry/ Sweet/ Very sweet	Producer	Name of Wine	Price
B.A.T.	California	SD	Christian Brothers	California Napa Rosé	$2.59
	Portugal	SD	C. Da Silva	Isabel Rosé	$2.79
	France	SD	Moc-Baril	Rosé d'Anjou	$2.98
	France	SD	Chanson	Rosé des Anges (Anjou)	$2.50

$3 to $3.49

Rating*	Region/ Country of Origin	Dry/ Semi- dry/ Sweet/ Very sweet	Producer	Name of Wine	Price
	France	SD	Sichel	Amourosé (Anjou)	$3.19
	Spain	VS	Bodegas Bilbainas	Brillante Vino Rosado	$3.29

* See p. 26 for rating code.

Food and Wine

Enjoying Wine with Food

There are many classical combinations of wine and food. Even the most traditional, however, have notable exceptions. Everyone knows that red wine should not be drunk with fish, yet Scandinavians, who rank among the greatest fish eaters in the world, regularly do just that, and Germans generally drink white wine with everything. You should experiment until you find the combinations you like. The best way to approach the subject is to realize that wine is another food and it must complement the meal with which it is served. Try different wines with the same dish, just as you may sometimes eat a hamburger with mustard and catsup, and at other times with relish and onions.

There are some guidelines. Daily simple fare requires simple wines, such as generic Chablis or Burgundy from California. Hot weather calls for lighter wines, cold weather for heavier and fuller. You would choose a Côtes-du-Rhône or Gamay Beaujolais with your steak in summer but a Gevrey Chambertin in the middle of winter. The most important rule is that wine and food should not overwhelm each other. Delicate dishes like blue trout or veal piccata are complemented by delicate wines such as a light Moselle or a Chenin Blanc. Spicy food, on the other hand, requires big wines that will stand up to it and cut through the spice, which is why so many Italian reds that are too tannic by themselves show beautifully with tomato sauces and garlic. All the various cheeses must also be matched with compatible wines, as it would be a pity to have one overshadow the other. Few taste affinities are as ideal as the perfect marriage of cheese and wine.

Traditional combinations are given in the wine chapters as well as in the Food and Wine Chart (pp. 212–214) and the Cheese and Wine Chart (pp. 215–216).

Finally, there are some dishes that do not go with wine at all: chocolate desserts, for example, artichokes, asparagus, hot curry, or heavily smoked fish, and some people even consider salad antagonistic to wine if there is vinegar in the dressing. Soups are also uncongenial because of the incompatibility of hot and cold liquids. Interestingly enough, though, wine goes very well *in* the soup and tends to improve its taste.

This brings us to the subject of cooking with wine. "Cooking wine" is very bad. It reminds one of old ladies who drink cooking sherry on the sly. During the cooking process, the alcohol evaporates and all that remains are the taste components of the wine, which, if the wine is inferior, will certainly not enhance the food. This, of course, does not mean that you must cook with great wines. Ideally it should be the same one that will be served with the dinner.

Serving more than one wine during a meal, each chosen for a separate course, is interesting and fun. Two glasses at each plate on the table are pretty, and one white wine and one red need not cost any more than two identical bottles. When serving more than one wine, light wines precede heavy ones; dry precede sweet; white, red; younger, older; and lesser precede better ones, which is more or less common sense. Lighter food courses usually precede heavier ones and dessert is always last, so it's not too hard to match them all up.

The Germans drink their greatest wines without food, usually after dinner, lest any other taste detract from their full enjoyment. The great German Auslese, Beerenauslese, and Trockenbeerenauslese are indeed best by themselves, a relaxed atmosphere being better for their enjoyment than any food we can think of.

Our favorite pre-dinner white wines, besides Moselle and Chablis, are light German Rhine wines, and any wine made from the Chenin Blanc, Sauvignon Blanc, or Chardonnay, be it from California or France, but only the less expensive ones. The others are too assertive and big. Some light red wines are similarly suitable, usually the ones served slightly chilled, such as a young Beaujolais, Bardolino, or Zinfandel. Interestingly enough, most wines that are best by themselves are also good with picnics, cold food generally being less assertive than hot.

Many people drink white wine on the rocks. Watering wine is an unforgivable sin in the wine business, and we frown on it, unless the wine is so inferior that its taste improves with ice. In the summer, however, you may want to take a glass of white wine with soda water and ice, a spritzer, a thirst-quenching, refreshing drink.

There is, of course, the other problem of when, how, and with what you should drink that great bottle. It is our contention that a meal should have only one star, either the food or the wine. For great wines, have a simple dish made from the best ingredients. A great Bordeaux is best with roast baby lamb served in its own juice, boiled new potatoes, and fresh string beans. We would serve a great Burgundy with a broiled steak or rib roast, a great Moselle with blue trout, a great Sauternes with lemon mousse, and a great Rhine wine with a fine selection of cold cuts, home-baked bread, and sweet butter.

CODE FOR WINES LISTED IN THE FOOD/WINE AND CHEESE/WINE CHARTS

The wine types in this book have been assigned the following numbers for use in the Wine and Food Chart.

1 Bordeaux
  Bordeaux Supérieur

2 Médoc
  St. Emilion
  Graves, red
  California Cabernet Sauvignon

3 Côtes-du-Rhône
  Corbières
  California Pinot Noir

4 Red Burgundies
  California Petit Sirah
  Cru Beaujolais
  Individual Zinfandel

5 Côte Rôtie
  Châteauneuf-du-Pape

6 California Claret
  California Carignan
  California Burgundy
  California Mountain Red
  New York red wines
  Regular Zinfandel

7 Regional from Piedmont, Italy, or
    Dão, Portugal

8 Beaujolais
  Beaujolais Supérieur
  Beaujolais-Villages

9 Bardolino
  Valpolicella

10 Italian Chianti
   Italian Chianti Classico
   Italian Chianti Riserva

11 California Chianti
   California Barbera
   California red wines with
     Italian names

Argentine Barbera
Mexican red wines

12 Premium Zinfandel

13 Gamay Beaujolais
   Gamay Noir

14 German Rhine wines
   Liebfraumilch

15 Moselle
   California Emerald Riesling

16 Alsatian Riesling and Sylvaner
   California Riesling (also called
     Johannisberg Riesling)
   California Sylvaner (Riesling)
   California Grey Riesling

17 Alsatian and California
     Gewürztraminer

18 French
     White Burgundies
     Chablis
   California
     Chardonnay ⎱ Under $4.50
     Pinot Blanc ⎰
   New York State Chardonnay
   Loire Valley Muscadet

19 French
     White Burgundies ⎫
     Chablis   ⎬ Over $4.50
   California   ⎭
     Chardonnay

20 Italian Soave
   Italian Orvieto
   Portuguese Vinho Verde

21 Italian Frascati
   Italian Verdicchio

22 Spanish Rioja
 Spanish Panadés

23 California Chenin Blanc
 Loire Valley: Vouvray

24 California Rhine Wine

25 American Chablis
 American Sauterne
 American white wines produced
  east of the Rockies and
  Canadian white wines

26 White Bordeaux: Graves
 Loire Valley: Pouilly-Fumé
 California Sauvignon Blanc
 California Sémillon
 California Fumé Blanc

27 White Bordeaux:
  Entre-Deux-Mers
 White Bordeaux: Sauvignon Blanc

28 Dry Rosés:
 Eastern U.S. and Canadian dry
  rosés
 California Grenache Rosé
 California Gamay Rosé
 California Cabernet Sauvignon
  Rosé
 California Rosé
 France, Tavel Rosé
 France, Côtes de Provence Rosé
 Rosés of all other countries

29 Sweet Rosés:
 Eastern U.S. and
  Canadian sweet rosés
 California Grenache Rosé
 California Gamay Rosé
 California Cabernet Sauvignon
  Rosé
 California, Rosé
 France, Anjou Rosé
 Rosés of all other countries

30 French Sauternes, Barsac

Food and Wine Chart

The numbers listed below for wine types correspond to the numbers listed on pages 210–211. The first number listed is our preference.

BEEF

Barbecued   3, 14
Boiled   8, 15
Bourguignon   3, 4
Braised   1
Brisket   2
Chili con carne   6, 10, 11
Chipped, creamed   3, 8
Chop suey   26, 14
Goulash   10, 13
Hamburgers   6, 8, 9
Kabobs   6, 8, 9
Liver with bacon   1, 2
Meat loaf   6, 8, 9
New England
   boiled   17, 28
Pot au feu   3, 4
Pot roast   12, 13
Roast   2, 4
Roast beef hash   6, 11
Sauerbraten   7, 3, 17
Shepherd's pie   4, 6, 11
Short ribs   4, 6, 11
Steak and kidney pie   3, 4
Steak, broiled   2, 4
Steak, Swiss   1, 3
Stroganoff   8, 9
Stuffed cabbage   8, 9
Teriyaki   5, 7, 12

BOUILLABAISSE   18

CAESAR SALAD   6, 11

CAVIAR   Champagne

CHEESE   (*see* Cheese and
   Wine Chart, pp. 215–216)

CHEF'S SALAD   28, 14, 8

CHICKEN

à la King   23, 20, 18

Baked, broiled
   roasted, sautéed,
   stewed   1, 3, 7, 14
Baked in cream   23, 14, 16
Barbecued   14, 16
Braised in wine
   or coq au vin   4
Cacciatore   10, 9
Creole   12, 9
Croquettes   19, 23, 14
Curry   17, 26
Florentine   28, 14, 26
Fried, southern style   8, 9, 16
Hash   6, 11
Kiev   14, 18, 12
Livers sautéed with onions   9, 12
Paprika   22, 10, 11
Pot pie   14, 18
Tarragon   14, 18
Tetrazzini   9, 28 20

CHILI   17, 14

CHINESE FOOD   26, 14, 28

CLAMS

Baked or broiled
   on the half shell   19, 21, 22
Deviled   19, 21, 22
Fried   19, 21, 22
On the half shell, raw   19, 27
Steamed   19, 27

CORNED BEEF HASH   6, 11

CRAB

Deviled   18, 26, 27
Soft-shelled, broiled
   or fried   18, 26, 27

CRAWFISH   18, 15

DUCK

à l'Orange, Cerises   30, 14
Roast   4, 14
Wild   4, 5

EGGPLANT

Moussaka   1, 3
Parmesan   10, 9

EGGS AND EGG DISHES   15, 23

FISH

Abalone   15, 16, 22
Bass   14, 18
Broiled w/lemon and butter   18
Brook trout   15
Cod in cream sauce   14, 23, 15
Coquille St. Jacques   27
Flounder   18, 20, 26
Lobster (*see* Lobster)
Oysters (*see* Oysters)
Red snapper, baked   26
Salmon, poached   1, 28
Scallops (*see* Scallops)
Shad, broiled, or
   baked with roe   19, 14
Shrimp (*see* Shrimp)
Sole   18, 20, 26
Trout   18, 20, 26

FRANKFURTERS

w/baked beans   25, 6, 28, 24
w/sauerkraut   17

FROGS' LEGS   16, 18

FRUITS

Citrus   30
Peaches   1, 11
Apples   All wines
Pears   1, 30

GOOSE

Roast   5, 4, 12

HAM

Baked, barbecued, smoked   14, 22, 24

LAMB

Chops, broiled   2, 9, 10
Crown roast   2, 9, 10
Curry with rice   17, 14, 26
Irish stew   8, 9, 13
Roast leg   2, 7, 12
Shish kabob   3, 19, 9

LOBSTER

Baked, stuffed   19, 14, 26
Boiled, broiled with
   lemon and butter   19, 14, 26

MEXICAN FOOD

Arroz con pollo   10, 7, 11
Enchiladas   10, 7, 11

MUSSELS

Marinière, steamed   27, 18, 15

OYSTERS

Fried, on the half shell   18, 27, 15
Rockefeller   18, 27, 15

PAELLA   2, 9, 4

PARTRIDGE

Roast   2, 4, 12

PASTA

Canelloni   10, 7, 9
Fettuccine   9, 12, 13
Lasagne   7, 8, 10
Manicotti   9, 12, 13
Ravioli   10, 7, 9
Spaghetti
   w/clam sauce   20, 28, 9
   w/tomatoes and
      meat sauce   10, 7, 9

PEPPERS

Stuffed   28, 3, 9

PHEASANT

Roast   2, 4, 12
Young, broiled   2, 4, 12

PIGEONS AND SQUABS

Roasted   4, 2, 12

PIZZA   14, 26, 28

PORK

Chops   14, 19, 26
Crown roast   14, 19, 26
Goulash   9, 1, 8
Roast suckling pig   2, 4, 5
Roast w/sauerkraut   17, 16, 14
Sausage, hot   17, 16, 14
Sausage, cold   14, 28, 8
Spareribs, barbecued   14, 23, 18

QUAIL

Broiled, roasted   4, 2, 12

QUICHE, all types   18, 14, 23

RABBIT   8, 9, 20

SALAD NIÇOISE   8, 9, 25

SCALLOPS   18, 27, 15

SHRIMP

Boiled   18, 27, 15
Fried   18, 22, 26
Newberg   18, 23, 16

SNAILS   8, 4, 12

SOUFFLÉS

Cheese   8, 9, 12

Chicken   1, 8, 14
Fish   18, 26, 21

SWEETBREADS

Braised   8, 1, 2

TONGUE

Beef, corned or pickled   1, 4, 12
Veal   9, 12, 1

TUNA FISH

Casserole   26, 14, 23
Salad   25, 21, 20

TURKEY

Roast   2, 14, 4

TURTLE

Stew   5, 4, 2

VEAL

Birds   9, 12, 1
Blanquette de veau,
   in cream sauce   14, 8, 9
Kidney   1, 7, 12
Orloff   2, 4, 19
Piccata   18, 20, 16
Roast   2, 12, 14
Saltimbocco   2, 12, 14
Scallopini   18, 20, 16
Steak or Wiener Schnitzel   8, 16, 28

VENISON   4, 5, 2

WELSH RAREBIT   8, 1, 17

Cheese and Wine Chart

HARD CHEESES	APPROPRIATE WINES
Parmesan, Romano, Cheddar, Cantal.	Red 3, 8, 13 White 14, 16 Rosé 28

SOFT CHEESES, SHARP AND PUNGENT	APPROPRIATE WINES
Brie, Camembert, Boursault, Coulommiers, Crema Danica.	Red 4, 10, 7 White 19, 26, 22

BLUE CHEESES	APPROPRIATE WINES
Roquefort, Danish Blue, Gorganzola, Bleu de Bresse, Stilton.	Red 12, 5, 4 White 30, 17 Porto (Port Wine)

VERY PUNGENT CHEESES	APPROPRIATE WINES
Limburger, Liederkranz, Bierkäse (beer cheese), Handcheese, Reblochon	Red 2, 10, 11 White 17

SHARP AND GOAT CHEESES	APPROPRIATE WINES
Chèvres, Feta.	Red 1, 3, 9, 13 White 16, 14, 20 Rosé 28

FRESH AND CREAMY CHEESES	APPROPRIATE WINES
Cottage cheese, cream cheese, Mozzarella, Ricotta, Gervais.	Red 3, 8 White 23, 15, 27 Rosé 29

CREAMY AND SPICY CHEESES	APPROPRIATE WINES
Boursin.	Red 8, 3, 10

BLAND CHEESES, BUTTERY AND MILD	APPROPRIATE WINES
Bel Paese, Muenster (American), Taleggio, Fontina, Edam, Gouda, Samsoe, Bombel, Tilsit, Gourmandise, American Cheese.	Red 1, 6, 8 White 16, 21, 25 Rosé 28

SEMIHARD CHEESES, MILD

Swiss, Emmenthaler, Gruyère,
Cheshire, Monterey Jack, Pyrénées,
Jarlsburg.

APPROPRIATE WINES

Red   2, 7, 12
White   18, 20, 26
Rosé   28

SEMIHARD CHEESES, SHARP

Appenzell, Port Salut, Pont
l'Evêque.

APPROPRIATE WINES

Red   2, 10
White   26, 23, 14
Rosé   28

BACKGROUND

Storage, Decanting, Glassware, and
Bottle Shapes

STORAGE

There are three factors to be considered in wine storage: temperature, light, and vibration. Ideally, wine should be stored at about 55° F. Because white wines benefit from a slightly lower temperature, they ought to be kept in bins nearest the floor, where the temperature is lowest. Just as important, the temperature should be constant, even if it is somewhat higher or lower than ideal. Wines which are stored in too warm a place or which undergo frequent temperature changes will age prematurely and lose taste. Dry white wines are more susceptible to damage from poor storage, as they will turn brown. Most white wines we mention in this book need no aging. On the contrary, our advice is "The younger, the better." Buy them by the case, but no more than you can drink in three months.

Since wines should be protected from exposure to light, especially sunlight, most wine bottles are made of colored glass. Vibration also ages wine prematurely, so don't store it under stairways or in rooms which are frequently used. The decorative wine racks used in homes may display one's wines attractively, but it is difficult to imagine a device less conducive to keeping wines in good condition. For storing wine, no place is worse than a kitchen—the temperature goes up and down like a Yo-Yo, the light is too bright, and vibrations from appliances and family traffic are probably more excessive there than anywhere else in the house. Wine sealed with corks should be stored horizontally, or the corks dry out and air enters the bottle. Because wine can pick up odors through its cork, the storage area should be clean, free from strong smells, and well aired. A refrigerator is not ideal—

its temperature is too low and its compressor is a source of vibration. We have found that six weeks' storage of white, rosé, or sparkling wines is about as long as they should be kept in refrigerators.

Refrigeration, in the short run, slows aging. Therefore, if you have a partially consumed bottle of wine—white, red, or rosé—recork it and shove it into the icebox. If it is good to start with, it should keep at least a week. About an hour before you drink red wine, take the bottle out of the refrigerator to let it reach room temperature. If you can decant the wine into half-bottles, it will stay good even longer. Remember, the less air in the bottle, the longer the wine will keep.

DECANTING

Decanting red wine separates the wine from its sediment and enables the wine to breathe, which brings out its bouquet.

Simply put, decanting is pouring wine from its bottle into a decanter, carafe, or another bottle. If a bottle of red wine has been left long enough to have "thrown a sediment," bright, clear wine can be poured off in the following way:

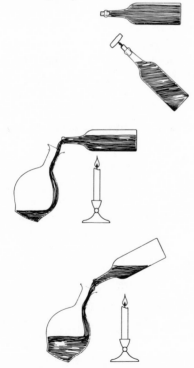

1. The sediment will have settled on the bottom side of the bottle. Move the bottle from its horizontal position with as little motion as possible and tilt it only slightly upright. We usually use a wine basket (the only time we find use for it).

2. Remove the cork slowly and gently. A mechanical corkscrew is desirable because it actually lifts the cork out of the bottle in the turning action.

3. Take the decanter in one hand and the bottle in the other, and hold the shoulder of the bottle over a candle or bright light so that you can see the light through the neck of the bottle.

4. Pour the wine slowly into the decanter until you see the sediment (it will look like a dark cloud) edging into the neck of the bottle. Stop pouring. You will leave a little wine in the bottle, but the enhanced quality of the wine will more than make up for the loss.

If the wine has no sediment and is being decanted only for aeration, the candle and the careful pouring are unnecessary.

GLASSWARE

Although much ado is made about the shapes of wine glasses, the basic requirements are really quite simple:

1. The glass should have a stem. This permits light to enter from every direction so that you can see the color of the wine. Furthermore, by holding the glass by its stem or foot you can drink the wine without warming it.

2. The glass should be clear so you can see the color of the wine.

3. The mouth of the glass should be slightly smaller than the body in order to hold the aroma.

TRADITIONAL WINE GLASS SHAPES

| Bordeaux* | Burgundy | Hock† | Alsace | Champagne |

*This makes a very good all-purpose glass.
†For Rhine, Hock and Moselle. The stem can be rust-colored for Rhine and green for Moselle.

Many wines are associated with particular shapes of glasses. While the shapes are the custom in the wine making regions, there is no reason why Burgundy should not be served in a Bordeaux-style glass, or vice versa.

However, if one doesn't mind the expense, it is a pleasant custom to serve different wines in their traditional glasses; the various shapes help make an attractive table setting.

BOTTLE SHAPES

A bottle shape often identifies the taste of a wine. The wine merchants of Bordeaux, Burgundy, Chianti, the Rhine, and Moselle were the first to develop their own distinctive bottles, and the shapes became identified with the wines. As other regions made wines similar to these, they put them in bottles that were commonly associated with the taste they tried to achieve. For example, French white Burgundies and Pinot Chardonnay from California both come in the traditional Burgundy bottle. The wines are similar. Another associated bottle shape is Bordeaux and California Cabernet Sauvignon. To some extent, to know the taste first associated with the wines of a particular bottle is to have a good idea of how other wines taste which appear in that shape bottle.

TRADITIONAL BOTTLE SHAPES

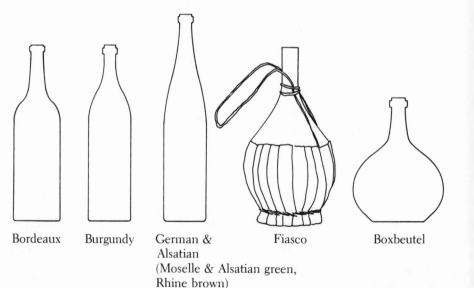

Bordeaux   Burgundy   German &
                        Alsatian
                        (Moselle & Alsatian green,
                        Rhine brown)

Fiasco   Boxbeutel

How to Give a Wine Tasting

Tasting is a fleeting sensory experience, like looking at a work of art or, even more accurately, listening to music. The impression must be captured and recorded while memory lingers.

To begin with, a wine must be compared against others, and you should not taste alone. By discussing a wine with others you will refine your tasting ability. Tastings can be highly structured educational sessions or rewarding social get-togethers. You might want to have a professional advise you and help you in organizing it. Obviously the purpose of a tasting is either to become acquainted with a new wine or to form an opinion on wines in taste categories with which you are familiar. One way to do this is to invite half a dozen friends and ask each to bring a bottle of his choice. This enables you not only to taste a variety of wines at little expense, but also to discuss them with your friends. The tasting might compare:

1. Wines from different subregions of the same general area. Thus, different red wines from Bordeaux—for example, Margaux, St. Emilion, St. Estèphe, and Graves—can be tasted against each other.

2. Wines of the same color, but from entirely different areas. For example, Pommard, Nuits St. George, Beaujolais, Côtes-du-Rhône, Corbières, and Barolo can form a group.

3. Wines of the same color but different grape varieties, such as Cabernet Sauvignon, Pinot Noir, Zinfandel, and Gamay Beaujolais.

4. Wines of the same color from the same area but of different pedigree, such as Mácon Blanc, Chablis, Chablis Grand Cru, Meursault, and Bâtard-Montrachet.

223

5. Wines of similar pedigree from the same region and of the same grape variety, such as several Cabernet Sauvignons from different California wineries, all within a given price range.

Other combinations can be used for tastings; there need only be some logical reason for comparison. A few guidelines for conducting the tastings should be observed:

Use a uniform set of glasses: clear, to see the color of the wine, stemmed, tulip-shaped, and of six-ounce capacity or larger to enjoy the bouquet of the wine.

All tasting should be blind, with labels covered and telltale bottle shapes disguised so that the taster will not be influenced.

The wines are tasted but not swallowed; they are spat into receptacles. The purpose here is to taste, not to get intoxicated. We use plastic buckets placed at intervals under or on the table. Ideally not more than four people should participate, in complete silence, making notes as they taste. Each participant should be able to concentrate fully on each wine, undistracted by the others, and all discussion should be postponed until the end of the tasting. These limitations are observed by professionals, but you might enjoy relaxing them.

Unless you are a professional, do not taste more than a dozen wines at a time. Big tastings are tiring and confusing.

The best time to taste is between ten and twelve o'clock in the morning, after an adequate breakfast, not on an empty stomach. A hungry taster is not critical enough, an overfed taster not sharp enough. The room should be well lit and well ventilated. If you wish to have the tasting at a more social hour, we would suggest before dinner.

If you like, drink water or eat a water biscuit between wines, to return your taste to neutral. We discount the theory that bland cheese eaten first will bring out the real flavor of the wine; rather, it tends to flatter the wine by neutralizing the astringent tannin. There is an old saying in the wine trade: "Sell on cheese, and buy on bread."

Always begin with the youngest wine and proceed to the oldest. When tasting white wines, move from the driest to the sweetest. In reds, from the lightest to the heaviest.

No smoking allowed!

Here is how you taste and what to look for: Fill the glass no more than half full. Holding its stem, lift the glass to examine color and clarity. Clarity is a prerequisite for a wine. If it is not clear, it has either been incorrectly treated by the bottler or it is an old wine that has thrown a deposit and should have been decanted before being served.

Color tells you something about the substance of a wine and its age. Ripe grapes make for substance. A 1966 red Bordeaux will always be deeper in color, not to say thicker, than an unripe year like 1968, where the color is almost rosé. Age shows in red wine by a distinct change of the hue from vibrantly, lively red in young wines to brown in old wines. The depth of color of a wine can be seen by standing over the glass and looking through the wine at a white surface. The color of a wine can best be studied by tilting the glass against a white surface to be able to study the color of the wine near the rim.

Put the glass back on the table and swirl it to release the bouquet. Lift it to your nose and inhale the aroma. Smell enables you to define a wine's fruit, sweetness, acidity, flower, lack of all these characteristics, or even faulty qualities. Many experts find that sight and smell almost completely reveal the ultimate taste of the wine.

Now take a sip and swish the wine inside your mouth to get the full flavor. We call this "chewing" the wine. Taste itself, of course, shows you the full quality, from first impression to "middle taste" to after taste. Perfect wines have all the elements, color, nose, and taste, in harmony.

Immediately and before they are forgotten, write down your impressions of the wine's appearance, aroma, and taste. These tasting notes form a valuable record for future reference, as well as a chronicle of your developing taste. Since the process is entirely subjective, each person will work out his own vocabulary for recording his reactions.

For your assistance in tasting and to help you understand our descriptions of wine, we have prepared a list of the most common adjectives used by experts to describe the appearance, color, bouquet, and taste of wine (see p. 227). We have also included a glossary of words used to describe wines (see Appendix, pp. 237–240). Words convey different meanings to different people, so adopt the ones you find most useful.

Many tasters assign each wine a numerical value, one for its overall quality, or as official California judging panels do, a series of ratings for different aspects of the wine. We believe this highly structured system can overrate a wine because the separate parts often add up to more than the value of the whole. Some tasters are able to use it accurately, however, and we reprint the California evaluation table for your information and possible use (see p. 226).

A word of caution: do not taste one wine against another that is outside its class. A boxing coach would not match a lightweight against a heavyweight. A $3 Cabernet Sauvignon from California may prove as good in its class as a $10 French wine in its. Generally, we are looking for a wine that is a champion in its own class, judged against fair competition.

Above all, keep an open mind and an open palate, essential equipment for tasting. Judge the wine as *you* taste it, not as you think someone else might apply his standards. Remember, one man's sweet is often another's poison.

For those of you interested in more detail, try J. M. Broadbent's *Wine Tasting.*

Organoleptic Evaluation Scoring Guide for Wine as Used by California State Fair Wine-Judging Panels

1. *Appearance*

   0—Cloudy
   1—Clear
   2—Brilliant

2. *Color*

   0—Distinctly off
   1—Slightly off
   2—Correct

3. *Aroma and Bouquet*

   1—Vinous
   2—Distinct but not varietal
   3—Varietal
   (Subtract 1 or 2 for off-odors, add 1 for bouquet)

4. *Vinegary (Acescence)*

   0—Obvious
   1—Slight
   3—None

5. *Total Acidity*

   0—Distinctly low or high

   1—Slightly low or high
   2—Normal, well balanced

6. *Sweetness*

   0—Too low or too high
   1—Normal

7. *Body*

   0—Too low or too high
   1—Normal

8. *Flavor*

   0—Distinctly abnormal
   1—Slightly abnormal
   2—Normal

9. *Bitterness*

   0—Distinctly high
   1—Slightly high
   2—Normal

10. *General Quality*

    0—Lacking
    1—Slight
    2—Impressive

RATINGS

17–20	Outstanding quality, fine wines
13–16	Sound commercial wines
9–12	Commercial with noticeable defect
6–8	Common, poor
1–6	Unsatisfactory

Adjective Selector for Describing Wines

Appearance	*Color*	*Bouquet*	*Taste*	
Brilliant	WHITE WINES	Acetic	Astringent	Insipid
Clear		Acid	Austere	Light
Cloudy	Pale green Young	Beery	Baked	Lively
Dull	Straw yellow	Black	Balanced	Long
Watery	Gold	currants	Big	Luscious
	Yellow-brown	Clean	Bitter	Maderized
	Brown Old	Corky	Body	Mellow
		Flinty	Breed	Metallic
	ROSÉ WINES	Flowery	Broad	*Nerveux*
		Foxy	Character	Noble
	Onion skin Young	Fruity	Clean	Oxidized
	Pink	Geraniums	Closed	Peppery
	Orange Old	Green	Cloying	*Petillant*
		Maderized	Coarse	*Piquant*
	RED WINES	Musty	Common	Ripe
		Peppery	Corky	Rounded
	Deep purple Young	Powerful	*Corsé*	*Sève*
	Ruby red	Smoky	Depth	Sharp
	Red	Spicy	Dry	Smooth
	Red-brown	Sulphury	Earthy	Soft
	Deep brown	Woody	Elegant	Sound
	Amber Old	Yeasty	Fat	Sour
			Finesse	Spicy
			Finish	*Spritzig*
			Flabby	Sulphury
			Flat	Sweet
			Flinty	Tannic
			Foxy	Tart
			Fruity	Thin
			Full	Velvety
			Grapy	Vigorous
			Green	Woody
			Harsh	Yeasty
			Heady	

APPENDIXES

Acknowledgments

To those listed below and to all the other unnamed people who assisted us with this work we are appreciative and grateful.

Fred and Eleanor Alger of New York

Gerald Asher, Monterey Vintners, San Francisco

Dr. Maynard A. Amerine, Department of Viticulture and Enology, University of California, Davis, California

Sam Aaron, Sherry-Lehman, Inc., New York

Sam and Pat Beard of New York

Robert Lawrence Balzer, Los Angeles

James Beckman, Guild Wineries and Distilleries, San Francisco

Michael Buller, Bell and Stanton Inc., New York

Arthur Brody, Gold Seal Vineyards, Inc., Hammondsport, N.Y.

Jamie Clark of New York

Charles Crawford, E. & J. Gallo Winery, Modesto, California

Tom and Frances Dittmer of Lake Forest, Illinois

Michael Dixon, Scottish and Newcastle Importers Co., San Francisco

Dan and Rae Emmett of Los Angeles

Anthony and Diane Espinoza of Asunción, Paraguay

Peter S. Friedman, Sonoma Vineyards, Tiburon, California

Alfred Fromm, Fromm and Sichel Inc., San Francisco

Robert Galichon, Liquor Control Board of Ontario, Canada

Ernest Gallo, E. & J. Gallo Winery, Modesto, California

Mary Ann Graf, Simi Winery, Healdsburg, California

Russel H. Green, Simi Winery, Healdsburg, California

Virginia Harrison of Washington, D.C.

Joe Heitz, Heitz Cellar, St. Helena, California

Raymond R. Herrmann, Jr., McKesson Wine & Spirits Co., New York

R. L. Hess, H. Sichel Söhne, Mainz, Germany

Robert Ivie, Guild Wineries and Distilleries, San Francisco

Pam Jackson, Four Seasons Sheraton, Ontario, Canada

Ian Kennedy, Canadian Wine Institute, Ontario, Canada

Sheila Kennedy, Canadian Wine Institute, Ontario, Canada

Hugh Knowlton, Jr. of New York

Perry and Memrie Lewis of Lake Forest, Illinois

Robert and Peggy Ley of Houston, Texas
Steve and Sharon Ley of Houston, Texas
Wendel and Audrey Ley
of Houston, Texas
Artur Meier, H. Sichel Söhne,
Mainz, Germany
Marilyn Melkonian of New York
Dr. Franz Werner Michel
of Mainz, Germany
Mark Miller, Benmarl Vineyards,
Marlboro, New York
Robert Mondavi, Robert Mondavi Winery,
Oakville, California
Peter Morrell, Morrell & Company,
New York
Alan Olson, German Wine Information
Bureau, New York
George E. Parducci, Parducci Wine
Cellars, Ukiah, California
Mrs. H. A. Potter of New York
Bob Pennington of Ontario, Canada
Dr. E. Peynaud of the Station Oenologique
de Bordeaux, France
Richard and Elizabeth Price
of Houston, Texas
R. E. and Ruth Robertson
of Houston, Texas
Robert Rose of Dallas, Texas
Robert and Pam Sakowitz
of Houston, Texas
John Salvi, Maison Sichel, Bordeaux,
France

John T. Sargent of New York
Harry Serlis, California Wine Institute,
San Francisco, California
Peter A. Sichel, Maison Sichel,
Bordeaux, France
Walter A. Sichel, H. Sichel & Sons Ltd.,
London
Steven Spurrier, Caves de la Madelein,
Paris
Rodney D. Strong, Sonoma Vineyards,
Tiburon, California
Edward S. Tauber, M.D., of New York
Roy W. Taylor, California Wine Institute,
San Francisco
Walter Taylor, Bully Hill Wine Co.,
Hammondsport, N.Y.
Guido Truffini, Schieffelin & Co.,
New York
Paul Violich of San Francisco
Jack Welsh, Christian Brothers,
San Francisco
Dennis A. Williams, H. Sichel & Sons
Ltd., London
Jim and Joan Wisner of San Francisco
Harold Wit of New York
Camilla Wood of New York
Julius Wile, Julius Wile Sons & Co.,
New York
Lea Yauner, Maison Sichel, Bordeaux,
France
Herbert J. Weiss, Schieffelin & Co.,
New York

The following people participated as members of our tasting panel:

Jerry Ayling of Ontario, Canada
John Beinecke of New York
Alexis Bespaloff of New York
Tex Bomba of New York
Jules Bond of New York
Gilbert Butler of New York
Fred Cherry of San Francisco
William B. Chivers of Ontario, Canada
William Clifford of Morris, Connecticut
John Couillard of New York
Mario Daniele of New York

Jean Delmas of Bordeaux, France
Margaret Dorsen of New York
Tim Enos of New York
Philip Erard of New York
Gerard Evaneaux of New York
William E. Findley of Ontario, Canada
David Fromkin of New York
Robert Haas of Vermont
Peter Hackenberger of Ontario, Canada
Edwin R. Haynes of Ontario, Canada
Virginia Hilu of New York

Bernhard Horstmann of New York
G. W. B. Hostetter of Ontario, Canada
F. Agustin Huneeus of New York
Barbara Kafka of New York
Geoffrey T. Kenway of San Francisco
Rudy Komon of Sidney, Australia
Harriet Lembeck of New York
Mary Libby of New York
Charles Mandelstam of New York
William and Dorothy Massee of New York
R. Keith Matthie of Ontario, Canada
Alexander McNally of
    Hartford, Connecticut
Otto Meyer of San Francisco
Robert Milligan of Miami, Florida
Robert Miltner of New York
Robert Misch of New York
Don Mohr of New York

Alfred Moran of New York
Charles Mueller of New York
Anthony Northrop of New York
Jack Oxley of New York
Percy Rowe of Ontario, Canada
Henry Rubin of San Francisco
Philip Scaturro of New York
Michael Schweitzer of New York
Timothy Seldes of New York
Stella Sichel of New York
Doris Tobias of New York
Richard Townsend of New York
Michael Vaughan of Ontario, Canada
Nicholas von Hoffman
    of Washington, D.C.
Lawrence and Pat Whitman
    of Philadelphia
Josie Wilson of New York

Wine as an Industry

Until twenty or thirty years ago, the grape grower in Europe or America was a small farmer who probably made his own wine and sold it to a merchant. Today, although most of the grapes are still grown on farms, the farmer sells the grapes to a merchant or to a cooperative winery with modern facilities for processing.

One step up is the farmer with more property or particularly fine vineyards, who not only grows grapes but also makes his own wine, selling it in bulk to a merchant/shipper or bottling it himself under his own label. It is then called château-bottled in Bordeaux and estate-bottled elsewhere in France, Germany, and the United States. Not all vineyards can produce a wine complete enough for the retail market, so it is the task of the merchant/shipper to take the raw wines from these farmers and blend them to a consistent product. This is the very heart of the wine business, because so much of our wine is the result of the shippers' prowess.

The wine broker is essential for getting the wine from the grower to the merchant/shipper. We shall take as an example the Bordeaux broker, the oldest one historically, acting as middleman between the 30,000 growers and the 200 merchants. The hundred or so main brokers each specialize either in one region or one type of wine. One will specialize in Sauternes, another in classified and lesser châteaux. His competence is in his ability to advise and counsel both parties. He keeps the farmer informed on the "taste" of the marketplace and the new innovations in grape growing and winemaking. For the shipper, he estimates movements in the market and developments in the wine trade, besides procuring hundreds of samples for tasting. The brokers are highly respected for their knowledge of the market and their integrity. When they become dishonest, as a few have at times, they can cause major disasters.

Next in line is the merchant, also called shipper. Through the brokers he buys young wines which he then blends for consistency, ages and bottles the wine, and ultimately ships it. He also buys bottled wines from estates, or, as in our case (Sichel Shippers), grapes that he crushes to make wine. In Europe, especially in France and Germany, it is rare for a merchant/shipper himself to own a vineyard. If he does, it is usually a prestige property, a small vineyard of high reputation that helps publicize his other products. The rest of the time he devotes to marketing and selling, promotion and advertising. With the zeal of a missionary, he makes endless efforts to spread the knowledge of wine among the public with tastings, lectures, and books.

WINE PRODUCTION IN THE UNITED STATES

BIG CONSUMER-WINE PRODUCERS

These are large operations that make mostly generic wines for everyday consumption, in sizes from half-bottles to gallons. Their mass-oriented products, at their best, represent excellent values. The market is dominated by Gallo and includes such other companies as United Vintners, Guild, and Franzia. Making a large quantity of consistently similar wine under one label, e.g., a generic Burgundy, is an art requiring great skill from a technical standpoint, for it is harder to make one million cases of uniform wine than one hundred cases of great wine.

PREMIUM WINERIES

These are somewhat smaller operations, making wine in lesser quantities from finer grapes, much in the manner of the French shipper, and like their European counterparts, they try to field a line of wines for every taste and pocketbook. The three leaders are Almadén, Paul Masson, and Christian Brothers. Actually, the wine market is shifting so rapidly that it is hard to categorize companies precisely; the big consumer wineries are experimenting with finer wines, and the premium wineries with mass-oriented products.

SUPER-PREMIUM WINERIES

These are small wineries that are devoted to quality and whose production is big enough to be a national factor. Although in many ways the super-premium wineries are similar to the premium companies, they produce wines of higher quality (and price) because of their smaller size and the strong leadership of a single personality. A typical example is the Robert Mondavi Winery, which reflects the individual character of its owner; searching continually for quality, he nevertheless limits himself to a few wine-types, recognizing that he cannot be all things to all men.

INDIVIDUAL ESTATES AND WINEMAKERS

This catch-all category includes wines made from grapes grown on individual estates as well as wines made by individual winemakers who either buy fine grapes from growers or grow their own. While estate-bottled wine is no guarantee of quality, wine made by a knowledgeable winemaker enjoys a definite advantage. One such example is Joe Heitz, who runs his own operation and produces some of the best wines on the market.

American wineries are generally able to control their product more strictly than their European counterparts because of their more integrated operations. Science plays a larger role in the art of winemaking here, so American wine is more likely to be stable and less subject to damage during movement or storage than many European imports.

THE PRICE OF WINE

Like everything else, the price of wine is determined by supply and demand, further accentuated here by the fact that wine is a luxury item and its sales volume depends on the amount of discretionary income the public is willing to spend. Fashions in wine, a sudden demand for a product that has caught the public's fancy, can also be a determining factor, as can worldwide demand, particularly in the case of French and German wines.

The first thing that affects the price you pay is the price of the grapes at harvest time, although some vineyards have gained such a reputation that the price of their wine no longer bears any relation to the cost of production.

As soon as the grapes or new wine arrive in the winery, the cost begins to go up. The shipper must recover for wine lost in evaporation, for money immobilized during aging, for investment in the work and equipment for processing the wine, and finally for bottling and casing. A single markup usually covers overhead expenses plus profit. In America the markup can be even higher if the winery has its own marketing organization or a prime distributor. An independent prime distributor marks up about 30 percent for his services, the wholesaler between 20 and 30 percent, and the retailer between 30 and 50 percent. Using average figures, this raises the price of a bottle of wine worth $2 at the winery to $2.60 in the hands of the prime distributor, $3.25 at the wholesaler's, and $4.55 at your friendly wine store.

Within the wide range of prices keyed to quality, some wines are handled by fewer middlemen before they reach the consumer and therefore are less expensive. Large wineries with mass production have an economic advantage that is reflected in lower market prices, but the buyer is also deprived of individuality in the wines.

Grapes or raw wine from a region that entitles the end product to a valued name or appellation command such high prices that the commercial situation can be blown totally out of proportion. For some regional Bordeaux, for example, raw-wine prices rose 400 percent in only three years, then dropped by 50 percent the following year.

Since the wines vary so much in price and quality, it is up to the merchant to see that there is a realistic relationship between the two. His survival in the market depends both on quality and value for money, and he has to balance these all the time. There are good values in every price bracket, from $1.49 California Burgundy to a superb $10 Bordeaux of a good year. Ultimately, it is a matter of taste. In the wine business, taste is truth.

Words Used to Describe Wine

Acetic Describes a sour, vinegary odor referred to as volatile acidity, too much of which will make the wine undrinkable.

Acid The sharp, tart effect of the green fruit of young wine on both the nose and tongue.

Aroma The perfume of fresh fruit. It diminishes with fermentation and disappears with age to be replaced by the "bouquet."

Astringent The rough, puckery taste sensation caused by an excess of tannin in especially young red wines. It diminishes with age in the bottle.

Baked Quality of red wine made in a very hot climate from very ripe grapes.

Balanced Having all natural elements in good harmony.

Beery The odor of stale beer from a white wine that is over the hill—usually in old Moselles.

Big Full of body and flavor; high degree of alcohol, color, and acidity.

Bitter Self-descriptive. Sign of ill-health caused by inferior treatment such as excessive stalks during crushing or even metal contamination.

Black currants The slight smell and taste of black currants often found in Bordeaux wines.

Body The weight and substance of the wine in the mouth; actually a degree of viscosity largely dependent on the percentage of alcoholic and sugar content.

Bouquet The fragrance a mature wine gives off once it is opened. It develops further after the wine is in the glass. "Nose" is the term that encompasses the two aspects of the olfactory sensations—aroma and bouquet.

Breed Having the character, type, and qualities of its origin.

Brilliant Bright and sparkling in appearance so that one can see the light through the wine. Opposite of dull and cloudy.

Broad Full-bodied but lacking in acidity and therefore also lacking in finesse.

Character Positive and distinctive taste characteristics giving definition to a wine.

Clean A well-constituted wine with no offensive smells or tastes. *See* Sound.

Clear Transparent and luminous appearance. Any sediment rests on the bottom of the bottle.

Closed Not showing any character yet, usually because it has been recently bottled.

Cloudy Unsound condition of a hazy, dull-looking wine. Not to be confused with the condition of a recently shaken old red wine whose deposit hasn't settled yet.

Cloying Too much sweetness and too little acidity.

Coarse Rough texture; little breed or elegance.

Common Adequate but quite ordinary.

Corky Disagreeable odor and flat taste of rotten cork due to a defective cork in the bottle.

Corsé Body and consistency, having generous and powerful proportions.

Depth Rich, lasting flavor.

Dry Completely lacking sweetness. Should not be confused with bitterness or sourness.

Dull *See* Cloudy.

Earthy What the French call *goût de terroir*. The peculiar taste that the soil of certain vineyards gives to their wines; disagreeable when too noticeable.

Elegant Well balanced, with finesse and breed.

Fat Full-bodied but flabby, which in white wines is often due to too much residual sugar. When applied to red wines, it means softness and maturity.

Finesse The breed and class that distinguish a great wine.

Finish The taste that the wine leaves at the end, either pleasant or unpleasant.

Flabby Too soft, almost limp, without structure.

Flat Dull, unattractive, low in acidity. Applied to a sparkling wine, it means that the wine has lost its sparkle.

Flinty What the French call *goût de pierre à fusil*. Steely, dry wine, such as a Chablis, with an odor and flavor recalling gunflint.

Flowery The flowerlike bouquet that is as appealing to the nose as the fragrance of blossoms, as, for example, in a fine Moselle.

Foxy A pronounced flavor found in wines made from native American grapes; the same smell as in grape jelly.

Fruity The aroma and flavor of fresh grapes found in fine young wines. It diminishes with age.

Full Having body and color; often applied to wines that are high in alcohol, sugar, and extracts.

Geraniums Smelling of geraniums, an indication that the wine is faulty.

Grapy The strong flavor that certain grape varieties, such as the Muscat, impart to certain wines.

Green Harsh and unripe with an unbalanced acidity that causes disagreeable odor and a raw taste.

Hard Tannic without softness or charm. It can mellow with age.

Harsh Excessively hard and astringent. It can become softer with age.

Insipid Lacking in character and acidity; dull.

Light Lacking in body, color, or alcohol, but pleasant and agreeable.

Lively Usually young with fruity acidity and a little carbon dioxide.

Long Leaving a persistent flavor that lingers in the mouth. Sign of quality. Opposite of short.

Luscious Juicy and soft, filling the mouth without a trace of dry aftertaste. Usually attributed to sweet wines well balanced with acidity.

Maderized Flat, oxidized smell and taste reminiscent of Madeira. Term is applied to wines that have passed their prime and have acquired a brown tinge.

Mellow Softened with proper age.

Metallic The unpleasantly bitter taste a white wine can acquire from improper treatment that did not eliminate traces of the copper that was used to spray the vines.

Musty Disagreeable odor and stale flavor caused by storage in dirty casks or cellars; moldy.

Nerveux Having a lively impact on the palate; well balanced with a flavor that is neither too alcoholic nor too acid.

Noble Superior and distinguished; not only possessing the right credentials but also having an impressive stature of its own.

Oxidized Having lost its freshness from contact with air; *see* Maderized.

Peppery The aromatic smell of certain young red wines from hot climates.

Pétillant Effervescent with a natural light sparkle.

Piquant Dry and crisply acid, prickling the palate with its tartness.

Powerful Usually applied to robust red wines of great substance, such as a Châteauneuf-du-Pape, or to white wines with a full, assertive bouquet, such as a big white Burgundy.

Ripe Full; tasting of ripe fruit, without a trace of greenness.

Rounded Well balanced and complete.

Sève The sap of a great wine; the concentrated aromatic savor of a luscious and ripe sweet white wine of inherent quality.

Sharp Excessive acidity, a defect usually found in white wines.

Short Leaving no flavor in the mouth after the initial impact; *see* Long.

Smoky Self-descriptive for the particular bouquet of certain Loire wines, such as Pouilly-Fumé, made from the Sauvignon grape.

Smooth Of a silky texture that leaves no gritty, rough sensation on the palate.

Soft Suggests a mellow wine, usually low in acidity and tannin.

Sound Healthy, well balanced, clean-tasting.

Sour Like vinegar; wine that is spoiled and unfit to drink.

Spicy Definite aroma and flavor of spice arising from certain grape varieties (Gewürztraminer). The aroma is richer and more pronounced than what we call "fruity."

Spritzig A pleasant, lively acidity and effervescence noticeable only to the tongue and not to the eye and mostly found in young wines.

Sulphury Disagreeable odor reminiscent of rotten eggs. If the smell does not disappear after the wine is poured, it is an indication that the wine is faulty.

Sweet Having a high content of residual sugar either from the grape itself or as the product of arrested fermentation.

Tannic The mouth-puckering taste of young red wines particularly from Bordeaux. Too much tannin makes the wine hard and unyielding but also preserves it longer. Aging in the bottle diminishes the tannin and softens the wine.

Tart Sharp, with excessive acidity and tannin. In the case of a young red wine, this may be an element necessary for its development.

Thin Lacking body and alcohol. It is too watery to be called light, and will not improve with age.

Velvety A mellow red wine with a smooth, silky texture that will leave no acidity on the palate.

Vigorous Healthy, lively, firm, and youthful. Opposite of insipid and flabby.

Watery Thin and small without body or character.

Woody Odor and flavor of oak due to long storage in the cask. Often found in Spanish wines.

Yeasty Smelling of yeast in fresh bread. Sign that the wine is undergoing a second fermentation, possibly because it was bottled too early, and is therefore faulty.

The Best Vineyards and Estates of the German Wine Regions

RHEINPFALZ—THE RHENISH PALATINATE

The finest vineyards in *Forst*: Freundstück, Jesuitengarten, Kirchenstück, Pech-stein, Ungeheuer; in *Wachenheim*: Gerümpel, Goldbächel, Rechbächel; in *Ruppertsberg*: Hofstück (now a Grosslage), Nussbien, Hoheburg; and in *Deide-sheim*: Hohenmorgen, Leinhöhle, which are as much sought after in Germany as the finest wines from Nierstein and Hattenheim. There are many outstanding estates, such as the three B's—von Buhl, Bürcklin-Wolf, and Bassermann-Jordan—and a number of cooperatives, among which the ones in Deidesheim, Dürkheim, Wachenheim, and Forst make wines as outstanding as those of the great estates.

RHEINHESSEN

There are many famous vineyards in *Nierstein*, the best and best-known being: Auflangen (a Grosslage under the new German wine law), Glöck, Heiligenbaum, Kranzberg, Ölberg, Orbel, Zehnmorgen, Rehbach (another new Grosslage), Hip-ping, Pettenthal, Hölle, and Paterberg. To the north of Nierstein, in the direction of Mainz, are the communities of *Nackenheim, Gau Bischofsheim, Bodenheim,* and *Nieder-Olm,* all of which make fruity and elegant wines. Although their names are hardly ever seen in the export trade, it is these communities, along with the ones listed below following Oppenheim, that furnish most of the wines sold under the labels of *Bereich Nierstein* and *Liebfraumilch,* or even under such Grosslage names as *Niersteiner Gutes Domtal.* Next in importance is the town of *Oppenheim,* which makes big and firm wines second only to the wines of Nierstein, and in great years every bit their equal. Its most famous vineyards are Kreuz, Sackträger, and Zuckerberg. The communities of *Dienheim, Guntersblum,* and *Alsheim* to the south of Oppenheim grow wines of great charm, and again these wines are more likely to appear in America under the label of *Bereich Nierstein* or *Liebfraumilch* or under the Grosslage name of *Oppenheimer Krötenbrunnen.*

There are two communities that deserve to be mentioned separately: *Bingen,* at the very north of the region, just opposite Rüdesheim, at the place where the Nahe flows into the Rhine; and *Worms,* a city made famous by Luther and the Niebelungen. The wines of Bingen are earthier and more robust than those of the rest of the region, and yet maintain their charm. The best vineyards in Bingen are on the *Rochusberg* and *Scharlachberg,* the two hills within the city limits. In Worms, a vineyard called Liebfrauenstift-Kirchenstück, surrounding the Liebfrauen Church, is reputed to be the source of the designa-tion Liebfraumilch. The vineyard makes the finest wines in Worms, but because the vineyard is on a plain, the wines cannot compete with those of Nierstein and Oppenheim.

Rheinhessen is also famous for some of the finest estates of Germany, among which the following are noteworthy: Franz Karl Schmitt, Freiherr Heyl zu Herrnsheim, Gustav Adolf Schmitts'sches, Louis Guntrum, Winzermeister Heinrich Seip, J.u.H.A. Strub, all of which are in Nierstein. The little town also has one of Germany's finest cooperatives specializing in selectively harvested wines. It is but one of many outstanding cooperatives in the Rheinhessen.

RHEINGAU

To describe the different communities of the Rheingau, let us start with the ones close to the river, and then those situated farther up the slopes. The former were planted during the Carolingian dynasty, the latter many centuries later after the Frankish kings no longer ruled. For simplicity's sake, we will enumerate the villages, followed by their best vineyards and a short paragraph citing the famous estates or notable characteristics of the wines grown in the community.

HOCHHEIM

Best vineyards: Domdechaney, Kirchenstück, Hölle.
Notable estates: Staatsdomäne, Geheimrat Aschrot, and Domdeschant Werner.
    The wines of Hochheim are heavier and earthier than most wines of the Rheingau. The vineyards being on the Main River, the wines are somewhat different from those of the rest of the region.

ELTVILLE

Best vineyards: Taubenberg, Sonnenberg.
    Count Eltz and Baron Langwerth von Simmern have their mansions and cellars in Eltville.

ERBACH

Best vineyards: Markobrunn (often spelled "Marcobrunn"), Hohenrain.
Notable estates: Prinz von Preussen, Baron von Oetinger.

HATTENHEIM

Best vineyards: Hassel, Mannberg, Nussbrunnen, Wisselbrunnen, Engelmannsberg.
    Hattenheim wines are firm, solid, and long-lived, and have great bouquet. The estate of Count von Schönborn is in Hattenheim.

OESTRICH

Best vineyards: Doosberg, Lenchen.

The wines of Oestrich have great body but sometimes lack elegance; in the best years, they show superb vinosity and juice.

WINKEL

Best vineyards: Hasensprung, Jesuitengarten (not to be confused with the vineyard of the same name in the Palatinate).

The wines are fragrant and elegant here. The von Brentano estate is in Winkel.

GEISENHEIM

Best vineyards: Kilsberg, Schlossgarten, Klaus, Klauserweg.

The world-famous oenological institute bottles wine here from its vineyards.

RÜDESHEIM

Best vineyards: Berg Roseneck, Berg Rottland, Berg Schlossberg, Bischofsberg.

The vineyards being terraced on steep hills facing south, the wines are big and heavy, yet have great elegance.

RAUENTHAL

Best vineyards: Baiken, Gehrn, Wülfen, Rothenberg.

Great body and great bouquet. Certainly some of the best wines of the region come from here.

KIEDRICH

Best vineyards: Wasseros, Gräfenberg, Sandgrub.

Lively and delightful wines, comparable to the best in great years. The von Ritter and Dr. Weil estates are situated here.

STEINBERG

A single vineyard always carrying only this name, without geographic designation. It is one of the greatest vineyards in the world, belonging to the State of Hesse, and in good years it makes wines of superlative quality.

HALLGARTEN

Best vineyards: Schönhell, Jungfer, Hendelberg.
Notable estate: Fürst zu Löwenstein.

Fine and big wines, particularly in great years. Otherwise, they tend to be a little austere.

SCHLOSS VOLLRADS

The wines are bottled under the name of Schloss Vollrads (same as château in French) and a system of colored capsules too complicated to describe here. The wines, once among Germany's finest, have distinguished themselves in recent years more by price than breed.

JOHANNISBERG

Best vineyard: Schloss Johannisberg.

This wine, too, carries only the name of the estate with a complicated system of colored capsules denoting the different qualities. Once indisputably Germany's finest wine, it went into an eclipse after the incomparable 1953 vintage. It has greatly improved in recent years, though it may not yet justify the price it demands for its name.

Other great vineyards in Johannisberg: Hölle, Mittelhölle, Klaus; closely followed by Schwarzenstein, Vogelsang, Hansenberg, Goldatzel.

THE NAHE

The best-known communities of this region are *Bad Kreuznach, Schloss-Böckelheim, Langenlonsheim,* and *Niederhausen.* The largest single grower is the state. It owns a superb central winery above a vineyard in Niederhausen and makes some of the finest wines of the region. There are many smaller estates and cooperatives, all of which make wines of charm and elegance. Notable among these are Reichsgraf von Plettenberg, Rudolf Anheuser, August Anheuser, and Finkenauer.

MOSEL-SAAR-RUWER

The viticultural district of the Mosel-Saar-Ruwer consists of the Moselle River from Trier to Koblenz and its two small tributaries, the Saar and the Ruwer. The Moselle is further divided into the upper, middle, and lower Moselle; the upper and lower Moselle mainly produce wine for local consumption and sparkling wines. This leaves only the middle Moselle, with the Saar and Ruwer, for production of quality wines. This is the region with the most individual character. The main river and its two tributaries cut their way tortuously through steep hills of slate, terraced on their southern exposure and planted almost exclusively to Riesling. Although in recent years many vineyards in the valley have planted Müller-Thurgau, the wines for which the region is justly famous are all made from the Riesling grape. They are distinguished by an incredible delicacy, bouquet, flavor, and softness perfectly balanced by a pleasant acidity, crispness, and a slight sparkle, which makes them unique. The wines are very low in alcohol, between 8 and 10 percent by volume, which only accentuates their fleeting charm. They are really best as simply Qualitätswein, Kabinett, or Spätlese, the lightness, softness, and flower lending themselves only reluctantly to Auslese and greater selection.

Mosel

The villages that make the best wines in this region are:

KLUSSERATH

Best vineyards: Bruderschaft and Königsberg.

TRITTENHEIM

Best vineyards: Altärchen and Apotheke.

DHRON

Best vineyards: Hofberger and Roterd.

PIESPORT

Best vineyards: Goldtröpfchen, Günterslay, and Falkenberg).

Some of the finest wines of the Moselle come from Piesport. They tend to have a little more body and substance. They also live longer than wines from other villages.

BRAUNEBERG

Best vineyard: Juffer.
Wines from Brauneberg are noted for their ripeness and full flavor.

BERNKASTEL

Best vineyards: Bratenhöfchen, Doctor, Graben, Lay, Matheisbildchen.
Notable estates: Witwe Thanisch, Deinhard, Lauerburg.
The Doctor is the premier vineyard of the Moselle, its wines fetching prices

similar to Grand Cru Bordeaux wines. Bernkastel and its adjoining villages of Wehlen, Graach, Zeltingen, Erden, and Ürzig down the river grow the finest and most distinguished wines on the Moselle.

WEHLEN

Best vineyards: Nonnenberg and the famous Sonnenuhr (a sundial is indeed in the middle of the vineyard).
Notable estates: Bergweiler-Prüm and Joh. Jos. Prüm.

GRAACH

Best vineyards: Abtsberg, Domprobst, and Himmelreich.
   The estate of Josephshof is incorporated in the village, making the famous Josephshöfer wine. The estate makes wine that resembles more the rich and full-bodied wines of Wehlen than the more delicate and elegant wines of Graach.

ZELTINGEN

Best vineyards: Himmelreich, Schlossberg, and Sonnenuhr.

ERDEN

Best vineyards: Busslay, Herrenberg, Prälat, and Treppchen.

ÜRZIG

Best vineyard: Würzgarten.
   Other well-known villages of the central Moselle include: *Traben-Trarbach*, *Kröv*, and *Zell*, with its Schwarze Katz.
Other notable estates: Bischöfliche Weingüter and Güterverwaltung Vereinigte Hospitien.

Saar

The Saar in good years makes wines that are crisp and lively and have great flavor and bouquet. They are generally lighter and more delicate than the wines of the Moselle, but they do not succeed in lesser years. The villages that produce the best wines are *Serrig* with its Antoniusberg, Vogelsang, and Kupp vineyards; *Ockfen* with its Bockstein, Geisberg, and Herrenberg vineyards; *Ayl* with its famous Kupp; and *Wiltingen*, the premier village of the Saar, with its Scharzhofberger and Braune Kupp. The Scharzhofberg is owned by the Müller family, and its world-famous wines are usually sold without the name of the village.

Ruwer

This is the smallest tributary of the Moselle. It makes good wines only in good years; wines that are fresh and delicate but need time to develop their full bouquet and flavor. The main villages are *Waldrach* with its Hahnberg and Jesuitengarten vineyards; *Kasel* with its Nieschen and Kehrnagel vineyards; *Grünhaus*, an individual estate that belongs to the von Schubert'sche Gutsverwaltung (in former times having been the property of the St. Maximin Abbey of Trier), which produces some of the finest wines of the district—the wines are invariably labeled Maximin Grünhäuser; *Eitelsbach* with its *Karthäuser Hof*, whose fine vineyards belong to Werner Tyrell, president of the German wine growers association; and *Avelsbach*.

FRANCONIA

The least-known region of Germany to Americans is Franconia, the area that ships its wines in *Boxbeutel*, a round flacon. The vineyards are along the Main, the only major tributary besides the Neckar that flows into the Rhine from the east. The climate in this northern province of Bavaria is even less conducive to the production of wine than the rest of the Rhine Valley. Clay, chalk, and lime are the main ingredients of the soil. The main grape varieties are Sylvaner, the Mainriesling (a cross of Riesling and Sylvaner that ripens early), and the Müller-Thurgau. The wines are really dry here, and are often, and mistakenly, compared to Chablis. They share some of the dryness of Chablis, but none of its crispness and light liveliness. The Franconian wines have more body and substance than the Chablis, and lack some of the Chablis' freshness.

In great years, wines of great distinction are grown here: Auslese, Beeren-auslese, and Trockenbeerenauslese on some of the finest vineyards that are planted to Riesling. They resemble, in these great years, the finest of the Rheingau. Unfortunately, this area is not so fortunate in lesser years, when most of the wines are dry and sturdy with a degree of elegance but not of charm. The best-known villages are *Iphofen, Escherndorf*, and the city of *Würzburg*, capital of the region. The two finest vineyards in Würzburg are Stein and Leiste. It is the Stein, Germany's largest single vineyard site (275 acres), that lends its name to the regional name of Franconian wines: Steinwein. Famous estates are Julius-spital, Bürgerspital, Hofkellerei, and Fürst Castell.

Important Burgundy Estates

R. Ampeau, Meursault
Marquis d'Angerville, Volnay
Henri Boillot & Fils, Volnay
Domaine Bouchard Père & Fils,
  Beaune
Domaine Camus, Gevrey-Chambertin
Chandon de Briailles
  (Comte de Nicolay), Savigny
Chapelle, Santenay
Domaine Clair-Daü, Marsannay
Domaine Felix Clerget, Pommard
Domaine Cosson, Morey
de Courcel, Pommard
Delagrange-Bachelet, Chassagne
Domaine Drouhin-Laroze,
  Gevrey-Chambertin
Domaine Faiveley,
  Mercurey and Nuits St. Georges
Fleurot-Laroze, Santenay
F. Gaunoux, Pommard
P. Gélin, Fixin
Gouges, Henri, Nuits St. Georges
Jean Gros, Vosne-Romanée
Marquis de LaGuiche, Chassagne

Henry Lamarche, Vosne-Romanée
Le Flaive, Puligny
Lequin & Fils, Santenay
Château Masson, Meursault
Prince de Merode, Ladoix
B. Michelot, Meursault
J. Monnier, Meursault
Ch. Noëllat, Vosne-Romanée
Domaine Pidault, Santenay
Château de Pommard (Laplanche),
  Pommard
Ponelle, Beaune
Domaine de la Pousse d'Or (Potel),
  Volnay
Ramonet-Prudhon, Chassagne
Rebourseau, Gevrey-Chambertin
Domaine de la Romanée-Conti,
  Vosne-Romanée
Roumier, Chambolle
A. Rousseau, Gevrey-Chambertin
Baron Thénard, Puligny and Givry
Domaine Trapet, Gevrey-Chambertin
Comte de Vogüé, Chambolle

Some Dependable Bordeaux Shippers

A. & R. Barrière Frères
Barton & Guestier
H. & O. Beyerman, S.A.R.L.
Albert Bichot
Birkedal Hartmann & Cie.
William Bolter & Company
Bolter & Schneider
Borie-Manoux
Paul Bouchard et Cie.
Bouchard Père et Fils
J. Calvet & Cie.

Chantecaille & Cie.
D. Cordier, S.A.
Coron Père & Fils
Cruse & Fils Frères
L. Danglade & Fils & Cie.
A. Delor & Cie., S.A.
Descas Père & Fils
Dourthe Frères
Louis Dubroca
Dulong Frère & Fils
Louis Eschenauer

Gilbey, S.A.
Ginestet
Grenouilleau-Aurélien
Nathaniel Johnston & Fils
Jouvet
Ed. Kressmann & Co.
La Bergèrie—Baron Philippe de
  Rothschild, S.A.
A. Lalande & Co.
Alexis Lichine & Co.
A. de Luze & Fils
Mähler-Besse & Cie.

Marnier Lapostolle
Mestrezat-Preller
A. Moueix & Fils, Ltd.
Prats Brothers
Les Fils de Marcel Quancard
Daniel et Alain Querre
Quien & Cie., S.A.
Schroder & de Constans
Schroder & Schÿler & Co.
Maison Sichel
Woltner Frères

Reliable Burgundy Shippers

A. Barolet
Barton & Guestier
A. Bassereau & Cie.
Albert Bichot
Boisseaux-Estivant
Bouchard, Ainé & Fils
Paul Bouchard et Cie.
Bouchard Père et Fils
Lionel Bruck
J. Calvet & Cie.
Chanson Père & Fils
F. Chauvenet
Coron Père et Fils
Etablissements Cruse
Charles Drapier & Fils
Joseph Drouhin
Georges Duboeuf
Dufouleur Frères
J. Faiveley
Geisweiler & Fils
Jaboulet-Vercherre & Cie.
Maison Louis Jadot
Maison Jaffelin
Louis Latour
Etablissements Leroy
Alexis Lichine & Co.
Liger-Belair & Fils

Lupé-Cholet & Co.
A. de Luze et Fils
Marnier Lapostolle
Prosper Maufoux
Moillard-Grivot
J. Mommessin
J. Moreau
Morin Père & Fils
de Moucheron & Cie.
Pasquier-Desvignes
Patriarche Père et Fils
Piat Père et Fils
Albert Pic
Pierre Picard
Poulet Père & Fils
A. Regnard & Fils
Jules Regnier & Cie.
Remoissenet Père & Fils
J. H. Remy
Maison Antonin Rodet
Ropiteau Frères
Maison Sichel
Roland Thévenin
Maison Thomas-Bassot
J. Thorin
Etablissements Charles Viénot

Reliable Shippers of Rhine, Moselle, and Alsatian Wines

Anheuser & Fehrs.
Leon Beyer
E. Boeckel, S.A.
Deinhard & Co.
Dopff
Dopff & Irion
Drathen
Export-Union Deutscher Weingüter
F. W. Langguth Erben
Weingut Louis Guntrum
Arthur Hallgarten
Hauptkellerei Rheinischer
   Winzergenossenschaften
Carl Jos. Hoch
Jacob Horz
Adolph Huesgen
F. E. Hugel et Fils
Ernst Jungkenn
Julius Kayser & Co.
Hermann Kendermann
Leonard Kreusch

Langenbach & Co.
Richard Langguth
Rudolph Müller
Weingut Ferdinand Pieroth
Qualitätsweingut Jakob Gerhardt
Franz Reh, K.G.
Reichsgraf von Kesselstatt
Société Vinicole & Dist. Sainte Odile,
   S.A.R.L.
Weingut Gustav Adolf Schmitt
Georg und Karl Ludwig Schmitt'sches
   Weingut
Scholl & Hillebrand
Schulz & Wagner
H. Sichel Söhne
A. Steigenberger
F. E. Trimbach
P. J. Valckenberg
Wilhelm Wasum
Adolphe Willm

Alexis Lichine's Suggested Classification of the Grands Crus Rouges de Bordeaux

Rather than give you our own estimate of the comparative worth of Bordeaux individual wines, we have obtained the kind permission of Alexis Lichine to use his excellent and definitive assessment of the Bordeaux growths. It and other valuable information you will find in *Alexis Lichine's New Encyclopedia of Wines & Spirits*,[1] which we consider an essential book for any wine lover to have.

The wines of Bordeaux were officially classified in 1855 from First Growths to Fifth Growths. If the wine listed was so classified, we indicate the ranking after the name of the château.

The best wines of Graves were officially classified in 1953 and 1959 as Classed Growths, or *Crus Classés* (CC). If the wine listed here was so classified, we indicate this after the name of the Graves château.

The best wines of St. Emilion were officially classified in 1955 as First Great Growths, or *Premiers Grands Crus Classés* (PGC), and Great Growths, or *Grands Crus Classés* (GCC). If the wines listed here were so classified, we indicate this after the name of the St. Emilion château.

Pomerol has never been officially classified.

CLASSIFICATION DES GRANDS CRUS ROUGES DE BORDEAUX

CRUS HORS CLASSE (Outstanding Growths)

Médoc

Château Lafite-Rothschild
    (Pauillac) 1st
Château Latour (Pauillac) 1st
Château Margaux (Margaux) 1st
Château Mouton-Rothschild
    (Pauillac) 2nd

Graves

Château Haut-Brion (Pessac,
    Graves) 1st, CC

Saint-Emilion

Château Ausone PGC
Château Cheval Blanc PGC

Pomerol

Château Pétrus

---

1. From *Alexis Lichine's New Encyclopedia of Wines & Spirits*. Copyright © 1967, 1974 by Alexis Lichine. Reprinted by permission of Alfred A. Knopf, Inc.

CRUS EXCEPTIONNELS (Exceptional Growths)

Médoc

Château Beychevelle (Saint-Julien) **4th**

Château Brane-Cantenac (Cantenac-Margaux) **2nd**

Château Calon-Ségur (Saint-Estèphe) **3rd**

Château Cos d'Estournel (Saint-Estèphe) **2nd**

Château Ducru-Beaucaillou (Saint-Julien) **2nd**

Château Gruaud-Larose (Saint-Julien) **2nd**

Château Lascombes (Cantenac-Margaux) **2nd**

Château Léoville-Barton (Saint-Julien) **2nd**

Château Léoville-Las-Cases (Saint-Julien) **2nd**

Château Léoville-Poyferré (Saint-Julien) **2nd**

Château Lynch-Bages (Pauillac) **5th**

Château Montrose (Saint-Estèphe) **2nd**

Château Palmer (Cantenac-Margaux) **3rd**

Château Pichon-Longueville [Baron] (Pauillac) **2nd**

Château Pichon-Longueville [Comtesse de Lalande] (Pauillac) **2nd**

Graves

Domaine de Chevalier (Léognan) **CC**

Château La Mission-Haut-Brion (Pessac) **CC**

Château Pape Clément (Pessac) **CC**

Saint-Emilion

Château Canon **PGC**

Château Figeac **PGC**

Château La Gaffelière **PGC**

Château Magdelaine **PGC**

Pomerol

Château La Conseillante

Château L'Évangile

Château Trotanoy

Vieux Château Certan

GRANDS CRUS (Great Growths)

Médoc

Château Branaire-Ducru (Saint-Julien) **4th**

Château Cantemerle (Haut-Médoc) **5th**

Château Cantenac-Brown (Cantenac-Margaux) **3rd**

Château Duhart-Milon-Rothschild (Pauillac) **4th**

Château Durfort-Vivens (Cantenac-Margaux) **2nd**

Château Giscours (Cantenac-Margaux) **3rd**

Château Grand-Puy-Lacoste (Pauillac) **5th**

Château d'Issan (Cantenac-Margaux) **3rd**

Château La Lagune (Haut-Médoc) **3rd**

Château Malescot-Saint-Exupéry
(Margaux) **3rd**
Château Mouton-Baron-Philippe
(Pauillac) **5th**
Château Pontet-Canet (Pauillac) **5th**
Château Prieuré-Lichine (Cantenac-
Margaux) **4th**
Château Rauzan-Gassies
(Margaux) **2nd**
Château Rausan-Ségla
(Margaux) **2nd**
Château Talbot (Saint-Julien) **4th**

Graves

Château Haut-Bailly (Léognan) **CC**

Saint-Emilion

Château L'Angélus **GCC**
Château Beauséjour-Bécot
Château Beauséjour-Duffau-
Lagarrosse **PGC**
Château Bélair **PGC**
Clos Fourtet **PGC**
Château Pavie **PGC**
Château Trottevieille **PGC**

Pomerol

Château Gazin
Château Lafleur
Château La Fleur-Petrus
Château Latour-Pomerol
Château Petit-Village

CRUS SUPÉRIEURS (Superior Growths)

Médoc

Château Batailley (Pauillac) **5th**
Château Boyd-Cantenac (Cantenac-
Margaux) **3rd**
Château Chasse-Spleen (Moulis)
Château Clerc-Milon-Rothschild
(Pauillac) **5th**
Château Gloria (Saint-Julien)
Château Grand-Puy-Ducasse
(Pauillac) **5th**
Château Haut-Batailley
(Pauillac) **5th**
Château Kirwan (Cantenac-
Margaux) **3rd**
Château Lagrange (Saint-Julien) **3rd**
Château Marquis d'Alesme-Becker
(Margaux) **3rd**
Château de Pez (Saint-Estèphe)
Château La Tour-Carnet (Haut-
Médoc) **4th**

Graves

Château Bouscaut (Cadaujac) **CC**
Château Carbonnieux (Léognan) **CC**
Château Fieuzal (Léognan) **CC**
Château Malartic-Lagravière
(Léognan) **CC**
Château Smith-Haut-Lafitte
(Martillac) **CC**

Saint-Emilion

Château Balestard-la-Tonnelle **GCC**
Château Cadet-Piola **GCC**
Château Canon-La Gaffelière **GCC**
Château La Clotte **GCC**
Château Croque-Michotte **GCC**
Château Curé-Bon-La-
Madeleine **GCC**
Château La Dominique **GCC**
Château Larcis-Ducasse **GCC**

Château Soutard **GCC**
Château Troplong-Mondot **GCC**

Pomerol

Château Beauregard
Château Certan-Giraud
Château Certan-de-May

BONS CRUS (Good Growths)

Médoc

Château d'Angludet (Cantenac-
Margaux)
Château Beau-Site (Saint-Estèphe)
Château Beau-Site-Haut-Vignoble
(Saint-Estèphe)
Château Bel-Air-Marquis d'Aligre
(Soussans-Margaux)
Château Belgrave (Saint-
Laurent) **5th**
Château de Camensac (Haut-
Médoc) **5th**
Château Cos-Labory (Saint-
Estèphe) **5th**
Château Croizet-Bages (Pauillac) **5th**
Château Dauzac-Lynch
(Labarde) **5th**
Château Ferrière (Margaux) **3rd**
Château Fourcas-Dupré (Listrac)
Château Fourcas-Hosten (Listrac)
Château Gressier-Grand-Poujeaux
(Moulis)
Château Haut-Bages-Libéral
(Pauillac) **5th**
Château Haut-Marbuzet (Saint-
Estèphe)
Château Labégorce (Margaux)
Château Labégorce-Zédé (Margaux)
Château Lafon-Rochet (Saint-
Estèphe) **4th**
Château Lanessan (Haut-Médoc)
Château Langoa (Saint-Julien) **3rd**

Clos l'Eglise
Clos de l'Église-Clinet
Châtean Le Gay
Château Lagrange
Château La Grave
Château Nenin
Château La Pointe

Château Lynch-Moussas
(Pauillac) **5th**
Château Marquis de Terme
(Marguax) **3rd**
Château Les Ormes-de-Pez (Saint
Estèphe)
Château Pédesclaux (Pauillac) **5th**
Château Phélan-Ségur (Saint-
Estèphe)
Château Pouget (Cantenac-
Margaux) **4th**
Château Poujeaux (Moulis)
Château Saint-Pierre (Saint-
Julien) **4th**
Château Siran (Labarde-Margaux)
Château du Tertre (Arsac-
Margaux) **5th**
Château La Tour-de-Mons
(Soussans-Margaux)

Graves

Château La Louvière (Léognan)
Château La Tour-Haut-Brion
(Talence) **CC**
Château La Tour-Martillac
(Martillac) **CC**

Saint-Emilion

Château L'Arrosée **GCC**
Château Baleau
Château Bellevue **GCC**

Château Cap-de-Mourlin **GCC**
Domaine du Châtelet
Château Clos des Jacobins **GCC**
Château Corbin (Giraud) **GCC**
Château Corbin-Michotte **GCC**
Château Coutet **GCC**
Couvent-des-Jacobins
Château La Fleur-Pourret
Château Fonroque **GCC**
Château Franc-Mayne **GCC**
Château Grand-Barrail-Lamarzelle-
   Figeac
Château Grand-Corbin
Château Grand-Corbin-
   Despagne **GCC**
Château Grand-Mayne **GCC**
Château Grand Pontet **GCC**
Château Grandes-Murailles **GCC**
Château Moulin-du-Cadet **GCC**
Château Pavie-Macquin **GCC**
Château Ripeau **GCC**
Château Saint-Georges-Côte-
   Pavie **GCC**

Château Tertre-Daugay **GCC**
Château La Tour-Figeac **GCC**
Château La Tour-du-Pin-
   Figeac **GCC**
Château Trimoulet **GCC**
Château Villemaurine **GCC**
Château Yon-Figeac **GCC**

Pomerol

Château Clinet
Château Clos-Rene
Château La Croix
Château La Croix-de-Gay
Château l'Enclos
Château Feytit-Clinet
Château Gombaude-Guillot
Château Mazeyres
Château Rouget
Château de Sales
Château Taillefer

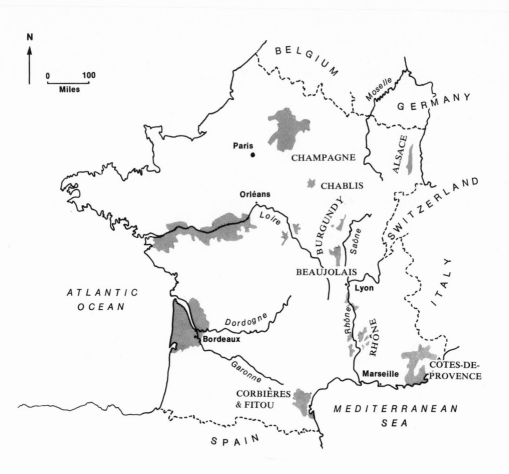

WINE PRODUCING REGIONS OF FRANCE

WINE PRODUCING REGIONS OF SPAIN AND PORTUGAL

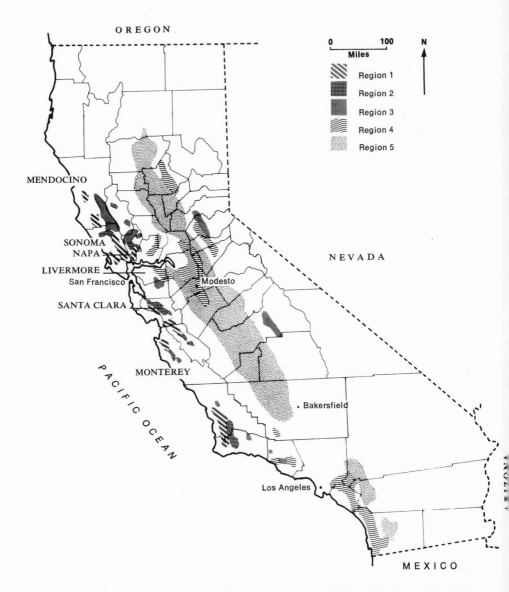

MAP OF CALIFORNIA SHOWING MAJOR WINE GROWING COUNTIES AND CLIMATE REGIONS

Bibliography

Adams, Leon D. *The Wines of America*. Boston: Houghton Mifflin, 1973.

Ambrosi, Hans. *Wo Grosse Weine Wachsen*. Munich: Gräfe u. Unzer Verlag, 1973.

———. *Deutscher Wein-Atlas*. Bielefeld, West Germany: Ceres-Verlag Rudolf-August Oetker K.G., 1973.

Amerine, Maynard A., and M. A. Joslyn. *Table Wines: The Technology of Their Production*. Rev. ed. Berkeley: University of California Press, 1970.

——— and W. V. Cruess. *The Technology of Wine Making*. Westport, Conn.: AVI Publishing, 1960.

——— and A. Winkler. *California Wine Grapes*. University of California, Division of Agricultural Sciences, 1963.

Balzer, Robert Lawrence. *Discovering Italian Wines*. New York: Ward Ritchie Press, 1970.

Beverage Media. New York: Associated Beverage Publications, 1974.

Born, Wina. *The Concise Atlas of Wine*. New York: Scribners, 1974.

Broadbent, J. M. *Wine Tasting*. London: Wine & Spirit Publications, 1970.

Cassagnac, Paul de. *French Wines*. London: Chatto & Windus, 1936.

Castillo, José del. *Los Vinos de España*. Bilbao: Proyección Editorial, 1971.

Chroman, Nathan. *The Treasury of American Wines*. New York: Rutledge-Crown, 1973.

Churchill, Creighton. *A Notebook for the Wines of France*. New York: Knopf, 1961.

———. *The World of Wines*. New York: Macmillan, 1964.

Cocks, Charles, and Edouard Féret. *Bordeaux et Ses Vins*. Bordeaux: Féret et Fils, 1969.

Cruess, W. V. *The Principles and Practice of Wine Making*. Westport, Conn.: AVI Publishing, 1947.

Dallas, Philip. *The Great Wines of Italy*. Garden City, N.Y.: Doubleday, 1974.

Deutscher Weinwirtschaftsverlag. *Weinfach Kalender 1974/75*. Mainz and Neustadt.

Engel, René. *Vade-Mecum de l'oenologue*. Paris: Ponsot, 1959.

Frumkin, Lionel. *The Science and Technique of Wine*. London: Lea & Company, 1965.

Gay, Charles. *Vouvray, Ses Vignes, Ses Vignerons*. Tours: Arrault & Cie., 1944.

Goldschmidt, Eduard. *Deutschlands Weinbauorte und Weinbergslagen*. Mainz: Verlag der Deutschen Wein-Zeitung, 1951.

Grossman, Harold J. *Grossman's Guide to Wine, Spirits, and Beers*. New York: Scribners, 1964.

"Harpers Directory and Manual." London: Harper Trade Journals, 1973/74.

Hillebrand, Walter. *Taschenbuch der Rebsorten*. Wiesbaden: Zeitschriftenverlag Dr. Bilz u. Dr. Fraud K.G., 1972.

Hogg, Anthony. *Off The Shelf*. Essex, England: Gilbey Vintners, 1972.

Hyams, Edward. *Dionysus, A Social History of the Wine Vine*. New York: Macmillan, 1965.

Jacquelin, Louis, and René Poulain. *The Wines and Vineyards of France*. Rev. ed. London: Paul Hamlyn, 1965.

Jeffs, Julian. *The Wines of Europe*. New York: Taplinger Publishing, 1971.

Johnson, Hugh. *Wine*. London: Thos. Nelson & Sons, 1966.

———. *The World Atlas of Wine*. New York: Simon & Schuster, 1971.

Klenk, Ernst. *Die Weinbeurteilung*. Stuttgart: Verlag Eugen Ulmer, 1960.

Larmat, Louis. *Atlas de la France Vinicole, Les Vins de Bordeaux*. Paris: Larmat, 1953.

———. *Atlas de la France Vinicole, Les Vins de Bourgogne*. Paris: Larmat, 1953.

Layton, T. A. *Winecraft, The Encyclopaedia of Wines and Spirits*. London: Harper & Company, 1959.

———. *Wines of Italy*. London: Harper & Company, 1961.

Lichine, Alexis. *Alexis Lichine's New Encyclopedia of Wines & Spirits*. New York: Knopf, 1974.

McMullen, Thomas. *Hand-Book of Wines*. New York: D. Appleton & Co., 1852.

Melville, John. *Guide to California Wines*. New York: Dutton, 1972.

Moisy, Robert. *Beaujolais*. Neuchâtel: Editions de La Baconnière, 1956.

Nègre, Edouard, and Paul Françot. *Manuel Practique de Vinification et de Conservation des Vins*. Paris: Flammarion, 1941.

Paronetto, Lamberto. *Chianti, The Story of Florence and Its Wines*. London: Wine & Spirit Publications, 1970.

Petel, Pierre. *Wine*. Montreal: Habitex Books, 1973.

Postgate, Raymond. *Portuguese Wine*. London: J. M. Dent & Sons, 1969.

Poupon, Pierre, and Pierre Fourgeot. *The Wines of Burgundy*. Paris: Presse Universitaire, 1971.

Puisais, Jacques, and R. L. Chabanon. *Précis d'Initiation à la Dégustation*. Paris: Institut Technique du Vin, 1967.

Rainbird, George. *Sherry and the Wines of Spain*. London: McGraw-Hill, 1966.

Ray, Cyril. *The Wines of Italy*. London: McGraw-Hill, 1966.

Renouil, Yves, ed. *Dictionnaire du Vin*. Bordeaux: Féret et Fils, 1962.

Renz, F. *Das Neue Weinrecht*. Stuttgart: Verlag Eugen Ulmer, 1969.

Rodier, Camille. *Le Vin de Bourgogne*. Dijon: L. Damidot, 1920.

Roncarati, Bruno. *D.O.C., The New Image for Italian Wines*. London: Harper Trade Journals, 1971.

Rowe, Percy. *The Wines of Canada*. Toronto: McGraw-Hill (Canada), 1970.

Rowsell, Edmund Penning-. *The Wines of Bordeaux*. London: Michael Joseph/International Wine & Food Society, 1969.

Schoonmaker, Frank. *Encyclopedia of Wine*. New York: Hastings House, 1973.

Shand, P. Morton. *A Book of French Wines.* London: Jonathan Cape, 1963.

Stanislawski, Dan. *Landscapes of Bacchus: The Vine in Portugal.* Austin: University of Texas Press, 1970.

Thompson, Bob, ed. *California Wine.* Menlo Park, Calif.: Sunset Books, 1973.

Veronelli, Luigi. *The Wines of Italy.* Rome: Canesi Editore, n.d.

Wines and Vines, Winery Listings 1973–1975. San Francisco: The Hiaring Company.

Younger, William. *Gods, Men, and Wine.* Cleveland: World Publishing/Wine & Food Society, 1966.

Yoxall, H. W. *The Wines of Burgundy.* London: Michael Joseph/International Wine & Food Society, 1968.

Index

Abbocato, 148
Acidity in wine, 18, 35, 36, 237; California generics, 137; and fruit balance, 12, 15, 107, 117; German wines, 107, 111, 117; Mâcon, 97–98; Muscadet, 132–133; Silvaner, 108; in southern wines, 147–148; and young Chablis, 95
Ackerman-Laurance, wine tastings:
  Ackerman Sauvignon, 129
  Ackerman Vouvray, 135
Adriatica, wine tastings:
  Rizling from Fruška Gora, 146
  Carbernet from Istria, 45
Aging of wine, 17–18, 31, 36–37, 50, 57–59, 87, 98–99, 101, 108, 127, 147, 218, 220. *See also* Storage of wine; Vintages
Alcohol in wine, 12, 16–17, 86–87, 163; Beaujolais, 66–68; Burgundy, 94; Châteauneuf-du-Pape, 56, 58; German wines, 107, 113; and Petit Verdot grape, 35; and Rosés, 153; in southern wines, 147, 149
Alexander Valley, 5, 37, 49
Algerian wines, 19, 57
Almadén Vineyards, 235; wine tastings:
  California Blanc Fumé, 128
  California Cabernet Sauvignon, 47
  California Chablis, 140
  California Chenin Blanc, 135
  California Chianti, 85
  California Dry Sémillon Sauterne, 129
  California Gamay Beaujolais, 93
  California Gewürztraminer, 117, 123
  California Grenache Rosé, 157
  California Johannisberg Riesling, 120
  California Mountain Grey Riesling, 145
  California Mountain Nectar Vin Rosé, 159
  California Mountain Red Claret, 45
  California Mountain Rhine, 146
  California Mountain White Sauterne, 140
  California Pinot Blanc, 105
  California Pinot Chardonnay, 105
  California Pinot Noir, 62
  California Sauvignon Blanc, 128
Aloxe-Corton, 54, 55
Alsatian wines, 107, 114, 115, 142–143; shippers of, 250
Alsheim (Rheinhessen), best vineyards, 241
Altärchen (Trittenheimer), 245
Amabile, 148
American wines (other than California), 5, 9, 160–161; tasting results, red: 163, 165; white: 166–168
Amerine, Maynard, 57

Ampelographers, 91
Andrés, wine tastings:
  Canadian Claret, 169
  Regency Extra Dry Vin Blanc, 170
  Richelieu Vin de Chaunac, 169
  Similkameen, 169
  Still Rosé, 171
  Vino Bianco, 170
  Vino Buono, 169
Angélus Ch. L', 253
Angludet, Ch. d', 254
Anheuser and Fehrs, wine tastings:
  Anheuser Bernkastel, 121
  Anheuser Johannisberger, 119
  Anheuser Liebfraumilch, 122
  Piesporter Michelsberg, 121
Anjou Rosé, 152, 153
Anjou Rosé de Cabernet, 153
Antinori, wine tastings:
  Bardolino Classico Superiore, 89
  Bianco della Costa Toscana, 151
  Est! Est! Est!, 151
  Santa Cristina Chianti Classico, 83
  Villa Antinori Chianti Classico, 83
Aperitifs and cocktail wines, 107, 127, 133, 138, 208–209
A. P. number (Amtliche Prüfungsnummer), 113
Appellation Contrôlée (A.C.), 6–7, 32, 51, 66–67, 77, 95, 124
Appellations; Beaujolais, 66–67; Bordeaux, 34–36; red Burgundy, 51, 54–55, 58; White Bordeaux, 124; White Burgundy, 95
Argentinian wine, 47, 142, 146
Aroma of wine, 225, 226, 237
Arrosée, Ch. L', 254
Aurora (grape hybrid), 161
Auslese, 11, 113, 118, 208, 247; vintage chart, 116
Ausone, Ch., 250
Austin, Nichols (importer), wine tastings:
  Ch. Guiraud-Cheval-Blanc, 46
  Ch. Simard, 48
Austrian wine, 142, 145
Auxey-Duresses, 54
Avelsbach (Ruwer), 247
Ayler Kupp, 246

Baco Noir (grape hybrid), 161
Baden, 110
Bad Kreuznach (Nahe), 244
Baleau, Ch., 254
Balestard-la-Tonnelle, Ch., 253
Barbaresco, 57
Barbera, 77, 80–82; tasting results, 84–85
Barberone, 77, 80–81
Barbier Blanco Seco, 151

Bardolino, 86–88, 92, 208; tasting results, 89
Barnes, wine tastings:
  Canadian Claret, 169
  Lake Niagara White, 170
  Lake Roselle, 171
  Medium-Dry Still Rosé, 171
  Ontario Country Rosé, 171
Barolo, 57, 223
Barsac, 125; vintages, 11, 126
Barton (Bordeaux shipper), 32
Barton & Guestier, wine tastings:
  Beaujolais St. Louis, 71
  Médoc, 47
  Prince Noir, 47
Bassermann-Jordan Estate, 241
Bassot, Thomas, wine tastings:
  Chantefleur Blanc de Blancs, 104
  Pinot Chardonnay-Mâcon, 105
  Pinot Noir Réserve des 3 Glorieuses, 63
Batailley, Ch., 253
Bâtard-Montrachet, 96, 223
Beaujolais, 18, 28, 81, 88, 132, 208, 233; red, 66–71, vintage chart, 68; compared to Gamay Beaujolais, 91; tasting results, 68–69, 70–71, 74, 92; white, 98
Beaujolais Blanc, 98, 101, 105
Beaujolais-Nouveau, 67–69
Beaujolais "St. Vincent," 5, 70
Beaujolais Supérieur, 66
Beaujolais-Villages, 67, 70
Beaujolais-Villages 1974, Tirage Primeur, 69
Beaulieu Vineyard, wine tastings:
  Beaumont Napa Valley Pinot Noir, 64
  Napa Valley Burgundy, 61
  Napa Valley Cabernet Sauvignon, 49
Beaune, 54, 55, 60
Beauregard, Ch., 254
Beauséjour-Bécot, Ch., 253
Beauséjour-Duffau-Lagarrosse, Ch., 253
Beau-Site, Ch., 254
Beau-Site-Haut-Vignoble, Ch., 254
Beerenauslese, 11, 113, 118, 208, 247; vintage chart, 116
Belair, Ch., 253
Bel-Air-Marquis d'Aligre, Ch., 254
Belgrave, Ch., 254
Bellevue, Ch., 254
Benmarl Vineyards, Hudson River Region Baco Noir, 165
Bereich, 112
Bereich Hochheim, 114
Bereich Johannisberg, 114
Bereich Nierstein, 114, 122, 241
Bereich Schloss Böckelheim, 114
Beringer Vineyards, wine tastings:
  Napa Valley Cabernet Sauvignon, 49
  Napa Valley Chardonnay, 105
  North Coast Grey Riesling, 146
Bernkastel (Mosel), 114, 118; best vineyards and estates, 245–246
Bertani, wine tastings:
  Bardolino Classico Superiore, 89
  Soave, 151
  Valpolicella Valpantena, 90
Beverage Media, 28

Beychevelle, Ch., 252
Bienvenue-Bâtard-Montrachet, 96
Bingen (Rheinhessen), best vineyards, 241
Bischöfliche Weingüter Estate, 246
Blanc Fumé, 125, 133
Blanchot (Grand Cru Chablis), 96
Blending of wine, 136, 161
"Blue Nun" Liebfraumilch, 5, 114
Bodegas Bilbainas, wine tastings:
  Brillante Blanco, 151
  Brillante Vino Rosado, 159
Bodegas y Viñedos López, wine tastings:
  Chateau Vieux, 128
  Rincón Famoso, 84
Bodenheim (Rheinhessen), wines, 241
Bolla, wine tastings:
  Bardolino Classico, 89
  Soave Classico, 151
  Valpolicella Classico, 90
Bonnes Mares, 54
Boordy Red Wine, 165
Bordeaux, France, 36–37, 223; chateaux, 30–31, 38, 79; map, 33; prices, 236; quality control, 34–35; shippers of, 32, 234, 248
Bordeaux Blanc, 124, 127
Bordeaux-style wine, 30–31, 35–36; tastings and results, 41–49, 167, 168, 170. *See also* California Cabernet Sauvignon
Bordeaux Supérieur, 30, 32, 35, 41, 43, 88
Bordeaux wine, French Red, 4, 20, 28, 37, 88, 209; Burgundy comparison, 30, 50, 94; description, 30–35; filtering and fining of, 18; Grands Crus classification, 246, 251–255; tasting results, 41–49; vintage chart, 40; vintages, 10–11, 38–39
Bordeaux wine, French White. *See* Graves, White
Vintages, 11, 125. *See also* Sauternes
Bottles and bottle shapes, 79, 87, 108, 130, 218, 222, 224, 247
Bottling and shipping, 18, 79, 98, 130–131, 147
Botrytis cinerea. See "Noble rot"
Bouchard Beaujolais Supérieur, 71
Bougros (Grand Cru Chablis), 96
Bourgogne, 58, 95; tasting results, 105
Bourgogne Grand Ordinaire, 58
Bourgogne Passe-Tout-Grains, 55, 91
Bouscaut, Ch., 253
Boxbeutel, 108, 247
Boyd-Cantenac, Ch., 253
Branaire-Ducru, Ch., 252
Brandy, 17
Brane-Cantenac, Ch., 252
Brauneberg (Mosel), wines and Juffer vineyard, 245
Bright, T. G., & Co., wine tastings:
  Aurora White Table Wine, 170
  Baco Noir, 169
  Blue Seibel, 169
  de Chaunac, 169
  DuBarry Medium-Dry Still Rosé, 171

Bright, T. G., & Co. (*continued*)
Manor St. David's Canadian Claret, 169
Manor St. David's Canadian Sauterne, 170
Pinot Chardonnay, 170
President's Canadian Burgundy, 169
President's White Table Wine, 170
Brillante, 150
Broadbent, J. M., *Wine Tasting*, 226
Brookside Vineyard California Vino Rosado, 157
Brotherhood New York State Chablis, 166
Brouilly, 67
Brown Vintners (importers), Ch. de la Chaize Brouilly, 70
Buena Vista Sonoma Zinfandel, 75
Buffavent, Ch. de (Schenley), 70
Buhl, von, Estate, 241
Bully Hill Vineyards, wine tastings:
Aurora Blanc, 139, 166
Bully Hill Red, 165
Chancellor Noir, 165
Seyval Blanc, 166
Bürcklin-Wolf Estate, 241
Bürgerspital Estate, 247
Burgundy, France, 3, 10, 19, 51, 91, 116; important estates of, 248; maps, 52–53; shippers of, 51, 54–55, 98, 249
Burgundy-style wine, 3, 50, 56–60, 235; tasting results, 59–65, 165, 166, 169, 170. *See also* California Pinot Noir; California Pinot Chardonnay
Burgundy wine, French Red; comparisons: with Bordeaux, 30, 50, 94; California Burgundy, 56; Claret, 42; description, 50–55; Grand Crus, 51, 54, 209; tastings, 59–65; vintage chart, 59; vintages, 10–11, 58–60
Burgundy wine, French White, 5, 94–103; vintage chart, 100–101, tastings, 101–102, 104–106

Cabernet Franc (grape), 34, 35
Cabernet Rosé d'Anjou, 153
Cabernet Sauvignon, 4, 7, 13, 35, 46–49, 160, 223. *See also* California Cabernet Sauvignon
Cabernet Sauvignon Rosé, 152–153
Cadet-Piola, Ch., 253
California, University of, 15, 57
California Growers Winery, wine tastings:
California Burgundy, 62
California Chablis, 141
California Varietals:
California Barbera and Barberone, 77, 80–82; tastings, 81, 84–85
California Burgundy, red, 5, 31, 42, 51, 57, 60, 72, 82, 93, 207
California Cabernet Sauvignon, 30, 37–38, 72–73, 224; tasting results, 41–49; vintages, 39
California Chablis, 4–5, 8, 103, 133, 136–141, 142–143, 150, 207
California Champagne, 130

California Chenin Blanc, 4, 127, 130, 138, 143; tasting results, 132–135
California Chianti, 31, 77, 80–82; tastings, 83–85
California Claret, 30, 31, 36–37; tastings, 42, 44–45
California Emerald Riesling, 108, 122, 131; tastings, 143–145
California French Colombard, 4, 130, 136–137; tasting results, 138–140
California Fumé Blanc, 102, 124–125, 133, 138; tasting results, 127–128
California Gamay Beaujolais, 4, 28, 74, 91–92, 207, 223; tasting results, 92–93
California Gewürztraminer, 107, 115–117; tastings, 156–159
California Grenache Rosé, 4, 152, 153; tastings, 156–159
California Grey Riesling, 4, 108; tastings, 142–146
California Johannisberg Riesling, 4, 107, 115; tasting results, 117–120
California Mountain Red, 50, 57, 59; tastings, 45, 61–62, 64
California Napa Gamay, 4, 91–92
California Petit Sirah, 40, 50, 58; tastings, 60
California Pineau de la Loire, 130, 135
California Pinot Blanc, 103; tastings, 104–105
California Pinot Chardonnay, 94, 99–100, 102; tasting results, 104–106
California Pinot Noir, 4, 50, 56–57, 58, 60, 223; tasting results, 61, 62, 64–65
California Pinot St. Georges, 56
California Rhine Wine, 108, 138, 142–144; tasting results, 146
California Riesling. *See* California Johannisberg Riesling
California Rosés, 72, 152–159; tasting results: dry, 156–157; other than dry, 158–159
California Sauterne, 125, 129, 133, 136–140
California Sauvignon Blanc, 124–127, 133, 138, 143; tasting results, 127, 128–129
California Sémillon, 4, 124–127, 143; tasting results, 128–129
California Sylvaner, 5, 108, 117; tastings, 142–146
California White Pinot, 130, 133
California Zinfandel, 42, 69, 72–74, 88, 208; tastings, 28–29, 75–76
California wine; compared to other American wines, 160–161; evaluation code, 225–226; industry, 4–5, 15–16, 19, 20, 98–99, 234–235; map, 258; regulations, 6–8; soil and climate effect, 13, 15, 72; vintage years, 9, 39
California Wine Association, wine tastings:
Fino Eleven Cellars California Cabernet Sauvignon, 47

California Wine Association (*continued*)
Fino Eleven Cellars California
Chablis, 141
Fino Eleven Cellars California Chenin
Blanc, 135
Fino Eleven Cellars California Claret, 45
Fino Eleven Cellars California Vin
Rosé, 157
Guasti California Chablis, 140
Guasti California Rhine, 146
L. & J. California Chablis, 140
L. & J. California Sauterne, 140
Vino Fino California Red Table Wine,
85
Vino Fino California White Wine, 141
California Wine Institute, 37, 72
Calona San Pietro Paisano, 169
Calon-Segur, Ch., 252
Calvet, wine tastings:
Domaine de St. Georges, Côtes-du-
Rhône, 63
Réserve Blanc, 129
Réserve (Bordeaux), 45
Camensac, Ch. de, 254
Canadian wines, 16, 160, 161–162; tasting
results, 164, 169–171
Canaiolo,79
Canon, Ch., 252
Canon-La Gaffelière, Ch., 253
Cantemerle, Ch., 252
Cantenac-Brown, Ch., 252
Cap-de-Mourlin, Ch., 255
Carbonnieux, Ch., 253
Carignan (grape variety), 37, 50, 57, 59,
72, 152–153
Carmel, wine tastings:
Avdat Red, 63
Israel Grenache Rosé, 158
Israel Sémillon, 128
Cartier St. Emilion, 47
Castle Ste. Michelle Château Rouge, 169
Central Valley, 39, 72
Certan-de-May, Ch., 254
Certan-Giraud, Ch., 254
Chablis (American), 3, 4, 8, 136–138,
150, 166; compared to Rhine wine,
142–143. *See also* California Chablis
Chablis (French), 3, 13, 94, 97, 99, 100,
208, 223; compared to American,
136; compared to Franconian wine,
247; description, 95–96; tastings,
101–102, 105; vintage chart, 101
Chablis Grand Cru, 95–96, 100, 223
Chablis Premier Cru, 96, 100
Chambertin, 54
Chambertin Clos-de-Beze, 54
Chambolle-Musigny, 54, 55
Chancellor (grape hybrid), 161
Chanson, wine tastings:
Beaujolais, 70
Beaujolais-Village St. Vincent, 70
Châteaneuf-du-Pape St. Vincent, 64
Côtes-du-Rhône, 63
Muscadet de Sèvre-et-Maine, 135
Rosé des Angers, 159
Chapelle-Chambertin, 54

Chapoutier, wine tastings:
Châteauneuf-du-Pape La Marcelle, 65
Tavel la Marcelle, 157
Chappellet Chenin Blanc, 132
Chardonnay, 4, 5, 13, 15, 125, 136, 149,
208; discussion of, 94–99; tastings,
101–103, 104–106; vintage and
charts, 100–101
Charmes (Meursault), 97
Charmes-Chambertin, 54
Chassagne-Montrachet, red: 54, 55;
white: 95, 97, 100
Chasse-Spleen, Ch., 253
"Château-bottled," 234
Château Cartier, wine tastings:
Canadian Burgundy, 169
Canadian Claret, 169
Gamay Beaujolais, 169
Johannisberg Riesling, 170
Jolly Friar Rosé, 171
Vin d'Or, 170
Vin Rosé, 171
Château Gai, wine tastings:
Canadian Sauternes, 170
Maréchal Foch, 169
Pinot Chardonnay, 170
Pinot Noir, 170
Rosé, 171
Seibel, 169
White Table Wine, 170
Châteauneuf-du-Pape, 4, 11, 50, 56, 60,
153; vintage information, 58; tasting
results, 64–65
Château Sauterne, 137
Châteaux of Bordeaux. See name of
château, e. g., Palmer, Ch.
Chauché Gris (grape variety), 143
Chaunac, Adhemar de, 163
Cheese and wine, 207, 224
Cheese and Wine Chart, 208, 215–216
Chelois (grape hybrid), 161
Chénas, 67
Chenin Blanc, 4, 127, 130–133, 136, 138,
143, 207, 208; tasting results,
134–135
Cheval Blanc, Ch., 251
Chevalier-Montrachet, 96
"chewing" the wine, 225
Chianti, 10, 68; description, 77–82; map,
78; tasting results, 83; vintage, 80
Chianti Classico, 77, 79–80, 82; tasting,
83
Chianti dei Colli Senesi, 77
Chianti Riserva, 11, 77, 80–81
Chianti Vecchio, 80–81
Chilean wines, 46, 59
Chiroubles, 67
Chorey-les-Beaune, 54
Christian Brothers, 235; wine tastings:
California Burgundy, 63
California Napa Rosé, 138
California Sauterne, 139
California Vin Rosé, 156
Chateau La Salle, 5
Napa Valley Cabernet Sauvignon, 49
Napa Valley Chenin Blanc, 134
Napa Valley Gamay Noir, 93

Christian Brothers (*continued*)
  Napa Valley Johannisberg Riesling, 120
  Napa Valley Pineau de la Loire, 135
  Napa Valley Pinot Noir, 65
  Napa Valley Pinot Saint George, 64
  Napa Valley Riesling, 146
  Napa Valley Zinfandel, 76
City Codes, 26–27
Clairet, 36–37
Claret. *See* California Claret
Classification of Red Bordeaux wines, 251–255
Clerc-Milon-Rothschild, Ch., 253
Climate and wine, 8, 12–15, 35–36, 56, 72, 80, 97, 112; and quality, 14; in warm countries, 147–148
Clinet, Ch., 255
Clos des Jacobins, Ch., 255
Clos de la Roche, 54
Clos de l'Eglise-Clinet, 254
Clos de Tart, 54
Clos de Vougeot, 54
Clos l'Eglise, 254
Clos-Rene, Ch., 255
Clos St. Denis, 54
Club Claret, 41, 44
Cocktail wines. *See* Aperitifs and cocktail wine
Color of wine, 16–17, 223–225, 226, 237
Comsommation Courante, 7
Concannon Vineyards California Chablis, 141, 150
Confrérie du Tastevin, 55
Cooking with wine, 208
Corbières, 50, 81, 223; vintage, 59
Corbin, Ch., 255
Corbin-Michotte, Ch., 255
Cordier Médoc, 49
Cornas (Côtes-du-Rhône), 56
Corton, 54, 96
Corton-Charlemagne, 96
Corvino (grape), 86
Cos d'Estournel, Ch., 252
Cosecha, 40
Cos-Labory, Ch., 254
Côteaux du Layon, 132
Côte Chalonnaise wines; red, 51, 54; white, 95, 97
Côte de Beaune-Villages, 54, 55, 58, 60
Côte de Beaune wines; red, 15, 51, 54, 56; vintages, 58–59; white, 95–97; vintage, 100
Côte de Blaye, 32, 41
Côte de Brouilly, 67
Côte de Castillon, 32
Côte de Nuits, 51, 54, 56; vintages, 58–59
Côte de Nuits-Villages, 55, 58; white, 96
Côte d'Or. *See* Burgundy, France
Côte Rôtie, 50, 56; vintage, 11, 58
Côtes de Bourg, 34, 41, 43
Côtes de Canon-Fronsac, 34
Côtes de Fronsac, 34
Côtes de Provence Rosé, 152, 153
Côtes-du-Rhône, 50, 51, 56, 69, 74, 207, 233; tastings and results, 60–65; vintage, 11, 58

Coutet, Ch., 255
Couvent-des-Jacobins, 255
Cresta Blanca, wine tastings:
  California Cabernet Sauvignon, 49
  California French Colombard, 139
  California Grey Riesling, 146
  California Petit Sirah, 62
  Mendocino Zinfandel, 76
Cribari & Sons Winery, B., wine tastings:
  Cribari California Burgundy, 62
  Cribari California Vino Bianco Da Pranzo, 141
  Cribari California Vino Fiamma Da Pranzo, 159
  Cribari California Vino Rosso Da Pranzo, 85
  Cribari California Zinfandel, 76
Criots-Bâtard-Montrachet, 96
Croix, Ch. La, 255
Croix-de-Gay, Ch. La, 255
Croizet-Bages, Ch., 254
Croque-Michotte, Ch., 253
Crozes-Hermitage, 56, 58
Cru Beaujolais, 60, 66–69; tastings, 70–71
Crus Classes (CC), 251
Cruse, wine tastings:
  Beaujolais, 71
  Bordeaux Roc Rouge, 46
  Châteauneuf-du-Pape, 65
  Grenache Rosé, 157
  Pouilly-Fuisse, 106
  St. Emilion "La Garderie," 49
  Tavel, 157
Curé-Bon-La-Madeleine, Ch., 253

Dão, 50, 59–60
Da Silva Isabel Rosé, 159
Dauzac-Lynch, Ch., 254
Decanting wine, 220–221
de Chaunac (grape hybrid), 161, 163
Deidesheim (Rheinpfalz), 110, 241
Deinhard, wine tastings:
  Bereich Bernkastel Green Label, 121
  Bereich Johannisberg Riesling, 119
  Hanns Christof Liebfraumilch, 114, 122
Delas Frères, wine tastings:
  Côtes-du-Rhône, 63
  Châteauneuf-du-Pape Saint Esprit, 64
Delor, wine tastings:
  Cabernet Sauvignon, 46
  LaCour Pavillon Médoc, 49
de Luze, A., wine tastings:
  Chablis, 105
  Club Claret, 44
  Pouilly-Fuisse, 104
Denominaciones de Origen, 7
Denominazione di Origine Controllata, 7, 77
Descriptive adjectives for wine, 225–226, 237–240
Dessert wines, 113–114, 118
des Tours, Brouilly, Ch. (Excelsior), 71
Desvignes Marquisat Beaujolais-Villages, 71
Dhron (Mosel) best vineyards, 245
Dienheim (Rheinhessen) wines, 241

d'Issan, Ch., 252
Doctor (Bernkasteler), 245
Domaine de Chevalier, 252
Domaine du Châtelet, 255
Dourthe Frères Grande Marque
  Bordeaux, 48
Drouhin, wine tastings:
  Beaujolais-Villages, 71
  La Forêt Mâcon-Villages, 105
  Pouilly-Fuissé, 104
  Soleil Blanc, 106
Dubroca St. Emilion, 49
Ducru-Beaucaillou, Ch., 252
Duhart-Milon-Rothschild, Ch., 252
Dulong, wine tastings:
  Ecu Royal Claret Reserve, 44
  Ecu Royal French Country White, 129
Durfort-Vivens, Ch., 252
Dürkheim (Rheinpfalz), 241
du Tertre, Ch., 254

Eau de vie de Marc, 17
Echézeaux, 54
Eiswein, 114
Eitelsbach (Ruwer), vineyards, 247
Eltville (Rheingau), best vineyards, 242
Emerald Riesling. *See* California Emerald
  Riesling
Enclos, Ch. L', 255
Entre-Deux-Mers, 124, 127
Erbach (Rheingau), best estates and
  vineyards, 242
Erden (Mosel), best vineyards, 246
Eschenauer (Bordeaux shipper), 32
Escherndorf (Franconia), 247
"Estate bottled," 153, 234; Burgundy, 98;
  California, 7–8, 99; Germany, 111
Evaluation Scoring Guide (California
  State Fair), 226
Excelsior (importer), Ch. des Tours, 71
Export Union, Wedding Veil
  Liebfraumilch, 122

Falkenberg (Piesporter), 245
Fazi Battaglia Titulus Verdicchio, 151
Federweise, 67
Fermentation, 12, 35, 79, 113, 124, 240;
  malolactic, 16–18
Ferrière, Ch., 254
Fetzer, wine tastings:
  Mendocino Carmine Carignane, 62
  Mendocino Gamay Beaujolais, 93
  Mendocino Zinfandel, 74
Feytit-Clinet, Ch., 255
Fiasco, 79, 87
Fieuzal, Ch., 253
Figeac, Ch., 252
Fleurie, 67
Folle Blanche (grape), 137
Fonroque, Ch., 255
Food and Wine Chart, 208, 212–214
Forst (Rheinpfalz), 110; best vineyards,
  241
Fould family, 31
Fourcas-Dupré, Ch., 254
Fourcas-Hosten, Ch., 254
Fourtet, Ch., 253

France, 17, 136, 143; map, 256; vintage
  years, 9–11; wine industry, 234;
  wine regulations, 6–7. *See also*
  Appellation Contrôlée
Franc-Mayne, Ch., 255
Franconian wines, 108, 110, 247
Franzia, 235; Vin Rosé of California, 158
Frascati, 147–148, 149, 150
Freemark Abbey Napa Valley Cabernet
  Sauvignon, 48
French Colombard. *See* California
  French Colombard
Frescobaldi Castello di Nipozzano
  Chianti, 83
Fumé Blanc. *See* California Fumé Blanc

G. & D., wine tastings:
  Fior di California Burgundy Scelto, 62
  Fior di California Barberone, 84
  Fior de California Chianti, 84
Gallo, E. & J., 57, 235; wine tastings:
  Barbera of California, 85
  Burgundy of California, 61
  Hearty Burgundy of California, 3, 57,
    63
  Prime Vineyard Rhine Garten,
    California, 146
  Prime Vineyard Vin Rosé of California,
    158
  Sauterne of California, 138, 139
  Zinfandel, California, 76
Gamay, 55, 66, 91–92, 152–153
Gamay Beaujolais. *See* California Gamay
  Beaujolais
Gamay Beaujolais Noir, 28, 74, 91
Gamay Beaujolais-Nouveau, 92
Gamay Rosé, 152
Garganega (grape), 147
Garnacha (grape), 36
Gattinara, 57–58
Gau Bischofsheim (Rheinhessen), 241
Gay, Ch. Le, 254
Gazin, Ch., 253
Gebiet, 112
Geisenheim (Rheingau), best vineyards,
  243
Generic wines, 3, 30, 50, 136–139,
  142–144
German-style white wines, 142–146
German wines, 5, 20, 94, 142–143, 208;
  best vineyards and estates, 241–247;
  compared to Alsatian wine, 114;
  discussion, 107–114; harvesting, 16;
  label word-meanings, 111–112;
  map, 108; tasting results, 115–123;
  vintages, 9–11, 115–116; wine
  classifications, 7, 113; wine industry,
  234; wine laws, 6, 7, 108, 113
Gevrey-Chambertin, 54, 55, 60, 207
Gewürztraminer, 4, 107–108, 115–118;
  tasting results, 123
Gigondas (Côtes-du-Rhône), 56
Ginestet, wine tastings:
  Bordeaux Vieux, 49
  Graves Extra, 129
  Médoc, 48
  Pomerol, 48
  St. Emilion, 49

Giscours, Ch., 252
Givry, 54
Glasses. *See* Wine glasses
Glockenspiel Liebfraumilch (Kayser),
114, 122
Gloria, Ch., 253
Glossary of wine terms, 237–240
Gold Chablis, 3, 139
Gold Seal, wine tastings:
Catawba Pink, 157
Catawba White, 167
Charles Fournier Chablis Nature, 166
New York State Rhine, 146
Goldtröpfchen (Piesporter), 245
Gombaude-Guillot, Ch., 255
Governo method, 79
Graach (Mosel) vineyards, 246
Graciano (grape), 36
Gräfenberg (Kiedricher), 243
Grand-Barrail-Lamarzelle-Figeac, Ch.,
255
Grand-Corbin, Ch., 255
Grand-Corbin-Despagne, Ch., 255
Grand Crus of Burgundy, 51, 54;
vintages, 58–59
Grand-Puy-Ducasse, Ch., 253
Grand-Puy-Lacoste, Ch., 252
Grands Crus Classés (GCC), 251
Grands Echezeaux, 54
Grão Vasco, Dão, 61
Grape hybrids, 160–161, 163
Grave, Ch. La, 254
Graves, Red: 30, 32, 34, 43, 223;
vintage chart, 40; tastings, 41;
Grands Crus classifications, 251–254
Graves, White: description, 124–125,
138; tasting results, 127–129; vintage
information and chart, 126
Graves Supérieures, 124
Great Western, wine tastings:
New York State Burgundy, 165
New York State Chablis, 166
New York State Chelois, 165
New York State Dutchess Rhine
wine, 167
New York State Rosé, 159
Green Hungarian, 4, 143
Grenache, 4, 36, 56. *See also* California
Grenache Rosé
Grenouilles (Grand Cru Chablis), 96
Gressier-Grand-Poujeaux, Ch., 254
Grey Riesling. *See* California Grey
Riesling
Griottes-Chambertin, 54
Groslot (grape), 153
Grosslage, 112, 241
Gruaud-Larose, Ch., 252
Guild Wine Co., 235; Tavola Red,
California, 85
Guiraud-Cheval-Blanc, Ch., 46
Guntersblum (Rheinhessen) wines, 241
Guntrum L., Niersteiner Holle Kabinett,
122

Hallgarten (Rheingau) best vineyards,
244
Hanns Christoff Liebfraumilch
(Deinhard), 114, 122

Hanzell Pinot Noir, 65 n.
Hattenheim (Rheingau), 111; best
vineyards, 242
Haut Bailly, Ch., 253
Haut Batailley, Ch., 253
Haut Brion, Ch., 30, 250
Haut-Médoc, 30, 32, 34, 35, 42
Haut Sauterne, 137
Hearty Burgundy (Gallo), 3, 57, 62
Heitz, Joe, 39–40, 235
Heitz Napa Valley Chablis, 140
Hermitage, 56; vintage information, 11,
58
Hochheim (Rheingau), 111, 114; best
vineyards and estates, 242
Hock, 86
Hospices de Beaune, 55
Hugel Gewürztraminer, 117, 123
Hungarian white wines, 13, 117

Individual Zinfandels, 73–74; tastings,
75–76
Inglenook, wine tastings:
Napa Valley Gamay Beaujolais, 93
Napa Valley Gamay Rosé, 156
Napa Valley Johannisberg Riesling, 120
North Coast Counties Vintage Chablis,
140
North Coast Counties Vintage
Zinfandel, 75
Institut National des Appellation
d'Origine des Vins et Eaux-de-Vie
(INAO), 6
Iphofen (Franconia), 247
Israeli wines, 51, 59, 158
Issan, Ch. d', 252
Italian Swiss Colony, wine tastings:
Burgundy, California, 62
California Gold Chablis, 139
California Grenache Rosé, 156
Chianti, California, 85
Pink Chablis of California, 157
Rhine, California, 145
Zinfandel, California, 76
Italian wines, 17, 20; map, 78; red:
50–51, 57, 77–83, 86–90, 92, 207;
white: 147–148, 150–151; vintage
information, 10–11; wine regulations,
6, 7, 77, 86. *See also* Chianti;
Bardolino; Soave; Valpolicella

Jaboulet-Vercherre Beaujolais Garelle, 71
Jacquin Selection, Little Rhine
Bear Liebfraumilch, 122
Jadot, Louis, 54–55; wine tastings:
Beaujolais Blanc, 105
Beaujolais-Village Jadot, 70
Mâcon Blanc-Villages Jadot, 104
Johannisberg (Rheingau), best vineyards,
244
Johannisberg Riesling (German), 4,
107–108, 111, 115–116; tasting notes
and results, 118–120; vintages, 114,
116. *See also* California Johannisberg
Riesling
Johnston (Bordeaux shipper), 32
Jordan, wine tastings:
Côte Ste. Catherine, 169

Jordan (*continued*)
  Santa Maria, 171
  Sauternes Canadien, 170
  Valley Red, 169
Josephshof Estate wines, 246
Jouvet Pouilly-Fuissé, 106
Juliénas, 67

Kabinett, 11, 113–114, 118
Kasel (Ruwer), best vineyards, 247
Kayser, Julius, Glockenspiel
  Liebfraumilch, 122
Kiedrich (Rheingau), best vineyards, 243
Kirwan, Ch., 253
Klusserath (Mosel), best vineyards, 245
Korbel, wine tastings:
  California Burgundy, 63
  California Cabernet Sauvignon, 48
Kressman (Bordeaux shipper), 32
Kreusch, Leonard, wine tastings:
  Bernkasteler Kufürstlay Riesling, 121
  Kröver Nacktarsch, 121
  Le Chat Noir Rouge Velouté, 172
  Liebfraumilch, 122
  Niersteiner Gutes Domtal, 122
  Piesporter Goldtröpchen Kabinett, 121
Kröv (Mosel), 246
Kröver Nacktarsh, 114, 118, 121
Krug, Charles, wine tastings:
  Napa Valley Burgundy, 61
  Napa Valley Chenin Blanc, 134
  Napa Valley Claret, 45
  Napa Valley Gewürz Traminer, 123
  Napa Valley Johannisberg Riesling, 119

Labégorce, Ch., 254
Labégorce-Zédé, Ch., 254
Labels, wine, 8, 111–112
La Bergèrie Mouton-Cadet, (red), 49,
  (white), 129
La Clotte, Ch., 253
La Conseillante, Ch., 252
La Dominique, Ch., 253
Lafite-Rothschild, Ch., 30, 251
Lafleur, Ch., 253
La Fleur-Petrus, Ch., 253
La Fleur-Pourret, Ch., 255
Lafon-Rochet, Ch., 254
La Gaffelière, Ch., 252
Lage, 112
Lagrange, Ch., 253
La Grave, Ch., 254
LaGuiche, Marquis de, Estate (Mâcon),
  98
La Lagune, Ch., 252
Lalande de Pomerol, 34
La Louvière, Ch., 254
La Mission-Haut-Brion, Ch., 252
LaMont California Vineyards, wine
  tastings:
  California Barbera, 85
  California Burgundy, 63
  California French Colombard, 141
  California Ruby Cabernet, 45
Lancers Vinho Branco, 151
Lanessan, Ch., 254
Langenbach Rheinkeller Liebfraumilch,
  122

Langenlonsheim (Nahe), 244
Langoa, Ch., 254
Languedoc, 59
La Pointe, Ch., 254
Larcis-Ducasse, Ch., 253
La Romanée, 54
Lascombes, Ch., 252
La Tâche, 54
Latour, Ch., 30, 35, 251
Latour, Louis, 55; wine tastings:
  Beaujolais Supérieur, 71
  Pouilly-Fuissé, 104
La Tour-Carnet, Ch., 253
La Tour-de-Mons, Ch., 254
La Tour-du-Pin-Figeac, Ch., 255
La Tour-Figeac, Ch., 255
La Tour-Haut-Brion, Ch., 254
La Tour-Martillac, Ch., 254
Latour-Pomerol, Ch., 253
Latricières-Chambertin, 54
Laws and regulations. *See* Wine laws and
  regulations
Lawton (Bordeaux shipper), 32
Le Flaive Estate, 98
Léoville-Barton, Ch., 252
Léoville-Las-Cases, Ch., 252
Léoville-Poyferre, Ch., 252
Les Amis du Vin, 20
Les Clos (Grand Cru Chablis), 96
Les Ormes-de-Pez, Ch., 254
Les Preuses (Grand Cru Chablis), 96
L'Evangile, Ch., 252
Lichine, Alexis, *Grandes Crus Rouges de
  Bordeaux classification*, 251–255
Lichine, wine tastings:
  Cabernet Sauvignon, 46
  Graves, 128
  Médoc, 47
Liebfraumilch, 114, 117, 118, 142, 241;
  tasting results, 122
Lirac Rosé, 153
Listrac, 30, 34
Llords & Elwood, wine tastings:
  Castle Magic Johannisberg Riesling,
    120
  Velvet Hill Pinot Noir, California, 65
Loire Valley wines, 124–127, 130–135,
  153; map, 131; tastings, 133, 135
Los Hermanos Mountain Chablis, 141
Lussac, 34
Lynch-Bages, Ch., 252
Lynch-Moussas, Ch., 254
Lyon, France, 66

Mâcon Blanc, 223
Mâcon Supérieur, 97
Mâcon-Villages, 5, 97, 100–101; tasting
  results, 104–105
Mâcon Viré, 97
Mâcon white wines, 5, 66, 94–95, 97–98,
  101–103; vintage chart, 100
Mâconnais, 15
Madeira, 102, 238
Maderization, 102, 238
Maehler (Bordeaux shipper), 32
Magdelaine, Ch., 252
Mainriesling (grape), 247
Main river, 113, 242, 247

Malartic-Lagravière, Ch., 253
Malbec (grape), 35
Malescot-Saint-Exupéry, Ch., 253
Malolactic fermentation, 17–18
Malvasia (grape), 79, 148
Manischewitz Cream White Concord, 168
Maréchal Foch (grape hybrid), 161
Margaux, Ch., 30, 251
Margaux wines, 30, 34, 39–40, 223;
   tastings, 41, 43
Marqués de Riscal Rioja, 49
Marquis d'Alesme-Becker, Ch., 253
Marquis de Terme, Ch., 254
Martha's Vineyard, Napa Valley, 5
Martini, Louis M., wine tastings:
   California Mountain Barbera, 84
   California Mountain Burgundy, 63
   California Mountain Cabernet
      Sauvignon, 48
   California Mountain Chablis, 141
   California Mountain Chianti, 5
   California Mountain Gewürz Traminer,
      123
   California Mountain Pinot
      Chardonnay, 104
   California Mountain Pinot Noir, 64
   California Mountain Red Wine, 63
   California Mountain Riesling
      (Sylvaner), 146
   California Mountain Vin Rosé, 156
   California Mountain Zinfandel, 76
Masi, wine tastings:
   Soave Classico Superiore, 151
   Valpolicella Classico Superiore, 90
Masson, Paul, 235; wine tastings:
   Baroque, 5, 61
   California Burgundy, 61
   California Cabernet Sauvignon, 47
   California Chablis, 138, 139, 150
   California Pinot Blanc, 104
   California Pinot Chardonnay, 104
   California Pinot Noir, 61
   California Riesling, 145
   California Vin Rosé Sec, 157
   California Zinfandel, 76
   Emerald Dry, 146
   Rubion, 44
Mateus Branco, 151
Maufoux Beaujolais-Villages 1974,
   Tirage Primeur, 69
Maximin Grünhäuser, 247
Mazeyres, Ch., 255
Mazis-Chambertin, 54
Mazoyères-Chambertin, 54
Mazuelo (grape), 36
Médoc wines, 30–32, 34–35; vintage
   information, 38–40; chart, 40;
   tastings, 41–42, 43, 46–49; Grandes
   Crus classifications, 251–254
Meier's, wine tastings:
   Isle St. George Haut-Sauternes, 168
   Isle St. George Sauternes, 168
Melini Chianti Classico, 83
Melon de Bourgogne (grape), 132
Mendocino, California, 56, 72–73
Mendoza Barbera, 85
Mendoza Malbec, 45

Merchants, wine, 19–20, 236; merchant-
   shippers, 234
Mercurey, 54, 55, 60
Merlot (grape), 35, 37
Merode, Prince de, 51
Meursault, 95, 97, 99, 223; vintage
   chart, 100; tasting note, 103
Meursault Premier Cru, 100
Mexican wines, 77
Michigan State; wine industry, 160;
   Rosé, 159
Mid-varietal wines, 4
Mirassou, wine tastings:
   Monterey Gewürztraminer, 123
   Monterey Pinot Noir, 65
   Monterey Riesling, 146
   Monterey White Burgundy, 139
Moc-Baril Rosé d'Anjou, 159
Moillard-Grivot, 55
Molinara (grape), 86
Mondavi, Robert, 39–40, 235
Mondavi & Sons, C., wine tastings:
   C. K. Mondavi California Zinfandel, 75
   C. K. Mondavi Chablis, 139
Mondavi Winery, Robert, wine tastings:
   Napa Valley Cabernet Sauvignon, 48
   Napa Valley Chardonnay, 105
   Napa Valley Chenin Blanc, 134
   Napa Valley Fumé Blanc, 128
   Napa Valley Gamay, 93
   Napa Valley Gamay Rosé, 136
Montagne, 34
Montagny, 97
Monterey, California, 7, 16, 37, 56–57,
   72–73
Monterey Vineyard, wine tastings:
   Del Mar Ranch White Monterey, 141
   Monterey Chenin Blanc, 134
   Monterey Gamay Beaujolais, 93
   Monterey Johannisberg Riesling, 119
Montlouis, 132
Montrachet, 96–97
Montrose, Ch., 252
Morey St. Denis, 54
Morgon, 67, 68, 69
Moselblümchen, 114, 118
Moselle River valley, 10, 13, 111; best
   vineyards and estates, 244–246
Moselle wines, 86, 107, 110–115, 207,
   208, 209; compared with White
   Burgundy, 94; tasting results, 116,
   118, 121; vintage chart, 116
Mosel-Saar-Ruwer region; shippers of,
   250; vineyards, 244–247
Moser Tytell Lipizzaner, 145
Moucheron, Comte de, 51
Moulin-à-Vent, 67, 68, 69
Moulin-du-Cadet, Ch., 255
Moulis, 30, 34
Mountain Red wines. *See* California
   Mountain Red
Mouton, Ch., 30
Mouton-Baron-Phillipe, Ch., 253
"Mouton Cadet" Bordeaux, 5, 41, 49, 129
Moutonne, 96
Mouton-Rothschild, Ch., 251
Müller-Thurgau (grape), 108, 110, 245,
   247

Muscadelle (grape), 125, 143
Muscadet, 130, 132; tastings, 133, 135
Muscadet Côteaux de la Loire, 132
Muscadet de Sèvre-et-Maine, 132
Musigny; red, 54; white, 96

Nackenheim (Rheinhessen) wines, 241
Nahe region, 110, 111, 114; communities
    and estates, 244
Napa Burgundy, 5, 60
Napa Gamay. *See* California Napa
    Gamay
Napa Valley, California, 5, 7, 37, 56,
    72–73; vintage years, 39
Nebbiolo (grape), 57
Nebbiolo d'Alba, 58
Nebbiolo di Canale, 58
Neckar, 113
Negrara (grape), 86
Nenin, Ch., 254
New York State, 160; red wines, 50, 59,
    162; tasting results, 163, 165; white
    wine tasting results, 166–168; wine
    industry, 16, 160, 163
Nieder-Olm (Rheinhessen) wines, 241
Nierstein, 110, 114, 117, 118; tasting
    results, 122; best estates and vine-
    yards of, 241, 242
Niersteiner Gutes Domtal, 241
Niersteiner Hölle Kabinett, 122
Noble (grape), 153
"Noble rot," 16, 113–114
Normandie White Table Wine, 170
North Coast Counties, California, 37
Norton, wine tastings:
    Mendoza Malbec, 45
    Mendoza Barbera, 85
Nuits St. Georges, 54, 55, 223; white, 96

Oakville Vineyards Napa Valley
    Sauvignon Blanc, 129
Oberrhein, 113
Ockfen (Saar) best vineyards, 246
Oestrich (Rheingau) wines and best
    vineyards, 243
Ohio wine industry, 160
Ontario, Canada, wine production,
    161–162; tasting results, 169–171
Oppenheim (Rheinhessen) wines and
    best vineyards, 241
Oppenheimer Krötenbrunnen, 114, 118,
    241
Organoleptic Evaluation Scoring Guide
    for wine, 226
Orvieto, 148

Palmer, Ch., 252; vintage quality and
    climate chart, 14, 15
Panadés wines, 148–149
Pape Clément, Ch., 252
Parducci Wine Cellars, wine tastings:
    California Zinfandel, 76
    Mendocino County Burgundy, 63
    Medocino County Cabernet Sauvignon,
        48
    Mendocino County Chablis, 139
    Mendocino County Chardonnay, 104
    Mendocino County Chenin Blanc, 134

Mendocino County Gamay Beaujolais,
    93
Mendocino County Petit Sirah, 65
Mendocino County Pinot Noir, 65
Mendocino County Sylvaner Riesling,
    145
Parsac, 34
Pastene, wine tastings:
    Mellow Burgundy, California, 61
    Mellow Red Burgundy, California, 63
Paternina, wine tastings:
    Gran Reserva, 49
    Rosado, 157
Patriarche, wine tastings:
    Bourgogne-Aligoté, 105
    Chablis, 105
Pauillac, 30, 34, 35
Pavie, Ch., 253
Pavie-Macquin, Ch., 255
Pédauque, Reine, 54–55
Pédauque Beaujolais, 71
Pedesclaux, Ch., 254
Pedrizetti Cabernet Sauvignon, 49
Pedroncelli, wine tastings:
    Sonoma County Burgundy, 62
    Sonoma County Cabernet Sauvignon,
        49
    Sonoma County Chablis, 139
    Sonoma County Chenin Blanc, 134
Pereire family, 31
Perrières (Meursault), 97
Petit Chablis, 96, 100–101
Petit Syrah (grape), 56–57. *See also*
    California Petit Sirah
Petit Verdot (grape), 35
Petit-Village, Ch., 253
Petrus, Ch., 251
Pez, Ch. de, 253
Phélan-Ségur, Ch., 254
Phylloxera, 31, 36
Piat Château de Saint Amour, 71
Pichon-Longueville (Baron), Ch., 252
Pichon-Longueville (Comtesse de
    Lalande), Ch., 252
Picking of grapes, 16, 112
Piedmont, 10, 50, 51, 57–58
Piesport (Mosel) wines and best vine-
    yards, 245
Piesporter Goldtröpfchen, 114, 118
Piesporter Michelsberg, 114, 118
Pineau d'Aunis (grape), 153
Pineau de la Loire, 130, 133, 135
Pinnacles, California, 37, 73
Pinot Blanc, 95, 130. *See also* California
    Pinot Blanc
Pinot Chardonnay (grape), 130
Pinot Chardonnay-Mâcon, 5, 101. *See
    also* California Pinot Chardonnay
Pinot Noir, 4, 13, 51, 55, 63, 66, 91.
    See also Burgundy, French Red;
    California Pinot Noir
Pinot Noir-Gamay, 58
Pinot St. Georges (grape), 56
Pomerol, 30, 34, 35, 41–43; Grandes
    Crus classifications, 251–255
Pommard, 54, 55, 223
Pontet-Canet, Ch., 253

Portuguese wines; map, 257; red, 50–51; rosé, 153–154; tasting results, 158–159; Vinho Verde regulations, 147, 149, 151
Pouget, Ch., 254
Pouilly-Fuissé, 4, 94–95, 97–98, 103, 125; tasting results, 103–106; vintage chart, 100
Pouilly-Fumé, 124–125; vintage information, 126–127
Pouilly-Loché, 98, 100
Pouilly-sur-Loire, 125
Pouilly-Vinzelles, 98, 100
Poujeaux, Ch., 254
Prats Médoc, 46
Prats St. Emilion, 47
Premier Cru appellation, 51, 54, 55, 58
Premières Côtes de Bordeaux, 32
Premiers Grands Crus Classés (PGC), 251
Premium Zinfandel, 73–74; tastings, 75–76
Price Categories of wines in Tasting Results Charts:
  Red Wines:
    Up to $1.99, 172–173
    $2 to $2.49, 174–175
    $2.50 to $2.99, 176–177
    $3 to $3.49, 178–179
    $3.50 to $3.99, 180–182
    $4 to $4.49, 183
    $4.50 to $4.99, 184
    $5 to $5.49, 185
    $5.50 to $5.99, 186
    $6 and over, 187
  Rosé Wines, Dry:
    Up to $2.99, 204
    $3 to $4.99, 205
  Rosé, Other than Dry:
    Up to $1.99, 205
    $2 to $3.49, 206
  White Wines:
    Up to $1.99, 188–189
    $2 to $2.49, 190–193
    $2.50 to $2.99, 194–195
    $3 to $3.49, 196–197
    $3.50 to $3.99, 198–199
    $4 to $4.49, 200
    $4.50 to $4.99, 201
    $5 to $5.99, 202
    $6 and over, 203
Price of wines, 25, 27, 235–236; of Bernkasteler Doctor, 245–246; and tasting panel, 28
Prieuré-Lichine, Ch., 253
"Produced and bottled by," 8
Prohibition, 161–162
Proprietary wine names, 5
Publicker (importer), Trovador Rosé, 158
Puisseguin, 34
Puligny-Montrachet, 95, 97, 99–100
Puligny-Montrachet Les Pucelles, 95, 97

Qualitätswein (Q.b.A.), 7, 113–114, 115, 118
Qualitätswein mit Prädikat, 7, 113

Racking, 18
Rating code for wine tastings, 26
Rauenthal (Rheingau) wines and best vineyards, 243
Rausan-Seglá, Ch., 253
Rauzan-Gassies, Ch., 253
Red Côtes de Provence, 81
Refractometer, 15
Refrigeration of wine, 219–220
Regional wines, 4–5. *See also* various wine types, e. g., Bordeaux, French Red; Beaujolais
Rheingau region, 110–111, 114, 247; villages, vineyards, and estates, 242–244
Rheinhessen region, 110, 114; villages, vineyards and estates, 241–242
Rheinpfalz region, 110; villages and vineyards, 241
Rhine wines (German), 107, 110, 208–209; compared to white Burgundy, 94; shippers of, 250; tasting results, 117, 122; vintages, 9–11; vintage chart, 116
Rhine wines (other than California), 3, 166. *See also* California Rhine Wine
Rhone Valley wines, 11, 51, 152. *See also* Côtes-du-Rhône
Ricasoli Brolio Chianti Classico, 83
Richebourg, 54
Ridge Vineyards, wine tastings:
  California Zinfandel Lytton Springs, 75
  York Creek Petite Sirah, 65 n.
Riesling (grape), 4, 5, 13, 72, 107–108, 110–111, 115, 142, 160, 244–245, 247. *See also* Johannisberg Riesling
Rincôn Famoso, 84
Rioja, 30–31, 35–36; tastings, 42, 49; vintages, 40; white wines, 148
Rioja Alavesa, 36
Rioja Alta, 36
Rioja Baja, 36
Ripeau, Ch., 255
Riscal, Marqués de, Rioja, 49
Riunite Bianco, 150, 151
Robust Burgundy, 3
Romanée-Conti, 51, 54
Romanée St. Vivant, 54
Roma Winery, wine tastings:
  California Pink Chablis, 157
  California Vin Rosé, 158
  California Zinfandel, 76
  Vino D'Uva of California Country Red, 84
Rondinella (grape), 86
Rosé wines, 10, 37, 149; aging, 17–18; and tannin, 16–17; French and Portuguese, 153–154; tastings for dry rosé, 156–157; tastings for semi-dry, 158, 159; tastings for Canadian, 171
Rothschild family, 31
Rouget, Ch., 255
Ruby Cabernet, 4, 30, 37, 45
Ruchottes-Chambertin, 54
Rudesheim (Rheingau), 111; wines and best vineyards, 243

Ruffino, 81; wine tastings:
Bardolino Classico Superiore, 89
Chianti, 83
Soave Classico Superiore, 151
Valpolicella Classico Superiore, 90
Rully, 97
Ruppertsberg (Rheinpfalz), 110; best
vineyards, 241
Russian River, California, 37, 72
Ruwer, 110, 111, 244–245; villages and
vineyards, 247

Saar, 110, 111, 244–245; wines and
villages, 246
Sables, 34
St. Emilion, 30, 34, 35; Grands Crus
classifications, 251–256; tastings,
41–43, 47–49; vintage information,
38–39; chart, 40
St. Emilion "La Garderie," 49
St. Estephe (Médoc), 30, 34, 223
St. Georges (St. Emilion), 34
Saint-Georges-Côte-Pavie, Ch., 255
St. Joseph (Côtes-du-Rhône), 56
St. Julian, wine tastings:
Continental Michigan Rhine, 166
Continental Michigan Sauterne, 167
La Salle Club Michigan Mello White,
168
La Salle Club Kastel Rhine, 168
St. Julien (Médoc), 30, 34, 39–40;
tastings, 41
Saint-Pierre, Ch., 254
St. Véran, 97, 100
Ste. Michelle Vintners, wine tastings:
Washington State Grenache Rosé, 159
Washington State Johannisberg
Riesling, 120
Sales, Ch. de, 255
Sangioveto (grape), 79
San Martin Vineyards, wine tastings:
California Gamay Beaujolais, 93
California Mountain Burgundy, 61
California Mountain Chablis, 140
California Mountain Vin Rosé, 159
California Petite Chablis, 139
California Pinot Noir, 65
California Sylvaner Riesling, 146
California Zinfandel, 76
Santa Clara Valley Emerald Riesling,
145
Sémillon Sauterne, 129
Santa Barbara, California, 56
Santa Sofia, wine tastings:
Bardolino Classico Superiore, 89
Soave Classico Superiore, 151
Valpolicella Classico Superiore, 90
Santenay, 54, 55
Saumur, 132
Sauterne (American), 125, 133, 136–140,
150, 163; compared with American
Rhine wine, 143–144; tastings, 129,
137–140. *See also* Canadian wines
Sauternes (French), 3, 124–125, 127,
136–137, 209; compared to American
Sauterne, 125; vintages, 11, 126
Sauvignon Blanc, 102, 208. *See also*
California Sauvignon Blanc

Savigny-les-Beaune, 54, 55
Scharzhofberger (Saar), 246
Schenley (importer), wine tastings:
Ch. de Buffavent, 70
Valmont Cabernet Sauvignon, 47
Schloss Böckelheim, 114
Schloss Johannisberger, 244
Schloss Vollrads, 244
Schroder & Schyler (Bordeaux shipper),
32
Sebastiani, wine tastings:
North Coast Counties Barbera, 84
North Coast Counties Gamay
Beaujolais, 93
North Coast Counties Green
Hungarian, 145
North Coast Counties Mountain
Chablis, 140
North Coast Counties Pinot
Chardonnay, 105
North Coast Counties Vin Rosé, 157
Northern California Mountain
Burgundy, 62
Sonoma Zinfandel, 75
Secco, 148
Secrestat Chambord, 169
Selo de Origem, Comissão de Viticultura
de Região dos Vinhos Verdes, 149
Sémillon. *See* California Sémillon
Serrig (Saar) vineyards, 246
Shippers of wine, 98, 234, 236; of
Bordeaux, 32; of Burgundy, 249; of
Rhine, Moselle, Alsatian, 250
Sichel, wine tastings:
Amourosé, 159
Beaujolais, 70
Bereich Bernkastel, 121
Bereich Johannisberg Riesling, 119
Bereich Nierstein, 122
Blanc de Blanc Sauvignon Sec, 128
Blue Nun Liebfraumilch, 122
Chablis Special Selection, 105
Châteauneuf-du-Pape, 65
Côtes-du-Rhône, 61
Graves Supérieures, 128
My Cousin's Claret, 48
Pinot Chardonnay-Mâcon, 105
Rosé de Provence, 157
St. Emilion, 48
Zeller Schwarze Katz, 121
Sichel Shippers (Bordeaux), 32, 234
Silvaner, 107–108, 110. *See also* Sylvaner
Simi Winery, wine tastings:
Alexander Valley Cabernet Sauvignon,
49
Alexander Valley Pinot Chardonnay,
105
North Coast Carignane, 62
North Coast Chablis, 140
North Coast Pinot Noir, 65
Siran, Ch., 254
Smith-Haut-Lafitte, Ch., 253
Soave, 86, 147; tasting results, 150–151
Soil and wine, 36, 56, 57, 87, 107–108,
111; wine quality chart, 14; minerals,
13, 15, 107
Sonoma County, California, 5, 37, 39,
49, 56–57, 72–73

Sonoma Vineyards, wine tastings:
California Petit Sirah, 62
Sonoma County Cabernet Sauvignon, 49
Sonoma County Chardonnay, 104
Sonoma County French Colombard,
138, 139
Sonoma County Grenache Rosé, 156
Sonoma County Grey Riesling, 145
Sonoma County Pinot Noir, 65
Sonoma County Sauvignon Blanc, 128
Soutard, Ch., 254
South America, wine blends, 142. *See
also* Argentinian wines
Souverain of Alexander Valley, wine
tastings:
Johannisberg Riesling, Sonoma, 119
Mendocino County Grey Riesling, 146
North Coast Burgundy, 63
North Coast Chablis, 141
North Coast Dry Chenin Blanc, 135
Sonoma Chardonnay, 105
Souverain of Rutherford, wine tastings:
Napa Valley Dry Chenin Blanc, 134
Napa Valley Cabernet Sauvignon,
48
Napa Valley Mountain Zinfandel,
75
Napa Valley Petit Sirah, 64
Napa Valley Pinot Noir, 65
Spanish wines, 5, 51, 57; map, 257; red,
35, 36, 38; vintage information, 40;
tastings, 42, 49; regulations, 7, 36;
white, 147, 148–151
Spanna, 58, 59
Spätlese, 11, 113, 115, 118
Spritzer, 208–209
State wine and liquor stores, 20–21
Steinberg (Rheingau), 243
Steinwein (Franconia), 247
Storage of wine, 17–18, 36, 37, 98–99,
131, 218, 220; wood barrels and
casks, 17, 36, 37, 101, 124, 240
Sugar in wine, 7, 16–17, 112, 117, 118,
239
Sulphur in wine, 101–102, 239
Sunshine and wine, 13–15, 147–150. *See
also* Climate and wine
Sweetness, 107, 112–114, 118, 124–125,
127, 130, 133, 150, 161, 163, 239
Sylvaner, 5, 108, 117, 142, 247. *See also*
California Sylvaner
Syrah, 56

Tafelwein, 7, 113
Taillefer, Ch., 255
Talbot, Ch., 253
Tannin, 16–17, 31, 35, 37, 50, 77, 224,
239
Tastevin, Confrérie du, 55
Tasting Results Charts, 26
Bardolino and Valpolicella, 89–90
Beaujolais, 70–71
Bordeaux, red, Bordeaux-style and
California Cabernet Sauvignon,
44–49
Bordeaux, white, Sauvignon Blanc and
Sémillon, 128–129
Burgundy, red, Burgundy-style and
California Pinot Noir, 61–65

Burgundy, white and California Pinot
Chardonnay, 104–106
California Chenin Blanc and lower
Loire wines, 134–135
Canadian wines, 169–171
Chablis and Sauterne (American),
139–141
Châteauneuf-du-Pape and Côtes-du-
Rhône, 61–65
Chianti (Italian and California), 83–85
Gamay Beaujolais and Napa Gamay,
93
Gewürztraminer, 123
Moselle, 121
Rhine wine, 122
Riesling, 119–120
Rioja, 44–49
Rosés, dry, 156–157; other than dry,
158–159
U.S. wines produced East of the
Rockies, 165–168
White German-style wines, 145–146
White Italian, Spanish and Portuguese,
151
Tavel Rosé, 152–154
Taylor Wine Co., wine tastings:
New York State Burgundy, 165
New York State Claret, 165
New York State Lake Country Pink, 159
New York State Lake Country Red, 165
New York State Lake Country White,
167
New York State Rhine, 166
New York State Rosé, 157
New York State Sauterne, 168
Tempranillo (grape), 36
Tertre, Ch. du, 254
Tertre-Daugay, Ch., 255
Tokay (grape), 13
Topping, 18
Traben-Trarbach (Mosel), 246
Trebbiano Tuscano (grape), 79, 147–148
Trimoulet, Ch., 255
Trittenheim (Mosel), best vineyards, 245
Trockenbeerenauslese, 11, 113, 118, 208,
247; vintage chart, 116
Troplong-Mondot, Ch., 254
Trotanoy, Ch., 252
Trottevieille, Ch., 253
Trumpeter Cabernet-Malbec, 47
Turner, wine tastings:
Bon Appetit, 169
Heritage White Table Wine, 170
Tytell, wine tastings:
Bereich Bernkastel
Liebfraumilch, 122
Médoc, 47
Moselblümchen, 121
St. Emilion, 47
Zeller Schwartze Katz, 121

United States; laws and regulations, 4, 5,
6, 7, 21, 136, 161; wine marketplaces, 26; wine industry, 16, 160,
234–236
United Vintners, 235
Ürzig (Mosel) vineyards, 246
Utah state liquor stores, 21

Valmur (Grand Cru Chablis), 96
Valpolicella, 86–88; tasting results, 90
Vaudésir (Grand Cru Chablis), 96
Veneto, 10
Verdicchio, 148, 150, 151
Verdicchio Classico, 148
Verona, 86, 147
Verrazzano Chianti Classico, 83
Vieux Château Certan, 252
Villemaurine, Ch., 255
Vin de pays, 132
Vin de presse, 17
Vin ordinaire, 7, 138, 161
Viña Undurruga Cabernet, 46
Vines, 12–13, 91; harvesting, 15–16,
    112–113. *See also* Names of grape
    varieties; Names of wine regions
Vinho Verde, 149, 151
Vinification. *See* Wine making
Vins Délimités de Qualité Supérieure
    (V.D.Q.S.), 7
Vintages, 7, 8–11, 19, 25–26. *See also*
    name of wine for vintage chart
Vitis labrusca, 13, 160
Vitis riparia, 160
Vitis rupestris, 160
Vitis vinifera, 13, 72, 160–163
Vogüé, Comte de
Volnay, 54, 55
Vosne-Romanée, 54, 55
Vosne-Romanée Premier Cru Les
    Suchots, 54
Vougeot white, 96
Vouvray, 130, 132, 135; vintage, 132

Wachenheim (Rheinpfalz) wines and best
    vineyards, 110, 241
Waldrach (Ruwer) vineyards, 247
Warner Vineyards, wine tastings:
    Cask Michigan Mountain Red, 165
    Cask Michigan Mountain Rosé, 159
    Michigan Vineyard White, 168
Washington State wines, 115, 120, 124,
    159, 160
Wasum, Schloss Fürstenberger Riesling,
    119
Weibel Champagne Vineyards, wine
    tastings:
    California Cabernet Sauvignon, 49
    California Johannisberg Riesling, 20
    California Pinot Chardonnay, 105
    California Pinot Noir, 64
Weinexport Hattenheim, wine tastings:
    Madrigal Bernkastel Riesling, 121
    Madrigal Johannisberg Riesling, 119
    Madrigal Liebfraumilch, 122
    Madrigal Zeller Schwartze Katz, 121

Wente Bros., wine tastings:
    California Chablis, 141
    California Dry Sémillon, 128
    California Grey Riesling, 146
    California Pinot Blanc, 104
    California Pinot Chardonnay, 105
    California Pinot Noir, 65
White Pinot, 130, 133
White Riesling. *See* Johannisberg Riesling
Widmer's Wine Cellars, wine tastings:
    Naples Valley Delaware, 166
    Naples Valley Foch, 165
    Naples Valley Isabella Rosé, 157
    Naples Valley Vergennes, 166
    New York State Haut Sauterne, 168
    New York State Naples Valley Pink,
        159
    New York State Naples Valley Red,
        165
    New York State Sauterne, 167
    Sonoma/Napa Cabernet Sauvignon, 47
Wiltingen (Saar) best vineyards, 246
Wine: glasses, 221–222, 224; identifying
    terms, 3–4; industry, 234–236. *See
    also* California, wine industry; New
    York State, wine industry
Wine Codes for Food and Wine Chart,
    210–211
Wine laws and regulations, 4–7. *See also*
    California regulations; France, wine
    regulations; United States, laws and
    regulations
Wine making, 12–18, 79, 160. *See also*
    type of wine
Winemasters' Guild, wine tastings:
    California Gamay Beaujolais, 93
    California Chenin Blanc, 135
Wine Tasting (Broadbent), 226
Wine tastings, 223–227
Winkel (Rheingau) wines and best
    vineyards and estates, 243
Worms (Rheinhessen) best vineyard, 241
Württemberg, 110
Würzburg (Franconia) best vineyards, 247

Yon-Figeac, Ch., 255
Yugoslavia, 12, 45, 142, 146

Zell (Mosel), 246
Zeller Schwartze Katz, 114, 118, 246
Zeltingen (Mosel), best vineyards, 246
Zeltinger Münzlay, 114, 118
Zinfandel, 4, 42, 208, 223; rosé, 152–153.
    See also California Zinfandel